Wrox's Visual C#
Express Edition St

GW01417835

Wrox's Visual C# 2005 Express Edition Starter Kit

F. Scott Barker

WILEY

Wiley Publishing, Inc.

Wrox's Visual C#® 2005 Express Edition Starter Kit

Published by
Wiley Publishing, Inc.
10475 Crosspoint Boulevard
Indianapolis, IN 46256
www.wiley.com

Copyright © 2006 by Wiley Publishing, Inc., Indianapolis, Indiana

Published simultaneously in Canada

ISBN-13: 978-0-7645-8955-3

ISBN-10: 0-7645-8955-5

Manufactured in the United States of America

10 9 8 7 6 5 4 3 2 1

1MA/SZ/RS/QV/IN

Library of Congress Cataloging-in-Publication Data:

Barker, F. Scott.
  Wrox's visual C# 2005 Express edition starter kit / F. Scott Barker.
    p. cm.
  Includes index.
  ISBN-13: 978-0-7645-8955-3 (paper/cd-rom)
  ISBN-10: 0-7645-8955-5 (paper/cd-rom)
  1. C# (Computer program language) 2. Microsoft Visual BASIC. 3. BASIC (Computer program language)
  4. Microsoft .NET. I. Title.
  QA76.73.C154B42 2005
  005.13'3—dc22
                                      2005012036

About the Author

F. Scott Barker has worked as a developer in the database field for over 16 years, and with Visual Basic, SQL Server, and Microsoft Access for the last 14 years. Scott is a Microsoft MVP and holds a Bachelor of Science in Computer Science. Scott worked at Microsoft for two years as a member of the Microsoft Access and FoxPro teams. After leaving Microsoft, he started his own company, Applications Plus, and continued to consult for them by developing in-house tools. Scott has trained for Application Developers Training Company and throughout the United States, and is a frequent speaker at Microsoft Conferences in the United States, Canada, South Asia, and Europe. Through his classes and conferences, Scott has trained thousands of developers. Scott is a writer for a number of Microsoft Technical magazines, as well as a columnist for DotNetJunkies, and is the author of a number of books including topics such as ADO. NET, Visual Basic .NET, and InfoPath 2003.

Credits

Acquisitions Editor
Katie Mohr

Development Editor
Howard Jones

Technical Editor
Karli Watson

Production Editor
Felicia Robinson

Copy Editor
Joanne Slike

Production Manager
Tim Tate

Editorial Manager
Mary Beth Wakefield

Vice President & Executive Group Publisher
Richard Swadley

Vice President and Publisher
Joseph B. Wikert

Project Coordinator
Michael Kruzil

Graphics/Production Specialists
Joni Burns
Andrea Dahl
Mary Gillot
Lauren Goddard
Denny Hager
Barbara Moore
Melanee Prendergast
Alicia South

Quality Control Technicians
John Greenough
Leeann Harney

Permissions Editor
Laura Moss

Proofreading and Indexing
TECHBOOKS Production Services

Acknowledgements

Anytime you create a book that is shipping day and date with a product such as this one did, the project is much more complicated because of dealing with beta product right up until the end. There are a number of people I want to thank who have been working hard with me on this book for Wrox, including the following people who are at Wrox: Katie Mohr, who is the nicest acquisition editor (sorry Jim) there is. She can nag you about a deadline, and you thank her. Howard Jones, a great development editor who would put up with my late night submissions, and still made me look good. Felicia Robinson, the production editor who came in late in the process when we were short on patience, and made things easy for us.

I also want to thank Karli Watson, for taking the time to tech edit my book when I know he is busy with so much of his own work. I am honored to have you work on this book Karli.

Many thanks to Dan Fernandez, who is on the Microsoft C# Express team and Suzanna Moran, my MVP lead at Microsoft, for answering my many questions and making sure I had what I need to get this book done. Dan, you have a great amount of patience, and Suzanna, you rock when it comes to getting me connected with the right people.

As usual, my family has put up with me writing yet another book: Chris 17, Kari Anne 15, Nichole 12, David 10, Joseph 4, and my awesome wife Diana.

Dedication

To my beautiful and brilliant wife and friend, Diana. Besides being a strong woman of God who also demonstrates her belief in me every day, I can't think of anyone I would rather have by my side for the rest of my life, to guide my kids, and share many beautiful sunsets with.

Contents

Contents

Contents

Contents

Contents

Introduction

If you are picking this book up and seriously thinking about buying it, which you should, then you are likely just getting into software development for the first time. The Visual C# Express development environment is a great way to start since (a) it is free and (b) it rocks! To get some of the terms out of the way, Visual C# Express (call C# Express for short) is the IDE (Integrated Development Environment,) which consists of the editor you will use, and other tools for developing your projects. C# is the actual programming language. There will be lot of other terms that you will have to learn, but this is a good start.

I have been honored to have been able to teach literally thousands of developers, and have a written more than a few books on software development, but I am more excited about writing this development book than many others. The beauty of C# Express is that it introduces you to the power of C# but handles a lot of the frustrating and confusing tasks for you, thereby making your first experience in programming a far more pleasant one. When I first got into programming, I remember the excitement of creating my first applications and actually having them work. Nowadays a lot of time developers get so bogged down because of the environment they have to develop in. This is especially true when developing in lower-level programming language such as C.

The C# Express takes a lot of the pain away by providing design time objects using drag and drop, and writing some of the more tedious code for you. By the end of this book, you will feel confident in using the language of C# not only for the simple examples given here, but for moving forward into a lifetime of creativity developing software applications that seriously have no bounds.

Who This Book Is For

This book is for those of you who are just getting into programming for the first time, whether you are a high school student, hobbyist, or a professional looking to make a change. If you are already a software developer using another language such as Visual Basic, then you will also get benefits out of portions of this book, but it starts from square one for newbies.

Another group this book and C# Express is good for are those managers who want to get a handle on what C# is all about, without investing a ton of time and money involved in the full-blown version of Visual Studio .NET.

Although it is assumed that you have not had any kind of programming experience before, the book has been written such that you can skip Chapter 2 and miss the basic information on programming. After walking through the installation of C# Express, you will be given a chapter on what exactly is programming and how you get started.

What This Book Covers

This book covers the latest version (2.0) of the .NET programming language called C#, utilizing the development environment that is C# Express. C# combines a powerful editor with tools, wizards, and tutorials that help you create your first applications. The purpose of this book is to enhance your experience by giving other examples other that those provided in C# Express. Also covered is working with data using SQL Server Express, which is included in C# Express. SQL Server is a database product, used for managing information. C# Express provides tools for utilizing the data in your application, and this book will discuss the ways to take advantage of those tools in your programs.

How This Book Is Structured

In writing this book, I consider the logical steps you would have to take if you were taking a class on using C# Express. Broken into four parts, the book takes you all the way from introductory material and concepts to how to deploy applications you have created. In each chapter tasks are given so that you can take what you learn and put it to practical use. Following is the layout of the book and the order of topics discussed:

Part I: Introduction and Concepts introduces various programming concepts, as well as takes you through the Visual C# Express environment. Also covered are some of the base commands and concepts of the C# language itself.

❑ **Chapter 1—Starting Strong with Visual C# 2005 Express Edition.** This chapter walks you through installing the C# Express development environment and points out some of the various tools that are included in the IDE for your use. A discussion of how C# Express organizes files for projects and solutions is also included.

❑ **Chapter 2—Programming 101: A Quick Discussion.** Before you jump into the way commands are specified, the *syntax* of the C# language, it is a good idea to get a good overview of programming in general, as well as what is involved to program in the Windows environment. These items will be covered, as well as some of the major areas in the C# language.

❑ **Chapter 3—Quick Start Creating Your First C# Express Windows Project.** Before you jump into creating your own project, this chapter gives a quick overview of the starter kit that comes with C# Express, which is an application that creates screen savers. After examining the different types of possible applications you can create, you will create your first project, diving in and get use to the C# Express environment.

❑ **Chapter 4—Introducing .NET.** Although this sounds intimidating, the .NET Framework is made up of a number of assemblies and classes (which are explained in Chapter 2) that let you, the developer, handle literally any task you need to when programming your application. This chapter lists those .NET Assemblies and classes that are most commonly used in your development.

❑ **Chapter 5—Getting into C# Types.** One of the most common elements of any programming language is the use of variables for storing information in memory, and the types of data you can use. The concepts you learn in this chapter will be used throughout the rest of the book.

❏ **Chapter 6—Debugging Applications in C# Express.** When you are creating applications of any kind, there is a process that you follow of writing the code, then testing and debugging the code. This chapter shows you some of the tools that are available in the C# Express environment for tracking down bugs (errors) in your code. C# Express offers some new technologies for making the debugging task less onerous, including being able to stop the execution of code, edit the code, and continue on executing the code without restarting. (Current developers are going oohh, ahh at this point.)

❏ **Chapter 7—Selections, Iterations, and Catching Exceptions.** No matter how well you build your code, exceptions are going to occur. How you handle these exceptions affects the overall user experience in working with your applications. This chapter shows you how to handle exceptions effectively.

Part II: Creating Applications with C# Express takes what you have learned in the preceding chapter and shows you how to create user interface elements to create applications using Windows forms. C# Express provides many new enhancements in creating applications and even writing some of the code.

❏ **Chapter 8—Working with Forms and Controls.** This chapter shows how to utilize Windows forms and controls, such as the text box control and drop-down list boxes in your application. You will see some of the various controls that are available for your use, as well as what are properties, methods, and events that can be used with those controls. Lastly, you will learn how to add code for those forms and controls.

❏ **Chapter 9—Adding Dialog Boxes and Rich Text to Your Application.** There are a number of different dialog controls that make up standard Windows dialog boxes such as `FileOpenDialog` and `PrintDialog`. This chapter lists those controls and walks you through adding some of them to your own application by showing you how to create a quick Rich Text Note Pad application.

Part III: Using Data in Applications examines database concepts, data controls, SQL Server Express features, and ADO.NET.

❏ **Chapter 10—Introducing Database Concepts.** One of the things you are likely to have to do in creating C# applications is to work with data in your application. Before you jump into the mechanics of how you specifically do that, it is a good idea to get an overview of what a database is. This chapter will give you the overview you need so you can feel comfortable discussing tables, columns, and relationships and know what you are talking about.

❏ **Chapter 11—Using SQL Server Express Features within C# Express.** While it is great to be able to work in SQL Server Express, it is even better to be able to work in your database within C# Express. This chapter shows you how to use a data source for your project and take advantage of the visual tools within C# Express.

❏ **Chapter 12—Utilizing .NET Data Controls.** This chapter shows you the `DataGridView` control and other data controls that you now use on your forms.

❏ **Chapter 13—Working with ADO.NET.** While you will be able to create a lot of data applications without using code, there will undoubtedly come a time when you will need to use code with ADO.NET. This chapter explains how to utilize ADO.NET classes using code in your applications.

Part IV: Finishing Touches discusses the various ways to give your applications to other users to use.

❑ **Chapter 14—Getting More Experience with Controls.** This chapter creates a file browser using a `SplitContainer` control, a `WebBrowser` control, and more. Two of the tasks deal with various ways of working with date controls, status bars, and progress bars. This chapter includes about 10 different very useful controls.

❑ **Chapter 15—Using Web Services from Your C# Application.** Web services provide solutions to tasks that either don't make sense for you to create or even maintain the code for, or for which you would have to have access to outside data available from another company or facility.

❑ **Chapter16—Publishing Your Application and Next Steps.** Once you have created an application and want to deploy (distribute) it, you need to know what to do. This chapter will discuss additional steps to take once you have completed your first applications using C# Express.

What You Need to Use This Book

Everything you need to work with the examples of this book is included on book's Web site or on the CD in the back of the book. Beside the author's examples (available on the book's Web site), Microsoft has generously supplied a full copy of Visual C# Express on the CD, which also contains SQL Server Express.

Conventions

To help you get the most from the text and keep track of what's happening, I've used a number of conventions throughout the book.

> **Boxes like this one hold important, not-to-be forgotten information that is directly relevant to the surrounding text.**

Tips, hints, tricks, and asides to the current discussion are offset and placed in italics like this.

As for styles in the text:

❑ I *highlight* important words when we introduce them.

❑ I show keyboard strokes like this: Ctrl+A.

❑ I show filenames, URLs, and code within the text like so: `persistence.properties`.

❑ I present code in two different ways:

```
In code examples I highlight new and important code with a gray background.
```

```
The gray highlighting is not used for code that's less important in the present
context, or that has been shown before.
```

Source Code

As you work through the examples in this book, you may choose either to type in all the code manually or to use the source code files that accompany the book. All of the source code used in this book is available for download at www.wrox.com. Once at the site, simply locate the book's title (either by using the Search box or by using one of the title lists) and click the Download Code link on the book's detail page to obtain all the source code for the book.

> *Because many books have similar titles, you may find it easiest to search by ISBN; this book'sISBN is 0-7645-8955-5 (changing to 978-0-7645-8955-3 as the new industry-wide 13-digit numbering system is phased in by January 2007).*

Once you download the code, just decompress it with your favorite compression tool. Alternately, you can go to the main Wrox code download page at www.wrox.com/dynamic/books/download.aspx to see the code available for this book and all other Wrox books.

Errata

We make every effort to ensure that there are no errors in the text or in the code. However, no one is perfect, and mistakes do occur. If you find an error in one of our books, like a spelling mistake or faulty piece of code, we would be very grateful for your feedback. By sending in errata, you may save another reader hours of frustration, and at the same time you will be helping us provide even higher-quality information.

To find the errata page for this book, go to www.wrox.com and locate the title using the Search box or one of the title lists. Then, on the book details page, click the Book Errata link. On this page you can view all errata that has been submitted for this book and posted by Wrox editors. A complete book list including links to each book's errata is also available at www.wrox.com/misc-pages/booklist.shtml.

If you don't spot "your" error on the Book Errata page, go to www.wrox.com/contact/techsupport.shtml and complete the form there to send us the error you have found. We'll check the information and, if appropriate, post a message to the book's errata page and fix the problem in subsequent editions of the book.

p2p.wrox.com

For author and peer discussion, join the P2P forums at p2p.wrox.com. The forums are a Web-based system for you to post messages relating to Wrox books and related technologies and interact with other readers and technology users. The forums offer a subscription feature to e-mail you topics of interest of your choosing when new posts are made to the forums. Wrox authors, editors, other industry experts, and your fellow readers are present on these forums.

At `http://p2p.wrox.com` you will find a number of different forums that will help you not only as you read this book, but also as you develop your own applications. To join the forums, just follow these steps:

1. Go to `p2p.wrox.com` and click the Register link.

2. Read the terms of use and click Agree.

3. Complete the required information to join as well as any optional information you wish to provide and click Submit.

4. You will receive an e-mail with information describing how to verify your account and complete the joining process.

You can read messages in the forums without joining P2P, but in order to post your own messages, you must join.

Once you join, you can post new messages and respond to messages other users post. You can read messages at any time on the Web. If you would like to have new messages from a particular forum e-mailed to you, click the Subscribe to this Forum icon by the forum name in the forum listing.

For more information about how to use the Wrox P2P, be sure to read the P2P FAQs for answers to questions about how the forum software works as well as many common questions specific to P2P and Wrox books. To read the FAQs, click the FAQ link on any P2P page.

Part I

Introduction and Concepts

1

Starting Strong with Visual C# 2005 Express Edition

Okay, so the title of this chapter may be a little over the top. But to be honest, the Visual C# 2005 Express Edition, from now on referred to as C# Express, rocks as a starting development environment. If you are just starting out in developing, you don't realize how lucky you are to start with an environment such as C# Express, which really tries to walk you through getting into programming fairly gently. In the old days, just a few years ago (back when I had hair), you were handed an editor such as Notepad.exe and given-command line programs to compile and run your applications. That has all changed.

For C# being such a powerful language, Microsoft has worked hard to make the development environment that you use to create computer programs, even for seasoned developers, as painless as possible. Before, when developing with a lower-level language, such as C or Assembly, you had to put up with cryptic tools that were quite cumbersome to use for developing software. When you used the language, such as Visual Basic, the tools got easier, but then you had to put up with a less robust (i.e., less efficient) language. Now, with the .NET development languages, you get the best of both worlds. You will read more about programming languages in general and the differences between them in Chapter 2, "Programming 101: A Quick Discussion."

This chapter starts off the book by walking you through installing C# Express for the first time, along with SQL Server Express, which is the database component that you will mainly use with C# Express. In addition, this chapter will also

- ❑ Talk about differences between C# the language and C# Express.

- ❑ Discuss what it means to use an integrated development environment (IDE)?

- ❑ Give you an overview of C# Express development environment.

- ❑ Take a look at how C# Express structures solutions and projects and what the difference is between them.

What Is Microsoft Visual C# 2005 Express?

While I will be getting deeper into the various terminology and discussing what programming is in the next chapter, now is a good time to clear up a couple of items about C# Express. First, what exactly is C# Express? Exactly what is the difference between C#, the programming language, and C# Express?

The Differences between C# and C# Express

C# Express is actually what is called an *IDE*, or *integrated development environment*. What this means in plain English, or whatever language you are reading this in is that C# Express is a set of tools, including a special text editor that enables you to write computer programs in C#, the software development language. It also handles other necessary tasks such as building your application to either test for errors or release for people to use.

Microsoft wanted to come up with a way to get those who are not yet C# developers interested in programming, such as hobbyists and students. Prior to this, you could create your C# applications a couple different ways:

❑ **Use a simple note pad or third-party editor, and then use the command-line compiler.** Really, only long-time hardcore developers use this method, where you need no support for development and want to struggle through compiling the programs yourself.

❑ **Use Visual Studio .NET to development and maintain your C# code and application.** This is the preferred method if you can afford Visual Studio.

Now Microsoft has created the Express series to give you experience with developing using the last method but with pared-down features. The full-blown versions of Visual Studio contain supersets of commands found in the Express versions.

Members of the Express Series

In an effort to expose new developers of all kinds to their different products, Microsoft has created the Express series. The following products are part of this series and can be downloaded from the Web at http://lab.msdn.microsoft.com/express/default.aspx or, as with Microsoft Visual C# 2005 Express, can be found on the CD in the back of this book.

Besides C# Express, other products in the series include:

❑ Visual Basic 2005 Express

❑ Visual C++ 2005 Express

❑ Visual J# 2005 Express

❑ Web Dev 2005 Express

❑ SQL Server 2005 Express

The first three in this list are additional programming languages. Web Dev Express introduces you to Web development with ASP.NET and can be used with each of the four languages in the Express series. SQL Server Express is a scaled-down version of SQL Server, which is a database management system.

Since SQL Server Express is distributed with C# Express, and the other languages, all of Part III, "Using Data in Applications" features SQL Server in this book.

Before getting into what is included in the C# Express development environment, you need to install the product on your system. This is the purpose of this first Try It Out.

Try It Out   Installing Microsoft Visual C# Express

Taking the CD that came with the book:

1. Place the CD in the CD-ROM drive. An installation window appears, giving you the choice to install Microsoft C# 2005 Express.

2. Click Microsoft C# 2005 Express. The installation program begins, displaying a welcome page, as shown in Figure 1-1.

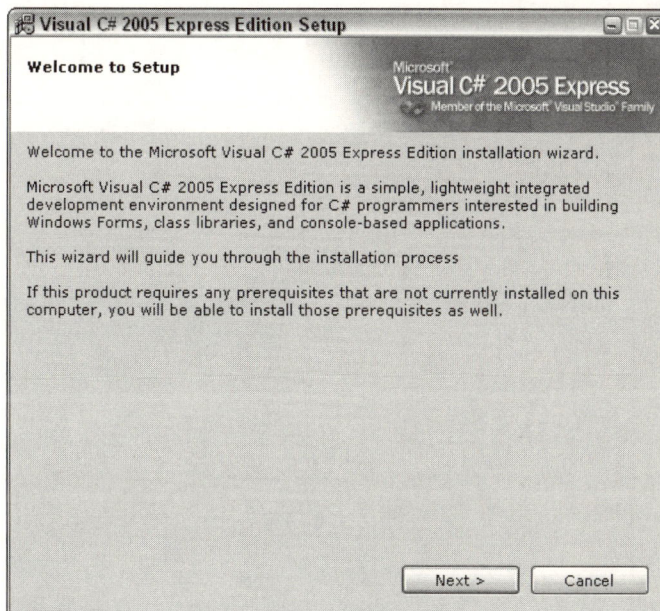

Figure 1-1

3. Click Next. The next page displays the EULA, or End User License Agreement.

4. After thoroughly reading the EULA (of course), place a check mark in the check box that reads "I accept the terms of the License Agreement," as displayed in Figure 1-2.

5. Click Next to continue the setup. You now have the option of installing SQL Server Express and the MSDN (Microsoft Developer Network) Express Library.

6. Place a check mark next to the additional two products, as shown in Figure 1-3.

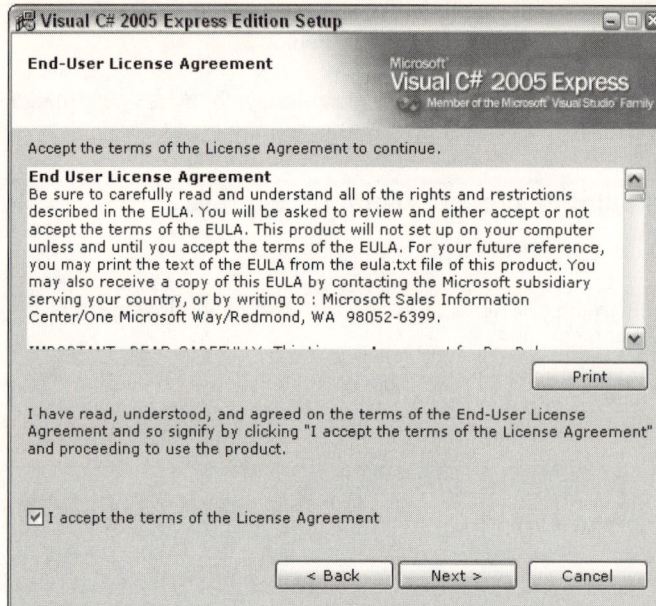

Figure 1-2

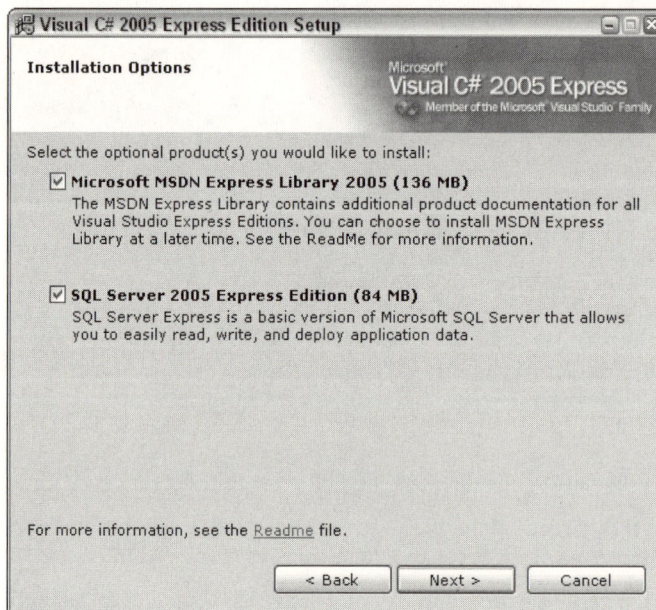

Figure 1-3

In addition to the products covered in the Express version of MSDN, MSDN contains a ton of articles and information for all the various Microsoft developer products, including an extensive knowledge base. So, in addition to installing the MSDN library version here for the Express products, check out the MSDN home page online at http://msdn.microsoft.com/. For the library area, go to http://msdn.microsoft.com/library/default.asp, where you can search the knowledge base for any issues and problems that come up.

If you have never loaded any software that required it before, you may have to load .NET Framework 2.0 as well.

7. Click Next to continue the setup. The next page, shown in Figure 1-4, displays where the C# Express applications will be installed.

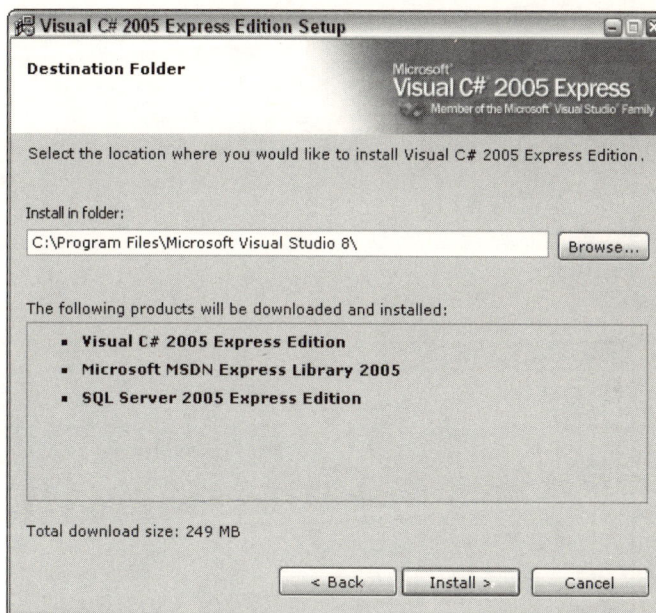

Figure 1-4

8. Click Install if you are OK with the default location; otherwise, click Browse and select where you want them placed. The installation program now sets up your three products, as shown in Figure 1-5.

The success page shown in Figure 1-6 appears. Setup is now complete.

9. Click Exit to close the setup dialog box.

C# Express has now been installed.

You can now choose Program Files → Visual C# 2005 Express from the Windows Start menu to see the starting page for Visual C# Express, as shown in Figure 1-7.

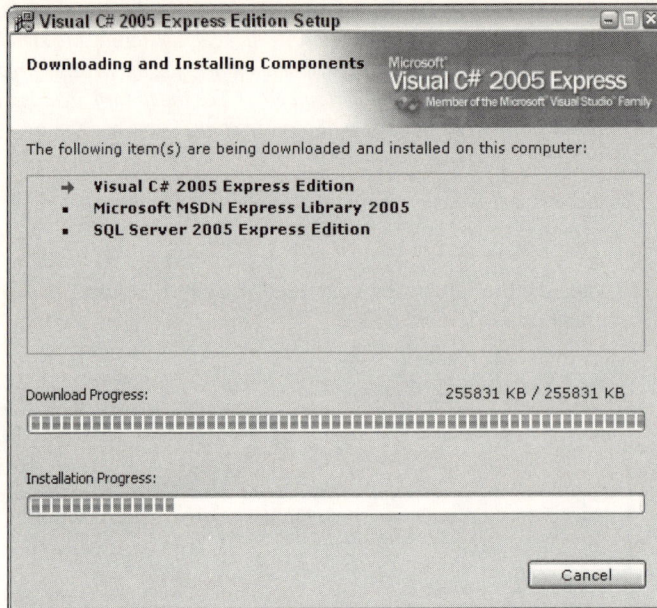

Figure 1-5

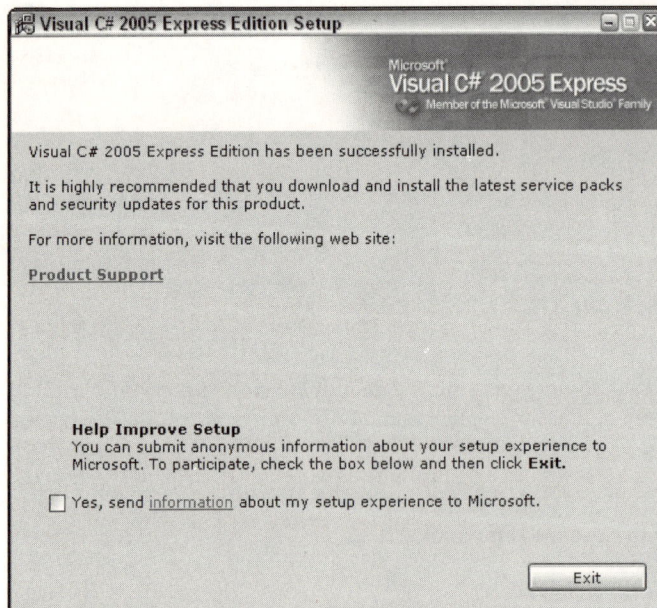

Figure 1-6

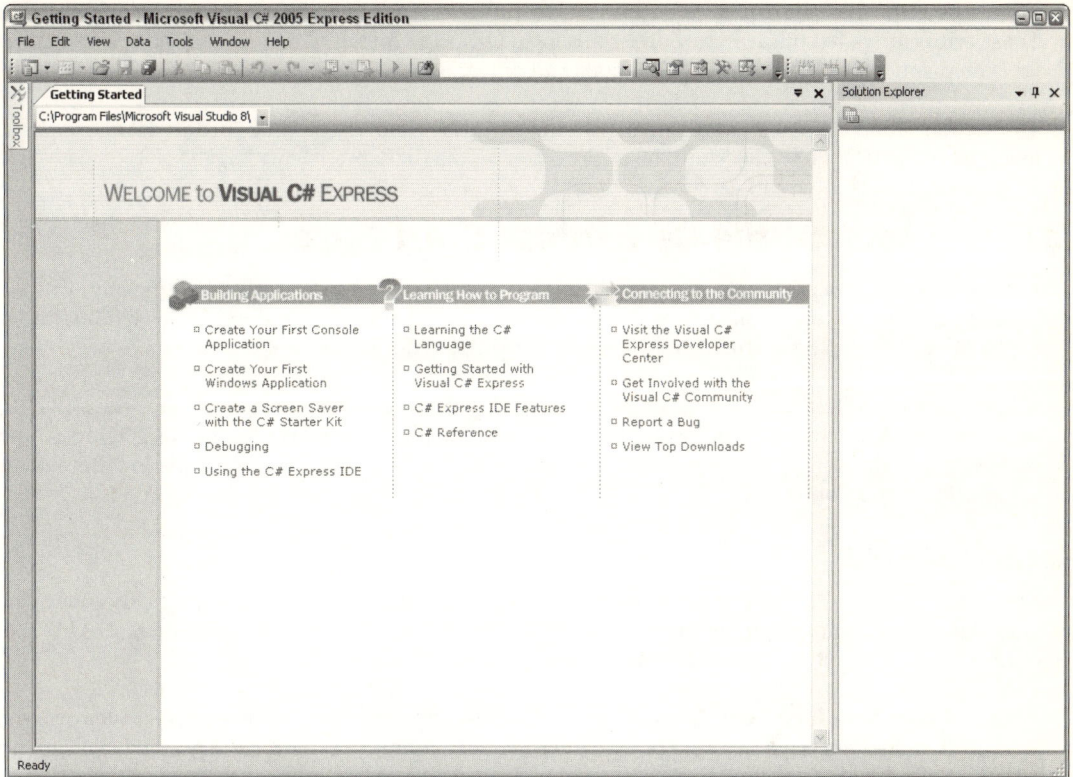

Figure 1-7

The following sections explain some of features of the C# Express development environment that you will be using first, along with some of the tools included.

Overview of C# Express Development Environment

The C# Express development environment takes almost as much time to learn as the C# language itself. OK, not really, but there are a lot of tools that can make your development experience more enjoyable and give you more control as you are creating applications. The first page to go over is the start page that appears when you first open the C# Express IDE. Herein lies a good question—what the heck is the IDE?

What Is the IDE (Integrated Development Environment)?

The Integrated Development Environment (IDE) is just what it sounds like: a development environment that includes an editor for writing your code, as well as integrated tools for managing your software projects.

When you write the commands for creating your application, called code, errors will invariably occur. These errors are called bugs. Some of the tools included help you with "debugging" your code. Other tools help you tie in data to your applications and organize your code projects

The section "Tools of the C# Express IDE" coming up in the chapter goes into further detail on what is included in the IDE. First, check out the information on the C# Express Start Page.

Taking a Look at the C# Express Start Page

Remember that C# Express was created to help new developers get comfortable creating applications. When you first go into the full version of Visual Studio .NET, you are placed in its IDE without much explanation. This can be confusing for new and experienced developers alike.

Microsoft has tried to alleviate some of the confusion by including help for new developers, as well as links for getting answers to issues that you may have. Looking at the Start page back in Figure 1-7, note that the page is broken up into three categories: Building Applications, Learning How to Program, and Connecting to the Community.

Getting Started

This category focuses on what it takes to create a project using C# Express. It doesn't really cover what goes into programming itself but rather what it takes to manage the code files and others. Here is the list of help topics covered, as seen under the Buildings Applications category:

❑ **Create Your First Console Application.** Console applications are a type of computer program that does not have any kind of user interface (e.g., forms) and performs specified tasks such as downloading data (taking information from the Web) or uploading data (putting information up on the web). Another example may be a print server, which sends documents to a printer without any user intervention.

❑ **Create Your First Windows Application.** Windows applications include forms for inputting data and prompting users. These can be tied to a database for managing data such as is used in accounting software or a mailing list. Video games are another example of Windows applications where you will create forms as a user interface.

❑ **Create a Screen Saver Project.** To help you get started in programming in C# using C# Express, Microsoft included a project template that helps you create a screen saver that can be used on your computer.

A project template is a project that has been started for you, to give you a jump start in writing the particular type of project, including various files needed for that type of project. A number of project templates are available; the first three are those just mentioned in the list. The other topic, Class Library, is discussed in Chapter 2.

❑ **Debugging.** This help topic takes you through the various ways to debug your project as you are building it. It points out the major tools to debug your project and how to use them. This topic is discussed in greater detail in Chapter 6, "Debugging Applications in C# Express."

❑ **Using the C# Express IDE.** This topic points out various tools included in the C# Express IDE — much like this chapter does in the "Tools of the C# Express IDE" section

Please note that these options don't cover everything that you can do with C#—a notable exclusion being ASP.NET code. The C# Express Environment gets you started using C# the language, but it doesn't provide all the possibilities for C#.

Learning How to Program

Whereas the previous category points out various features in the C# Express, this category on the Start page presents information on the C# language itself, as well as displaying additional features of C# Express.

Remember the distinction: C# is the language; C# Express is the set of tools created to help you write programs using the C# language.

Topics are as follows:

❑ **Learning the C# Language.** Just as the title says, this topic discusses getting going in the C# language, including structures of your programs and statements that you can use.

❑ **Getting Started with C# Express.** This topic overlaps other topics and also refers to other topics within this one. The topic discusses how C# is different from other programming languages, as well as how to get started creating your first C# application.

❑ **C# Express IDE Features.** The topic discusses various IDE features available to help you write and compile your C# applications.

After writing your code, C# Express compiles the code from the syntax that you understand to a language closer to what the computer understands. Compilers and compiled languages are discussed further in Chapter 2, "Programming 101: A Quick Discussion."

❑ **C# Reference.** This handy help topic contains a reference to the various commands (statements) within the C# programming language.

To be honest, I wouldn't recommend looking through this reference just yet. While the other topics use fairly easy to understand prose, the last just spits out the definitions of what the statements are. While this is great after you have been using the development language for a while and want to quickly find out a definition or syntax (various ways to write a particular programming statement), trying to take it all in when you are just starting out developing can be pretty intimidating. I would save this last topic for after you have read at least half of this book.

Connecting to the Community

While the last two categories of the Start page have been help topics that display static text to explain various parts of C# and C# Express, this section contains links to other Web sites that help support your coding. All of these links take you to sites under the MSDN (Microsoft Developer Network) main Web site.

❑ **Visit the Visual C# Express Developer Center.** This link takes you to the main Visual C# developer page and is loaded with great information. However, as with the last topic, I would hold off going to these links until you feel comfortable "speaking C#."

❑ **Get Involved with the Visual C# Community.** As you start developing in C# and are finding yourself running up against a wall as far as coming up with the proper commands, this link is a great resource. This link takes you to a number of newsgroups available on the MSDN site. Take advantage of them, but remember that most of the contributors are pretty advanced developers and may not have the patience to help you all the way through a solution. That being said, the majority of them are excited to help out new programmers, also called newbies. If you let them know you are new, often they will write the code themselves and send it to you. Another good suggestion is to read a bit and search for your topic in earlier posts before posting, because posting a topic that has already been amply addressed can sometimes annoy people.

❑ **Report a Bug.** Clicking this link takes you to the MSDN Product Feedback Center. Always looking to improve their products, Microsoft is constantly seeking feedback from users and developer on their products, so don't hesitate to go here if you have an issue with the product.

❑ **View Top Downloads.** Another very useful link, this one takes you to an MSDN page, shown in Figure 1-8, where you can download various examples and utilities.

Remember that this one is for both new and advanced developers, so you need to check the overview of the download to find the sophistication of the coding you want. Unfortunately, they are not labeled as such, and you can find yourself being quickly overwhelmed.

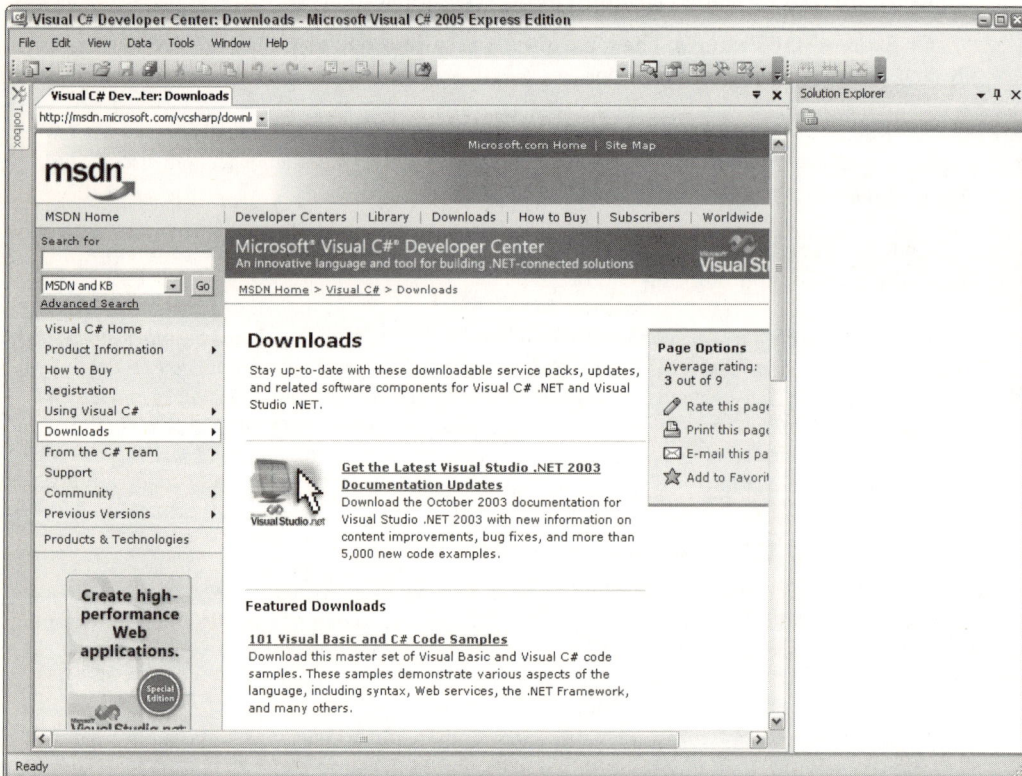

Figure 1-8

When you click a link and want to get back to the main start page, whether it is one of the help topics or a third category link, you can right-click and choose Back, as shown here in Figure 1-9.

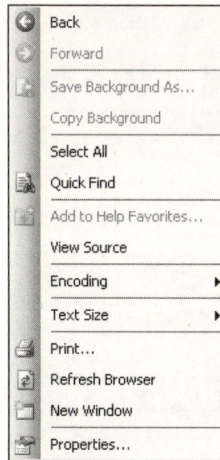

Figure 1-9

Besides the newsgroups and Web sites displayed in the Connecting to the Community category on the start page, a number of Web sites are dedicated to supporting C# and .NET developers. Two of the most active are www.GotDotNet.com and www.DotNetJunkies.com. (I happened to write a column for DotNetJunkies.com called "The First Hit," where I discuss various issues that you as a beginning developer face in the .NET world of programming.)

Before jumping in to the different C# Express IDE tools, you need to create your first C# project so that you have more of an idea of what you are doing when you finally get to work with the tools.

Try It Out   **Creating Your First C# Project**

1. Choose Program Files → Visual C# 2005 Express from the Windows Start menu. The IDE opens, and the Start Page is displayed.

2. Select New → Project from the Files menu. The New Project dialog box appears, giving you a choice of templates.

3. Highlight Console Application. Remember that this type of application doesn't have any forms or interface. It is also the easiest to start with.

4. Type in the name of the project you want to create. For this Try It Out, Chapter1Console was used, as shown in Figure 1-10.

5. Click OK. Your project is now created, as shown in Figure 1-11.

Alright! You have now created your first project. Notice I didn't say application, because this project really doesn't do anything. Before you add code to this, take a look at some of the tools available in the C# Express IDE.

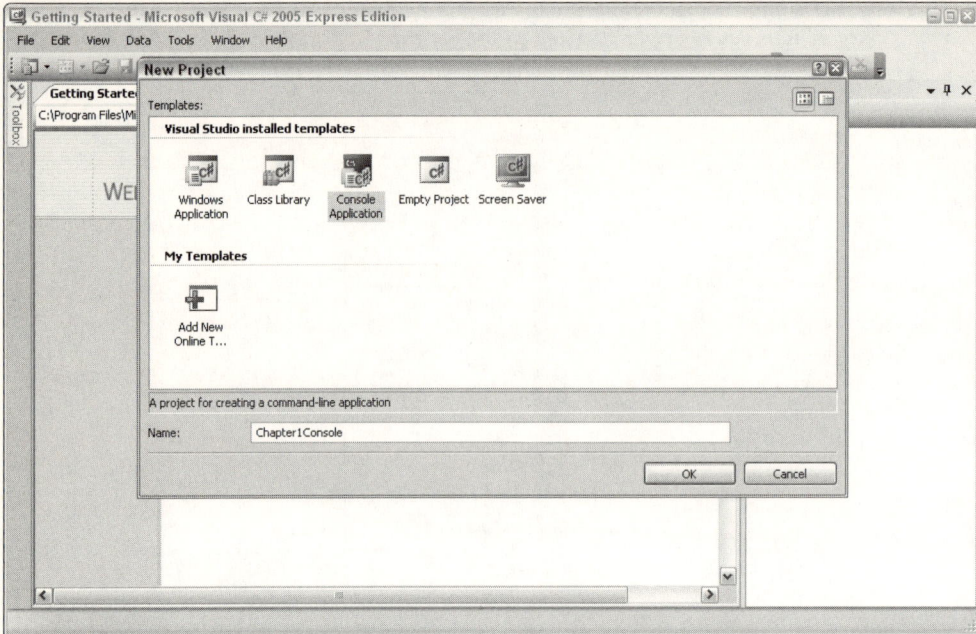

Figure 1-10

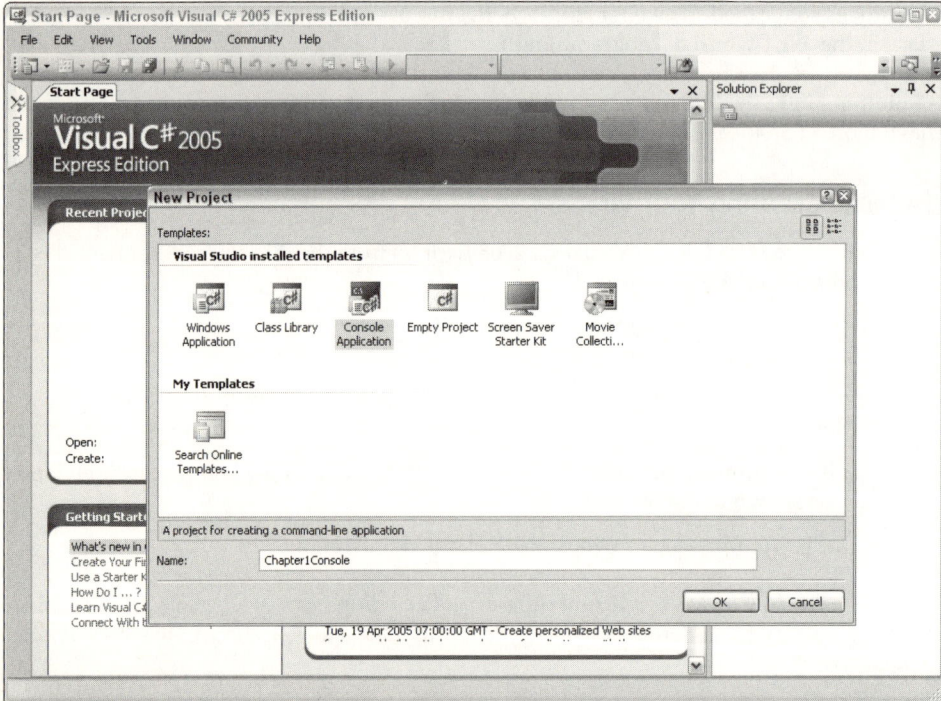

Figure 1-11

Tools of the C# Express IDE

In addition to the tools in Figure 1-11, I will introduce other tools throughout the rest of the book as needed. For starters, you can see some of those tools in the following list:

❏   **Main Editor.** This tool is the one you will likely use the most when you are working with your C# Express projects, because you use it to edit the code and the majority of projects are made up of code files. You can see from the tabs at the top of the editor that you can have more than one code file open at the same time. And, in fact, you can display different types of files in the main editor page, as shown here with Program.cs and the Getting Started page.

When you have another file, such as a Windows form, note that you can have both the form and code files open at the same time. As shown in Figure 1-11, the editor actually helps you control your program when formatting your code. This will become more apparent as you perform more extensive coding.

Files are loaded as you double-click on them in the Solution Explorer. You use the Main Editor tool to edit both forms that you can drag and drop to design and code files.

❏   **Solution Explorer.** The Solution Explorer helps you to organize your projects by putting your files in the order C# Express thinks they should be in for the project type you are creating. For example, look at the Solution Explorer located left of the main editor in Figure 1-11. You will see an entry called References. If you click on the plus sign, you will see the files located under that "node" of the solution tree, as shown in Figure 1-12.

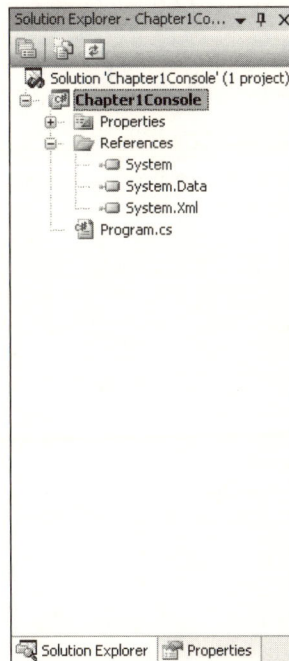

Figure 1-12

You can see the files that are referenced listed in Figure 1-12. These files are called .NET assemblies and contain classes that you will use to create your application. .NET assemblies and classes are both discussed further in Chapter 4, "Introducing .NET."

The following are additional tools that are not displayed but are used throughout the book:

❑ **Toolbox:** This pane contains controls that you add to your forms, and changes based on what type of applications you create.

❑ **Data Sources:** This tool helps you maintain and work with data in your application.

❑ **Console**: This is where you display output in both console applications and when debugging your applications.

❑ **Properties:** You use this tool to set various properties of different objects you will use in your projects. An example of an object could be the text of a label control, used to display literal values.

Note that some of the tools and their panes will appear as needed depending on where you are in the IDE. Now it's time to discuss how C# Express applications are structured in more depth.

Structure of C# Express Solutions and Projects

It can be kind of confusing as various terms are being whipped around. A couple of those terms are *solution* versus *project*. Are they the same? The answer is not really, but they can be. How is that for a definitive answer?

When you create a new project, a solution is created for you automatically. You can have multiple projects in a single solution. In fact, you can even have different types of projects, including different languages. For example: If I had a developer friend who has developed a useful tool that I want to include in my application, and it was created using Visual Basic .NET, I could still use it in my solution by creating a reference to it. I also could edit the code if needed by adding the existing project to the current solution. (For the majority of this book you will be using a single solution containing a single project.)

To finish off this chapter, you will add a line of code that performs the classic task of displaying the phrase "Hello World." The exact syntax that you are writing will actually be discussed later; I just want you to have the satisfying experience of creating and running an application.

Try It Out   Completing the First C# Express Project

With the project you created in the first Try It Out:

1. Place the cursor between the opening and closing brackets, under the line of code that starts with the word "static."

2. Type the command:

```
Console.WriteLine("Hello World");
```

The editor then changes the colors of the words appropriately. Editing your applications is discussed further in Chapter 3, "Quick Start Creating Your First C# Express Windows Project." The IDE then looks something like Figure 1-13.

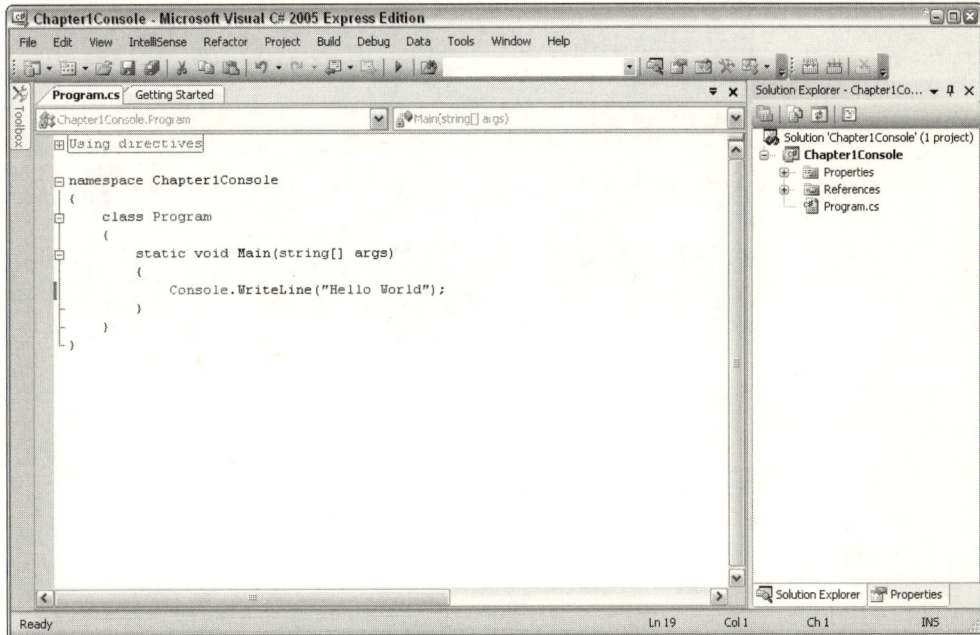

Figure 1-13

You have actually completed your first C# console application. Now you just have to build and compile it.

3. Select Debug → Start. This builds, compiles, and runs your application. Alternatively, you can press F5.

Now the Console window appears in the lower left corner of the IDE with the words "Hello World" displayed, as shown in Figure 1-14.

There you have it, your first application. Now it may not seem like much, but it is a start. What you did was tell the computer to print (WriteLine) the words "Hello World" into the Console window.

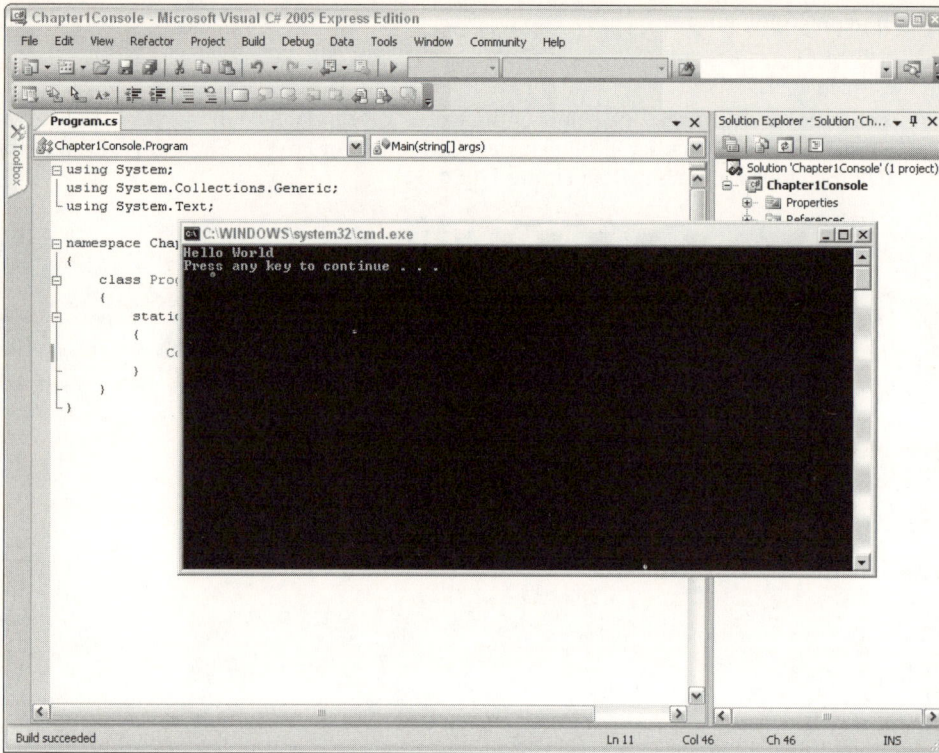

Figure 1-14

Summary

Microsoft Visual C# 2005 Express is one of a series of applications created to introduce you to the world of programming. You have now installed the C# Express IDE onto your system, and even know what the initials "IDE" stands for. You have also learned that with C# Express you can create different types of applications depending on which template you use.

When you first open C# Express, you are taken to the Getting Started page, which has three categories of help, as well as links to other Web sites with additional articles and downloads.

In C# Express, you create projects, which are part of an overall solution. You can manage your project using the Solution Explorer and edit code using the Main Editor window. In this chapter you created your first console application. Then you built, compiled, and ran it, displaying information in the Console window.

Exercises

1. What is the difference between Visual C# and Visual C# Express?

2. What are the three categories on the C# Express start page?

3. What does the acronym IDE stand for?

4. Name three of the tools available in the C# Express IDE.

5. What is the difference between a console application and Windows application?

2

Programming 101: A Quick Discussion

You, as the reader, may not be a computer scientist. In fact, I would bet my special edition version of HALO 2 that you aren't. If you were, you wouldn't deem it necessary to read an introductory book to anything. Therefore, since you have not probably studied software development to any extent, this is a good chapter for you. In fact, if your computer science teacher or professor were to read this chapter, they might cringe in their Birkenstocks, because this chapter briefly gives an overview of programming in general. There are whole series of books on the topic; I'm just trying to provide some understanding about why you have to perform some of the steps you do in programming.

When doing any kind of programming, you should first understand some of the terms and concepts behind it, and just what it entails. While the majority of the book will have you coding and creating actual programs, for this chapter you can sit back and relax in a nice comfortable recliner and read away. This chapter:

- ❏ Gives a history of programming and talks about software versus hardware.
- ❏ Discusses the differences being compiled and interpreted languages.
- ❏ Goes over Windows programming and discuss events.

What Is Programming?

Nowadays, even those who are just end users of computer have heard the term "computer programming". In the real world you heard about various cults which "program" their members into believing or behaving certain ways. Computer programming is basically the same thing, only it you, the new developer, telling the computer what to do. (The believe part doesn't carry over as well, but you get the idea.) Over the years there have been different ways to tell the computer what to do, and the exciting news is it is getting easier as time goes on.

This chapter talks about some of the "languages" that have been used to tell the computer what to do, and how it is accomplished today. To start, you need to know more about what it means to program a computer.

General Programming Overview

When you are programming a computer, you are giving commands to it. These commands come in the form of line of code called *statements* that are grouped together to form one or more tasks. An example is in accounting software when an end-of-month report must be created. Code would be written to accomplish this. In C# this code can be found in the form of methods that you write in programs and store on the computer's hard drive to perform again when needed. You will be hearing more on methods as you work throughout the book.

Hardware versus Software

This may seem like a simplistic topic, but some people when they start out programming still have a question about hardware versus software. Hardware is the physical computer components such as monitors, drives, and the box itself.

> *You can, in fact, program hardware, and C has been used for this purpose, but you are then creating software that runs on the hardware. When you are developing programming for hardware, you generally are writing programming for very low-level systems where the program is then put on the chip that is the CPU (central processing unit) of the computer itself, or on various peripherals such as printers, modems, and so on.*

There are different levels and types of software programs (applications) you can write. Following are some examples:

❑ **Operating system level.** This type is used to create programs that manipulate the operating system to perform a function.

❑ **Drivers and utilities.** Good examples of drivers are printer drivers. These work with various ports on the computers to help certain hardware work with various operating systems.

❑ **Video games.** This type of software takes a lot of skill and creativity; video game development, even though it sounds glamorous, is some of the toughest software to create.

❑ **Business applications.** Accounting applications and software such as Microsoft Office applications are used by the millions daily.

There are many more types of applications that you can create, and the cool thing is now you can write them all using C#.

Programming Then and Now

In the last 50 years of software development, there have been perhaps thousands of different software languages created. However, punch-card technology was used as far back as the 1800s. With this technology, holes punched in each card told the computer specific commands based on their locations and groupings. Unfortunately, you were in a lot of trouble if you dropped these cards, because an application could require hundreds of cards.

Some of the first hardware "programming" was performed by throwing switches on the front panel of a humongous (technical term) computer that can't even match the power of the simplest calculators nowadays. In the mid-1950s the first operating system was created, and programs were then able to be stored on magnetic tape, although punch cards were still used. From the 1950s on, other programming languages were created such as Assembler, COBOL, FORTRAN, and Pascal. Each language tended to lean toward one type of industry over another. For example, COBOL is mainly used for business applications, whereas FORTRAN is known for scientific applications. Assembler was designed for creating system-level utilities, as well as compilers for the other programming languages. Compilers are discussed in the next section. Some languages, such as Basic, are used in the various industries. Many versions of each language have been created.

When personal computers came out in the early 1970s, Microsoft then brought the Basic language to the Altair PC.

> *Two nerd trivia answers:*
>
> *—BASIC stands for Beginner's All-purpose Symbolic Instruction Language.*
>
> *—The Altair PC was named after the planet in* Star Trek.

C programming, the grandfather of C#, came into being right around 1970 and was originally created for the UNIX operating system. The C language was then brought over to the PC and not only took the place of other low-level languages such as Assembler but also was used for creating business-type applications. C++ was then created to take C into object-oriented programming (OOP), introducing inherited and black box programming (discussed further in the section called "What about OOP?" coming up in the chapter).

The majority of the programs were created using text editors, and the programming languages were then linked and compiled by using command-line instructions (remember the DOS prompt?). Then Microsoft and other companies came out with more visual tools for creating applications, with Microsoft calling their line of programming languages Visual Basic, Visual C++, and so on. Currently, Visual Studio.NET is their tool for editing and maintaining their various languages such as Visual Basic.NET and Visual C#.

With the .NET platform, the playing field has been leveled out for Visual Basic and C# so that developers can choose which language they are comfortable with based on their experience. While syntactically different, they use the same type libraries and compile down to the same language with .NET. The .NET Framework is discussed in greater detail in Chapter 4.

Compiled versus Interpreted

Besides purpose and ease of use, another difference between programming languages is whether they are interpreted or compiled. Before you learn how both compiling and interpreting works with programming, think about when somebody gives a speech in another language, such as Spanish. Sometimes a person will be beside the speaker repeating each sentence in English. This person is called an interpreter. If the speaker gives her speech in Spanish, and then someone writes it out or tapes it in English, then the speech is being *compiled* into English. The same works for programming.

Interpreted

When a programming language is interpreted, you write your code and run the application. Each line of code is then interpreted as it runs and is changed into machine code at that moment. The good thing was that you could run your code, have it break, fix it, and continue on from there. The language didn't require the linking and compilation time of other languages. The downside was these languages tended to be slower to run. The Basic language was an interpreted language when it started, but then compiled versions of the language began appearing in the 1980s. Most Web scripting is also interpreted today.

Compiled

Compiled languages would compile the code you wrote into executables (*.exe), which are more at the machine level and therefore much quicker to execute. However, this meant that you would have to write your code and link the application (now called building), which entailed specifying the various pieces of the applications to include, such as your code files and any other support files necessary. After linking the files, you then had to compile the applications. At the time of compiling, some errors would occur, and you would fix the application, then relink and recompile.

If the application got through the compile without any syntax errors, you could run the application. However, if errors occurred at that time, you would have to then find and fix the error and then relink and recompile.

C# Express

The awesome news is developers today have the best of both worlds. Visual C# Express does build and compile your applications, but it is:

❏ **Extremely quick and convenient.** By pressing F5 in the IDE, C# Express builds and compiles your solution, then runs the applications if no errors exist.

❏ **Very helpful with errors.** Now when you receive errors when building and compiling, those errors are listed in a task pane at the bottom of the IDE, and the errors are highlighted nicely in the code. It even provides additional help regarding the errors in the form of ScreenTips when you place the cursor over them.

❏ **Change code and continue.** Once only available in interpreted languages, if your application breaks when running, you can change the code and continue without having to reset the whole application. This feature rocks and will mean much more to you as you work through the rest of the book.

What about OOP?

OOP, or *object-orientated programming*, is a programming paradigm in which the developer focuses on objects, such as a form, that are derived from *classes*, which are like a cookie cutter for the objects. In C# a good example is *controls*, such as `TextBox` controls that you use. Each has *properties*, which describe something about the object created, such as the Width and Height properties, and *methods*, which perform actions with and for the objects, in this case, the `TextBox` controls.

The concept of black box programming means that you will be organizing your classes such that once you have created and tested them, the other parts of the program, or other developers, don't have to know about what commands are being used inside the class to use the methods and properties of that class. The class itself is like a "black box" to those using them.

With OOP you also get inheritance. *Inheritance* in this case means being able to create your own class based on another class, adding features to that new class. Say, for example, you want to create a new type of `TextBox` control with more features than the standard one.

The .NET framework is built around OOP features, and you can use its classes for your own use. Chapter 4 discusses this in more detail. For now, remember that even the forms you work with are actually classes with the above-mentioned properties and methods, as well as, which are discussed in the section called "Event Programming" later in this chapter.

Introduction to Windows Programming

With the introduction of Windows 3.0 in 1990, the programming world once again changed tremendously. With Windows programming came a whole new way of thinking for developers when developing applications.

Different Levels of Programming

Nowadays, when developing in the Windows environment, you have so much power because you not only have control over your application but also access to the very Windows system environment itself. In the past, application programming and system programming were very separate areas of development, but now the line has blurred quite a bit, especially with the introduction of the .NET development platform. I find myself performing system-level tasks such as logging errors into the Windows event log in my application programming. Following are different levels of programming:

- ❑ **Desktop application programming.** Involves programs that perform tasks such as business applications or video games. Included in the business category of development are applications you purchase such as Microsoft Word and Excel.

- ❑ **System programming.** Involves programs that are used "under the covers" by Windows to accomplish system-level tasks. Also, when the program manages a feature of Windows, system programming is being used.

- ❑ **Web development.** Created specifically to run in browsers, these applications can now utilize both HTML and programming languages to develop applications used across the Internet.

As mentioned, the lines between these three types of programming blur because you can now access the Web and perform system functions right from within desktop applications you create with very little effort. Web access from with your applications is discussed further in Chapter 15.

One of the terms synonymous with Windows programming is event programming.

Event Programming

Events in Windows are much like events in real life. An event occurs when an action takes place. When the day of your birth occurs once a year, a birthday occurs. The birthday is an event. In a Windows application, when a user clicks a button, an event occurs. There are events for many different actions that occur within Windows and Windows applications. Because Windows is a multitasking environment, how can you deal with multiple applications running simultaneously? Answer: With events — you only respond to what the user is currently doing; other code can wait "in the background" until it is needed

Which events exist depends on which Windows system you are working with, the development environment, or programming language you are using. With applications, depending on the language, you can create your own events on objects in the applications.

In the first chapter you created a Windows form using C# Express. Window forms have specific events built in, and because it is so flexible, you can create additional ones if needed. The following table describes some of the more common events you will use with forms.

Event	Description
Activate	Occurs when a form is activated, such as when the focus switches from another form onto the current form.
Close	Occurs when a form closes.
Load	Occurs when a form is loaded.
Deactivate	Occurs when the focus switches from the current form to another.

Controls used on forms also use events. The Click event of the button mentioned earlier in the section is an example. Developers can program code for these events. You will learn about the code throughout the rest of the book, starting with the next chapter.

Dynamic-Link Libraries

One of the features introduced with Windows programming are dynamic-link libraries. Prior to Windows, when applications were created, you could link libraries of routines into your own applications. The problem was that when a library changed that was used by many applications, all of those applications had to be relinked and recompiled.

With the dynamic-link libraries, which usually have the extension .dll, you can change routines in the library itself and recompile them, and all the applications would then be able to utilize them without having to be relinked and recompiled. You can use those libraries in various applications without having to rewrite the code.

Using DLLs is very convenient. However, as new versions of DLLs are introduced, problems can occur such as the application getting confused as to which version of the DLL to use. This is known as DLL hell, another technical term. Fortunately, .NET has solved a number of these issues by introducing versioning and wrapping up system DLLs for developers.

Summary

Since punch cards, computer programming has been developing for good number of years and has seen tremendous advances in the last 50 years. Programming languages can be interpreted or compiled, with benefits being seen in both. Microsoft has worked to take the best of both into their new .NET programming languages.

Windows programming has advanced software development with event programming and dynamic-link libraries. With events you can create applications that react to the user's needs and actions.

Exercises

1. What is the difference between hardware and software?

2. What are the differences between compiled and interpreted?

3. Name the three levels of Windows programming mentioned in the chapter.

4. What are dynamic-link libraries used for?

3

Quick Start Creating Your First C# Express Windows Project

The first couple chapters have given you a small taste of what it takes to use C# Express to create your applications. The applications haven't had any kind of user interface such as a Windows form involved. The various C languages in the past have been used for lower-level programming, such as creating compilers and other system-level programs that don't require interfaces. This is mainly because of the effort it takes to create those forms in the lower-level languages. Now with Visual C# Express and the professional Visual Studio .NET tools, creating business programs using C# having user interfaces is as easy as using other languages such as Visual Basic .NET. In fact, you will use the same .NET classes to accomplish creating the interfaces.

There are two kinds of interface programming templates: Web form applications and Windows (form) applications. However, in C# Express, only the latter is included. There are a lot of things to learn about creating and working with programming Windows applications using C#, and I want you to jump in and get some experience with it before delving deeper into how to program forms to a greater degree in Part II, "Creating Applications with C# Express."

In this chapter, you will learn:

- ❑ How to decide which type of application template to use.
- ❑ How to create your first Windows application.
- ❑ What makes up a Windows form.
- ❑ How to add text boxes and a button control to a Windows form.
- ❑ How to work with code on form and control events event.

Which Type of Application to Create: Windows or Console?

In Chapter 2, you learned what software development is about and got acquainted with Windows event programming. In C# you will use those concepts in just about all the applications you create, but there are some further distinctions that you need to understand first.

Differences between Using Windows and Console Applications

It is kind of a misnomer to say that Windows and console applications are that different just by their given name, since you are still going to be working with the Windows operating system in a console application and accomplishing tasks that a console application would perform within a Windows application. The real difference is the lack of including a user interface in console applications, meaning you aren't using forms to display or retrieve information.

Purposes for Using Windows and Console Applications

The real difference between the two types of projects is the purpose of your final application. C# Express includes templates for each type so that you can start out with only the necessary files in your project. Those types are Windows and console applications.

Console Application

Console applications, lacking the user interface, are great for utilities that need to run without user intervention. For example, I have used console applications for updating stock figures once a day from S&P 500 stocks into a SQL Server database. This capability is discussed further in Chapter 15, "Using Web Services from Your C# Application." Because this application is scheduled by the system to run at a certain time in the day and does not require a user to do anything, it is a perfect console application.

Windows Application

Windows applications cover a wide range of applications. Anything from business applications to utilities and video games are considered Windows applications. Basically, most of the applications that require user interfaces such as forms are Windows applications.

Getting Started with Windows Application Projects

When creating a Windows application project, you choose the Windows Application template from the list of templates in the New Project dialog box. Once you have supplied the name for the project and clicked OK, the new project is created. Unlike the Console Application project template, which takes you into a class module, when the Windows application project is created, a file representing a form is displayed. Before I address the various types of files used in an Windows application type project, take the time to create your first Windows application project.

Try It Out   Creating a Windows Project

Just to start nice and clean, close C# Express if you have it opened. Next:

1.   Open C# Express. The Start Page appears, as shown in Figure 3-1.

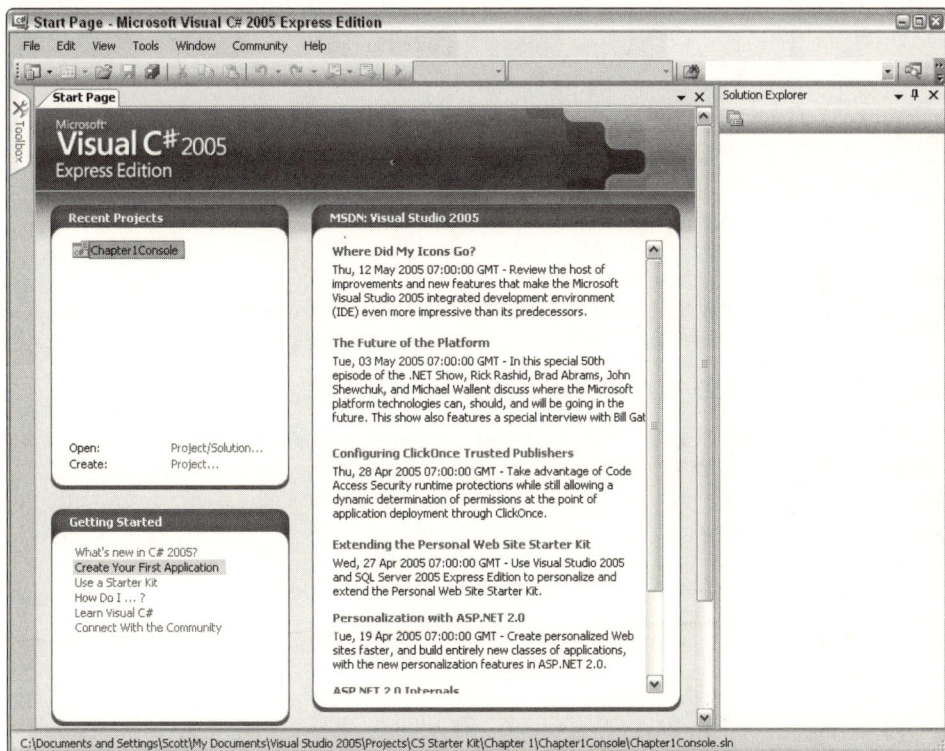

Figure 3-1

2. Choose Project from the File ⇨ New menu.

You may be tempted, as I was, to click the topic "Create Your First Application" in the Getting Started section. Don't. Remember, this is just the help topic and does not perform the task.

3. The New Project dialog box appears, displaying the various types of projects you can create. Highlight Windows Application.

4. In the Name field, type the name you want to call the project. For this example, Chapter3FirstWinApp was used, as shown in Figure 3-2.

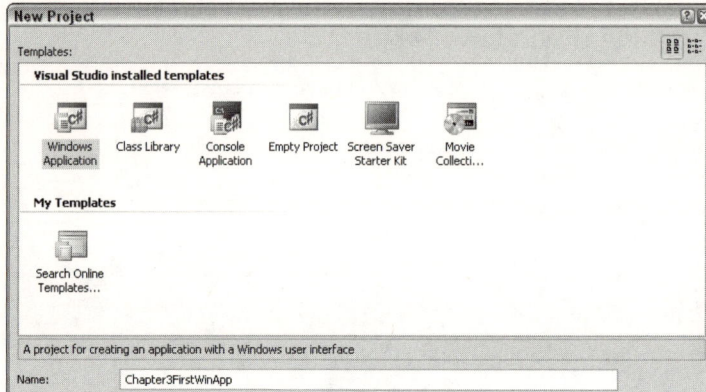

Figure 3-2

5. Click OK. The project files are created, and a form appears, as shown in Figure 3-3.

Setting the IDE up for a Windows Application Project

In a perfect world, the C# Express IDE would display all the panels you desire and need for a Windows application project. But it doesn't happen, because the IDE will open up with whatever settings you used the last time you were working in C# Express. If you were editing a console application project the last time, the editor is not set up for what you want to do this time.

Here are a couple of the items shown in Figure 3-3 and one that you will add.

❑ **Toolbox.** Needs to be pinned opened. The Toolbox contains controls that you will want to use on your forms.

❑ **Solution Explorer.** Can be expanded so you can see more of the various files used in the project.

❑ **Properties pane.** As with the Toolbox, this pane is used quite a bit with forms and controls, and is very handy to have displayed under the Solutions Explorer. You will add this in the following Try It Out.

Toolbox   Properties Pane   Solution Explorer

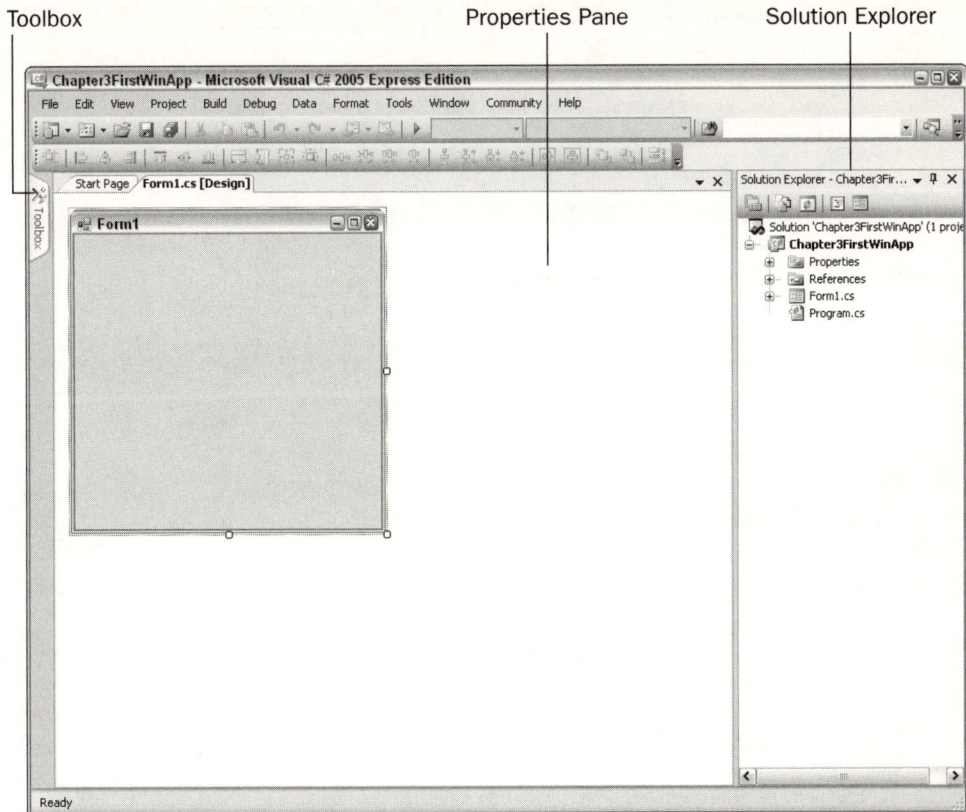

Figure 3-3

All of the settings listed in the preceding list are really up to your personal preferences. I happen to have found them to be particularly useful when working on Windows application type projects. Also, your IDE may be set up differently if you have been working on other projects, so some of the steps in the next Try It Out may not be necessary.

Now you will work through setting up the IDE as described in the prior list.

Try It Out   Setting up the IDE for a Windows Application Project

You will be using the project created in the first Try It Out. Again, because you are practicing opening C# Express and locating projects, close C# Express if it is opened. Now:

1. Open C# Express. The Start Page appears. This time, instead of using the New Project dialog box, you will open the existing project you created.

2. You will see the file you want to locate in the Recent Project pane on the Start Page and will see a hand cursor displayed when you placed over the file name, as shown in Figure 3-4.

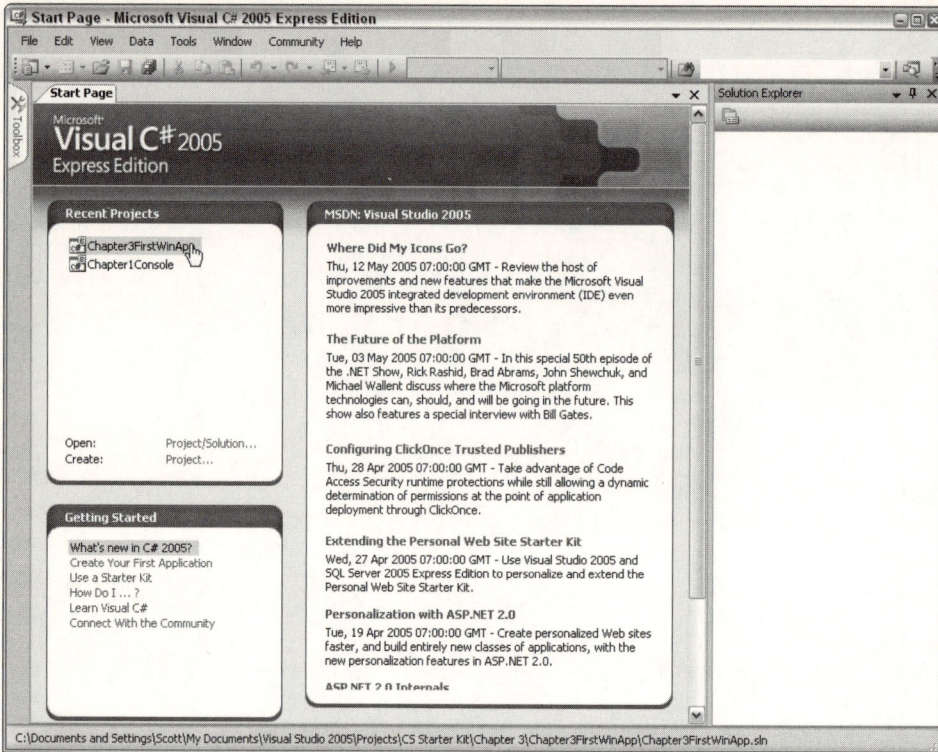

Figure 3-4

3. Select the project you want to use. The project is displayed again, with the settings as they were in Figure 3-3. It's time now to open the Properties pane.

4. Select View ⇨ Properties, the Properties pane will now be displayed as shown in Figure 3-5.

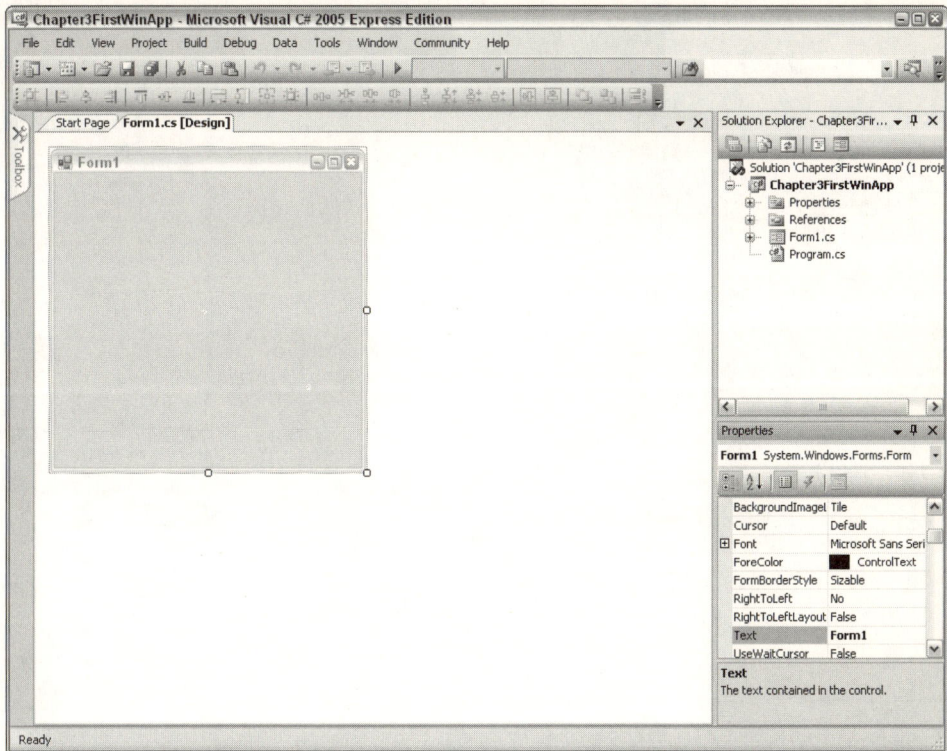

Figure 3-5

5.   Place the mouse on the left side of the Solution Explorer so that the mouse changes to the two arrows going up and down. See Figure 3-6.

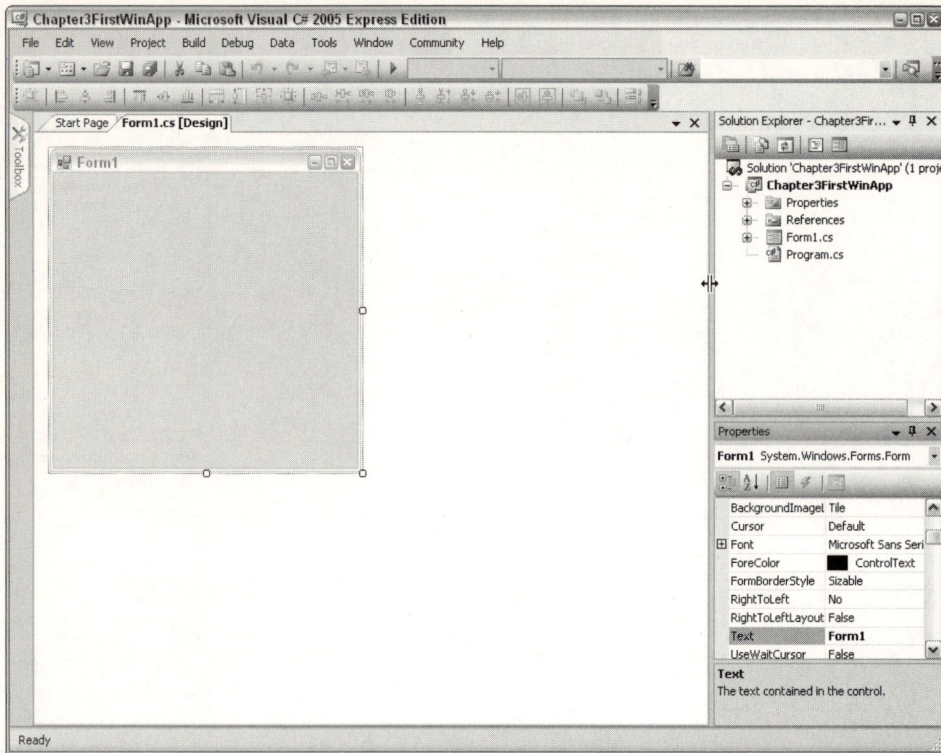

Figure 3-6

6. Press and hold the left mouse button, dragging the border of the pane to the left.

7. Release the mouse button when you can see all of the text in the Solution Explorer. Next it is time to open and pin the Toolbox.

8. Place the cursor over the Toolbox tag, located on the left side of the IDE. The Toolbox pane slides out.

9. Highlight the pin located next to Close button of the pane. In Figure 3-7, the pin is highlighted and the Auto Hide text is displayed. If you click this button, the Toolbox pane remains open.

10. Click the auto hide pin.

You are now ready to work on the Windows application project.

Right now if you run this application, you will just get a blank form, which is not very exciting on the surface. But a blank form in this context isn't completely unexciting when you consider what has been done. Despite being blank, C# Express has created a lot of Windows functionality — moving the form, resizing the form, minimizing, maximizing, and so on.

In a few pages, you will add a couple of controls and display the result. But first take a look at what is included when you created the form, and what is displayed in the Solution Explorer.

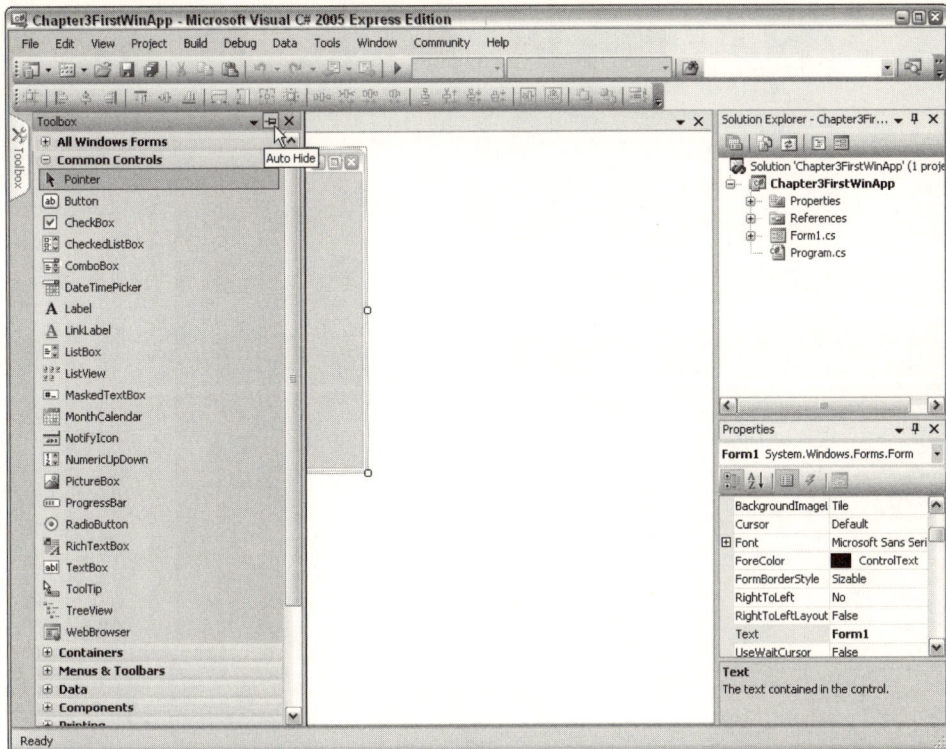

Figure 3-7

Overview of the Solution Explorer

The Solution Explorer was discussed briefly in Chapter 1, "Starting Strong with Visual C# 2005 Express Edition," explaining that it is the pane in the C# Express IDE that helps you maintain your projects.

Project Elements Controlled Using the Solution Explorer

With the Solution Explorer, you will:

❑ **View various files used in the project.** Projects are made up of multiple types of files, with extensions. The next section describes some of those types of files and their purposes. Besides double-clicking on a file with the left mouse button to edit a file, you can right-click a file and perform various tasks depending on the type of file.

❑ **Use references.** These references point to or include .NET assemblies, which are libraries of code that can be used to accomplish the tasks in your application. References can also be made to include other projects you have created and want to use in the current application. You will learn more about .NET assemblies in the Chapter 4, "Introducing .NET." You can see the references set up by C# Express by default in Figure 3-9.

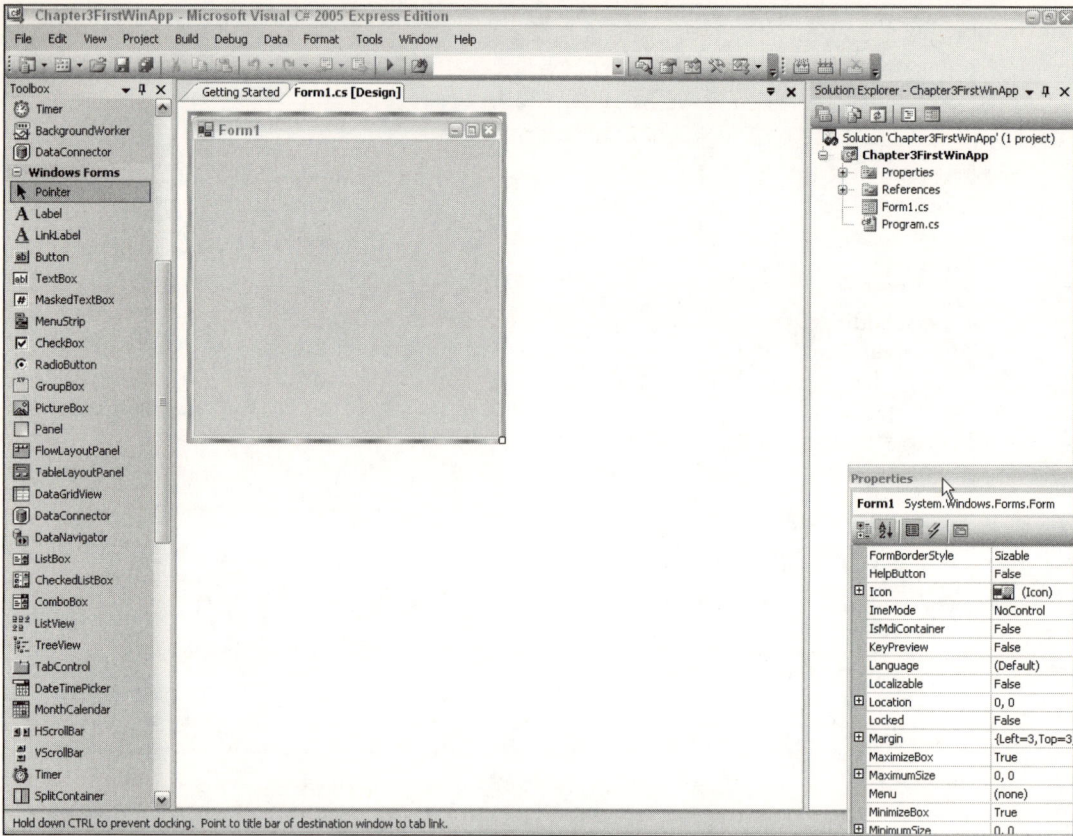

Figure 3-8

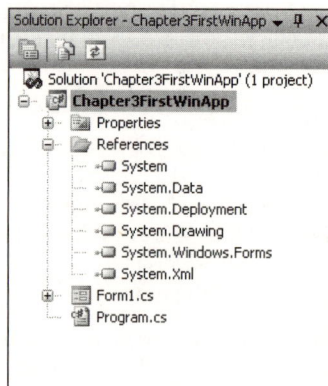

Figure 3-9

❑ **Use project properties.** Properties describe different aspects, or features, of whatever object they are on. For example, you can have properties that describe forms and controls, as explained further in the section titled "Discussion about Properties," later in this chapter. In the case of the project properties, various files are stored that describe various aspects of the project. The good news is you don't have to do anything with the files in the short term. Later on as you get more advanced in your programming skills, you may have to but not for a while.

Files Used in Windows Application Projects

Depending on which kind of project you are working with, you will have different file types displayed in the Solution Explorer. In the current type, you can see two files with the extension of .cs (C#). Notice also that even though both have the extension of cs, they have different icons representing the type of file they are.

You can create additional folders and store various types of the files, including graphic files or whatever you need for your project. Which files are used will totally depend on your project. Also, under the covers there are folders and files that are used for the project that aren't displayed by default. An example is that forms consist of two files: the code file and the designer information file. You can see these files by choosing Project ⇨ Show All Files. A plus (+) symbol appears by the form files. If you click the plus symbol, another file appears. In Figure 3-10 a couple of folders also are displayed.

Figure 3-10

For the most part, you really don't need to see all the files necessary for the project, because C# Express handles most of them for you and only has you deal with the necessary ones. But it is nice to know that you have the capability to track additional files and check out the ones that are there in the Explorer.

Discussion about Properties

Before jumping into adding to the Windows project you created, we should discuss properties in greater detail. As mentioned, properties, also called attributes, describe something about their object. A good example is the properties of the form you created in the first Try It Out. You can see some of those properties listed in the property sheet in Figure 3-11.

You can set properties for various objects such as controls and forms during both design time, as shown in Figure 3-11, and runtime, when the application is running. The various categories of properties for forms and controls are detailed in Chapter 8 "Working with Forms and Controls."

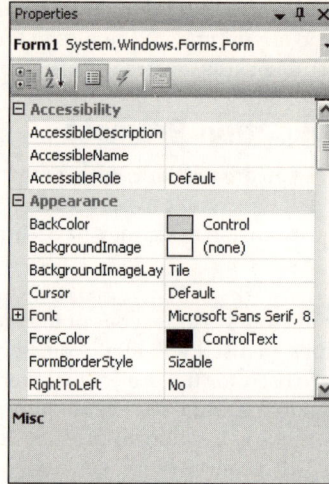

Figure 3-11

Try It Out   Change the Caption in a Form

You can see in Figure 3-11 that the value types in a Text property of a form is actually the caption displayed in the title bar of a form. Taking the project you create at the start of the chapter:

1. Double-click Form1.cs in the Solution Explorer if it is not already opened.

2. In the Properties pane, locate the Text property of the form.

3. Type **My First Form** in the Text property. You can see this in Figure 3-12.

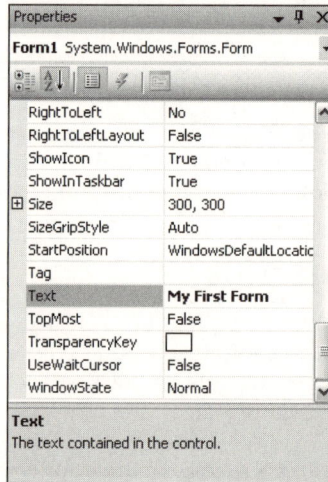

Figure 3-12

When you leave the property, you will see the caption change at the top of the form displayed in the design mode.

4. Press F5 to run the application. C# Express tests and builds your application for you, then runs it. The final form is shown in Figure 3-13.

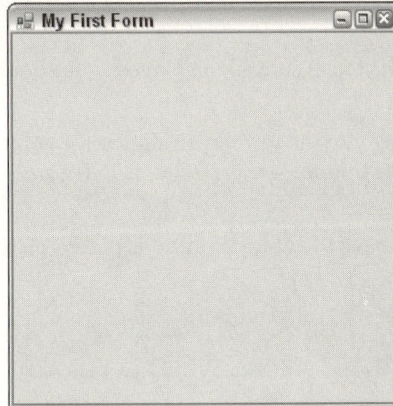

Figure 3-13

Not very exciting, but hey, you've got to start somewhere. Now it is time to add some controls to the form and make it a little more interesting. Click the Close button, which is the X in the top right corner of the form.

Adding Controls to the Form

A form doesn't do much good by itself without any controls to display or input data with. There are hundreds of controls that you can use on forms. Some of the most common controls are shown in the following list. These controls also are used in the rest of this chapter.

❏   **Text boxes.** Used for enabling input or display of text.

❏   **Labels.** Used to display text.

❏   **Buttons.** Also called command buttons, code can be attached to these to perform tasks.

Adding controls to your form using the designer is as simple as dragging and dropping them onto the form. Adding code to them and using events as described in Chapter 2 takes a little more work. Once you have added controls to a form, you can resize, move, and modify their properties as needed. These actions are discussed further in Chapter 8, "Working with Forms and Controls."

Because the purpose of this chapter is to get you going with creating the form, let's get busy. For the purpose of the remainder of this chapter, you will be adding three text boxes and a command button. In a separate Try It Out, you will then add code to the command button that will take the values entered into the first two text boxes and display them in the third text box.

Try It Out   Adding Three Labels and Text Boxes, and a Button to a Form

Although this seems like an ambitious task, adding these controls is really simple. Using the form you have been using this whole chapter:

1. Make sure that the Common Controls is the displayed category in the Toolbox by clicking the minus symbols of the other categories of tools, if they are displayed.

2. Place the cursor over the Label control, displayed in the Toolbox, and hold down the left mouse button.

3. Drag and drop the label onto the form by dragging the control from the Toolbox onto the form and releasing the mouse button. You can see this in Figure 3-14, just before the mouse button is released.

   Once the mouse is released, the Label control is placed on the form in the location you put it in.

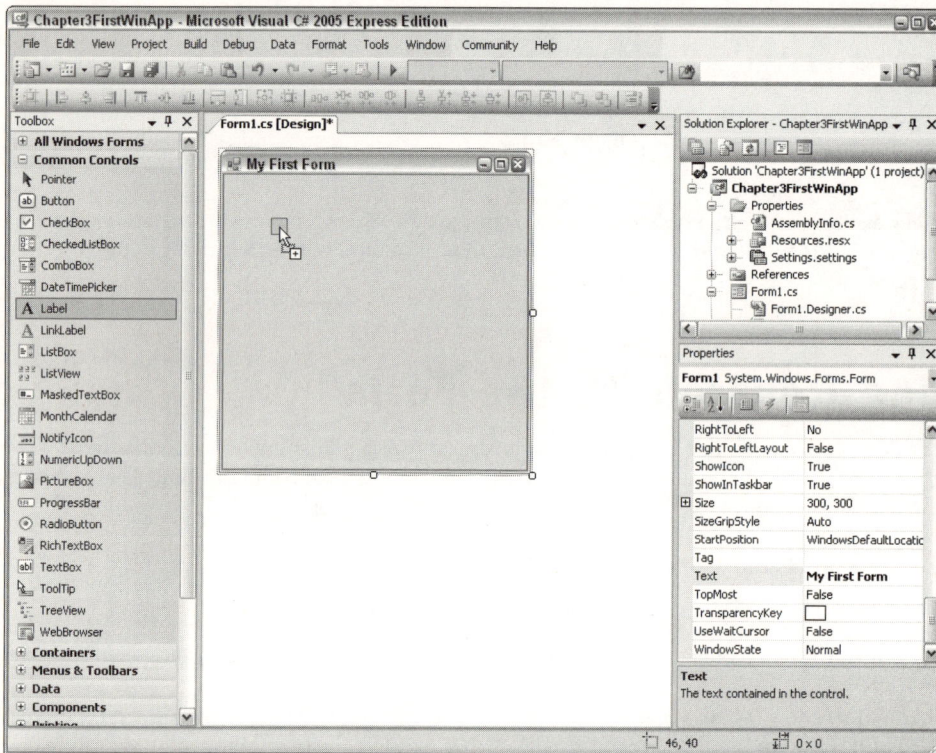

Figure 3-14

4. Locate the `Text` property of the `Label` control you place on the form.

5. Type **Value 1** for the `Text` property. If you press Enter or move out of the property, the text in the label is updated, as shown in Figure 3-15.

6. Drag and drop a `TextBox` control using the steps just described for the `Label` control on the form next to the `Label` control.

After you release the mouse button, you will then see the `TextBox` control shown in Figure 3-16.

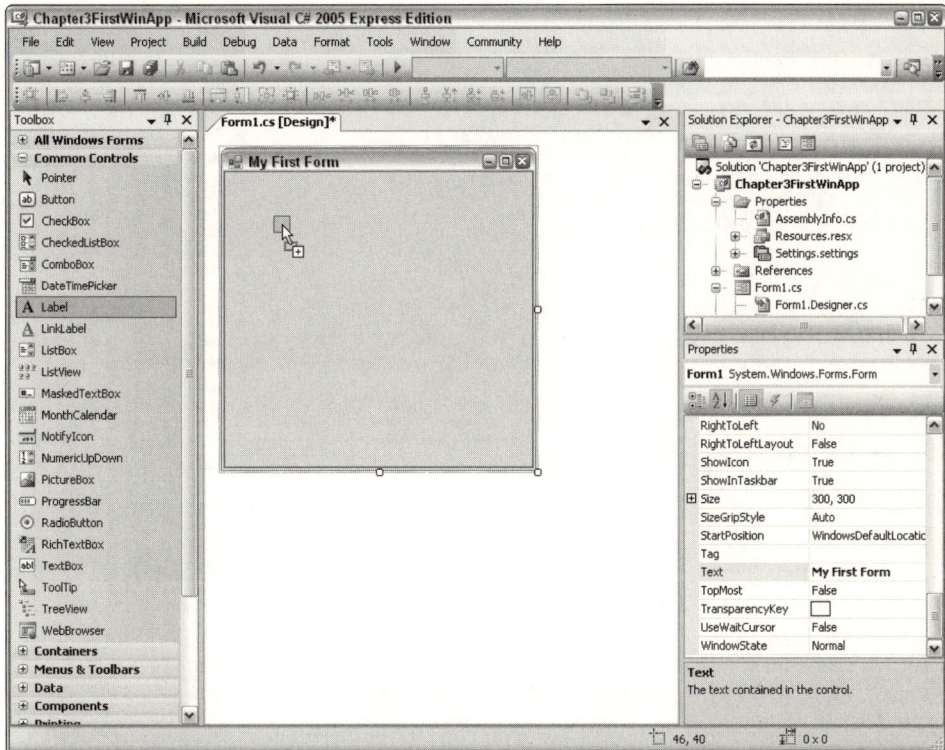

Figure 3-15

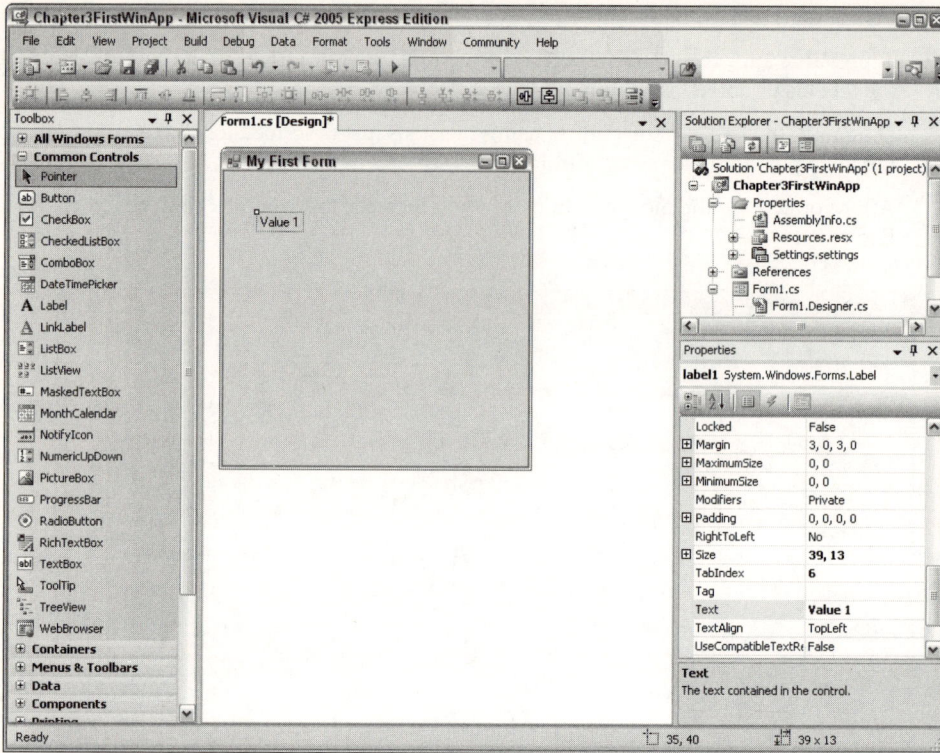

Figure 3-16

7. Repeat Steps 2 through 6 for two more `Label` and `TextBox` controls, setting the `Text` property for the `Label`s to "Value 2" and "Sum," and arrange them as displayed in Figure 3-17.

Normally you would be changing the names of controls to be a little more meaningful, but since the idea behind this chapter is to get you going quickly, I am holding off harping on that. This is discussed in more detail in Chapter 8.

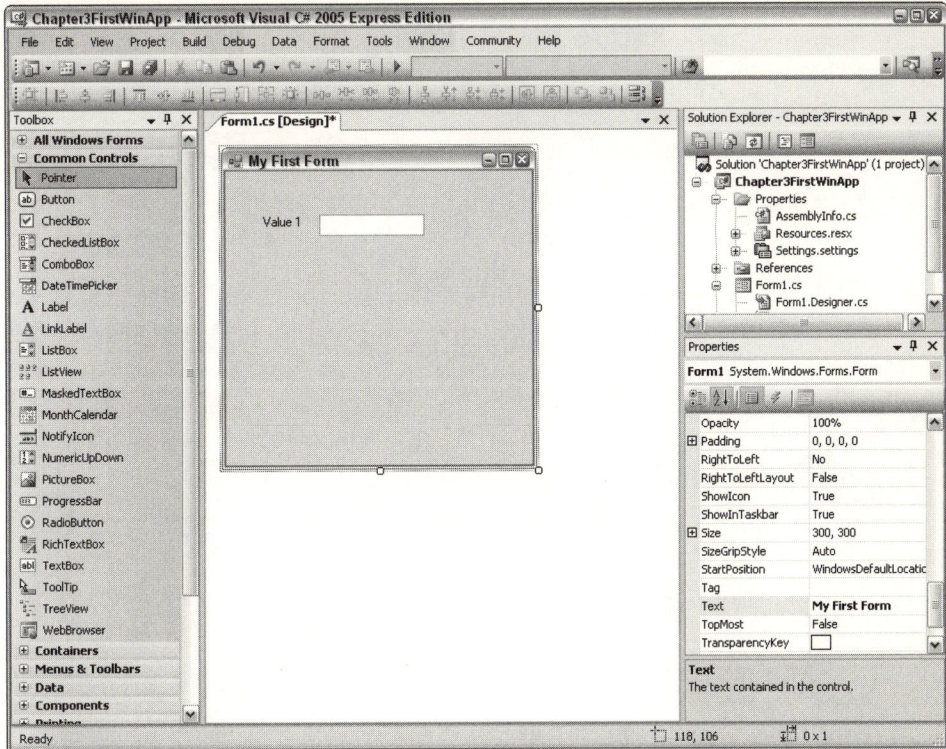

Figure 3-17

8. Drag and drop a `Button` control from the Toolbox on the form beside the last `TextBox` control you placed on the form.

9. Change the `Text` property of the button to be "Sum Values." The `Text` property of the button is actually the caption displayed on the button. You can see what the form now looks like in Figure 3-18.

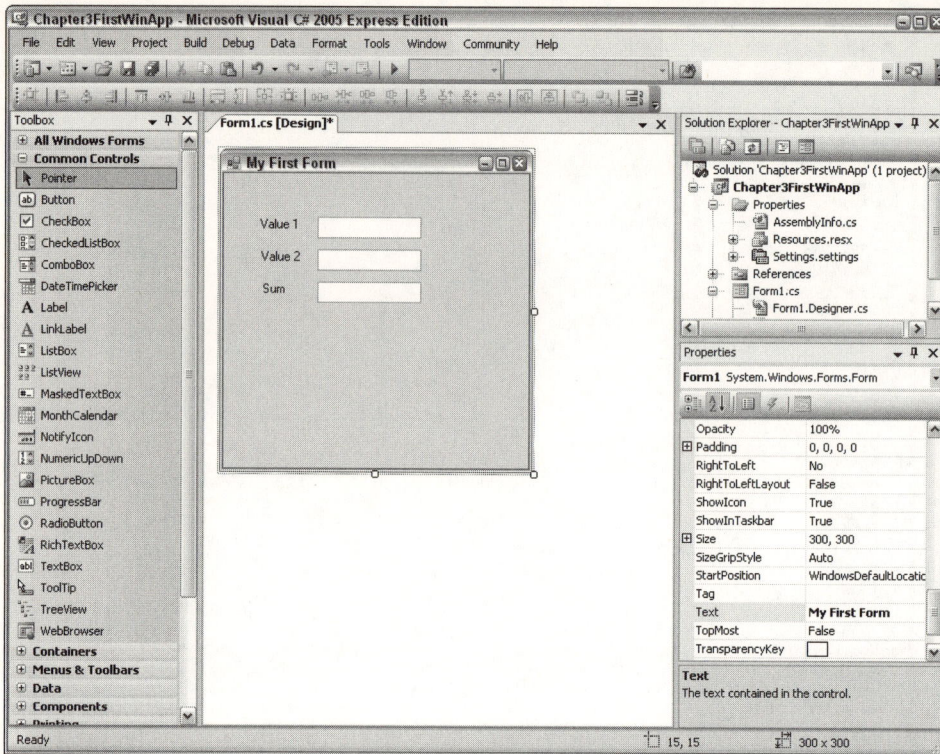

Figure 3-18

Okay, you have now created a form and placed controls on it. If you press F5 at this point, you would see the controls and could enter information into the three text boxes. You also could click the Sum Values button. However, nothing would happen, because you haven't told the computer, by using code, to do anything. To do so, you will write C# in an event on the button.

Working with Code on an Event

Events and the coding of the events were discussed in the last chapter, but they were not actually demonstrated. In this section you perform this task yourself. Although it sounds intimidating, it doesn't have to be. The list of events is discussed further in Chapter 8, but in this section you will use the `Click` event of the button to write code that will add the values entered into the first two text boxes into the third text box.

> Note that no error trapping of any kind is covered in this chapter. This means if you type nonnumeric values into your text boxes, or no values at all, errors will occur.

To add code to a default event of a control, you double-click the control in the designer. Most controls have default events. These events are those that are most likely to be used. For buttons it is the `Click` event.

After you double-click a button, you are taken into the code behind the form. You can see the code behind Form1 in Figure 3-19.

The editor places you on the spot where you need to be. Form class modules and the actual code syntax are discussed further in Chapter 8, but for now, focus on the lines that read:

```
private void button1_Click(object sender, EventArgs e)
{

}
```

C# Express wrote these lines of code, and additional code, so that you didn't have to. When you write C# commands, they are performed when the event, in this case the `Click` event, occurs. The commands can be anything from displaying a simple message to performing a number of intricate tasks, depending on your needs. In the case of the form you are working on, you will be adding the values entered into the text boxes together.

Now, in C# you can't just add two values together from text boxes. You need to convert the values, stored in the `Text` property of the text boxes, to a numeric type value. To accomplish this, you use the `ToInt16()` method of `System.Convert` .NET object. You then take the value returned from adding the text boxes together and convert it back to a string.

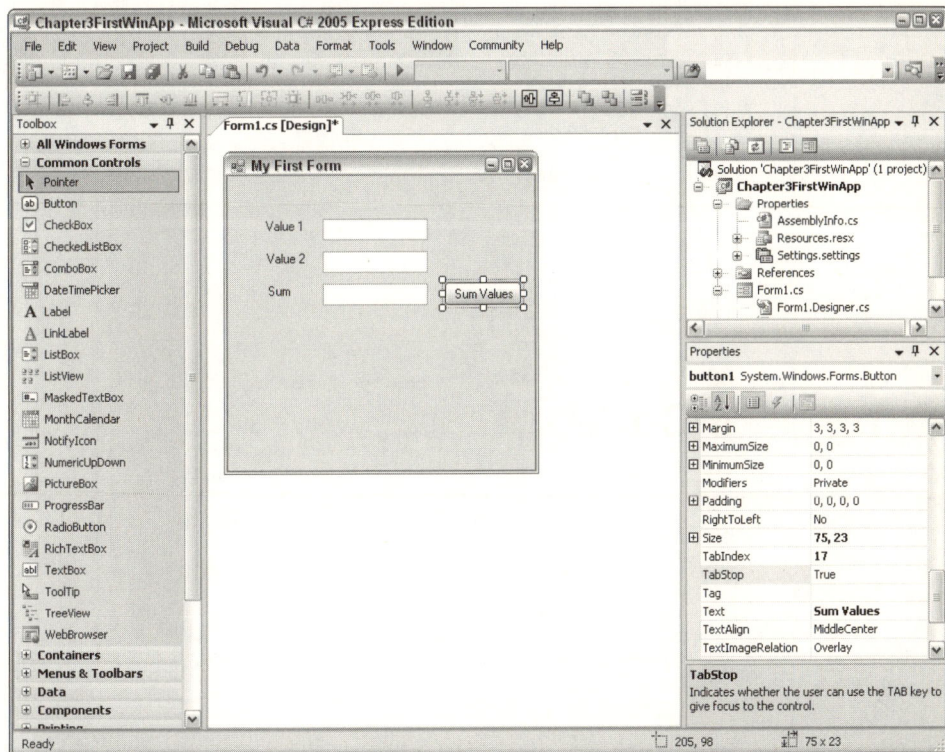

Figure 3-19

47

You may be thinking about throwing this book away reading this last paragraph, but don't worry; it is more complicated to describe what you are going to do than it is to just write out the line of code. The line of code you use looks like this:

```
textBox3.Text =
    Convert.ToString(Convert.ToInt16(textBox1.Text) +
                        Convert.ToInt16(textBox2.Text));
```

Again, please don't sweat the actual code itself at this time. I will be discussing C# types and .NET classes over the next few chapters. The point is to get you in and programming a Windows form.

One quick thing to note about this code is that you don't have to worry about continuing a command on more than one line. You just have to end your commands with a semicolon (;).

Try It Out   Adding Event Code to a Button and Testing the Form

You now have all the pieces you need to complete this chapter's task. You will add the code just displayed and run your new form.

1.   Double-click the Button control. The editor opens, as shown back in Figure 3-20.

```
using System;
using System.Collections.Generic;
using System.ComponentModel;
using System.Data;
using System.Drawing;
using System.Text;
using System.Windows.Forms;

namespace Chapter3FirstWinApp
{
    public partial class Form1 : Form
    {
        public Form1()
        {
            InitializeComponent();
        }

        private void button1_Click(object sender, EventArgs e)
        {
            textBox3.Text =
                Convert.ToString(Convert.ToInt16(textBox1.Text) +
                            Convert.ToInt16(textBox2.Text));
        }
    }
}
```

Figure 3-20

2. Type the following command in between the open and close brackets {} of the `button1_Click` method:

```
textBox3.Text =
            Convert.ToString(Convert.ToInt16(textBox1.Text) +
                        Convert.ToInt16(textBox2.Text));
```

The editor then looks as shown in Figure 3-20.

Okay, for the purposes of this task, you are done designing the form. Now you just need to test it out.

3. Press F5 to run the application.

4. Type numbers in the Value text boxes. For the purposes of this example, the values of 3 and 4 were entered into Value 1 and Value 2, respectively.

5. Click the Sum Values button. The sum of the two values is displayed in the third text box, as shown in Figure 3-21.

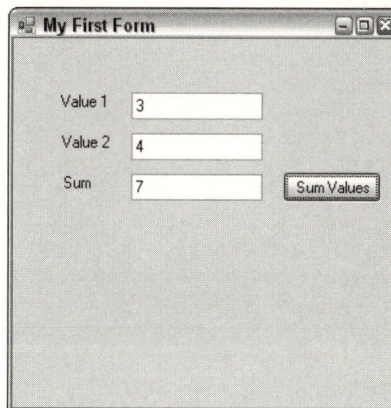

Figure 3-21

If for some reason your application does not build or run as it should, check the code to make sure it is typed exactly as it is in the example here. Next, make sure the Name properties of the fields are as they are in the example: textBox1, textBox2, and textBox3.

Summary

There are a number of types of projects you can create using C# Express. Two of the major types are console and Windows application project types. The main difference between the two is that the console applications don't usually include forms and other user interfaces. They are used for utility and system-level applications. Windows applications can include everything from database applications to video games.

The panes in the C# Express IDE can be rearranged as desired depending on what you are trying to accomplish and the type of project you are working on. In this chapter you saw how to create a Windows application including adding text boxes and buttons. In addition to adding the controls themselves, you saw how to create code that can be executed behind them at runtime.

Exercises

1. Can you include a Windows form in a Console application?

2. What is the extension of the file that is used for a Windows form?

3. What pane in the IDE contains the various controls used on a form?

4. `Height`, `Width`, and `Text` are _____ of a form.

5. What is the property that displays a caption on a button?

4

Introducing .NET

After programming for almost 20 years, I can honestly say that while not the easiest programming environment to work with, .NET is by far one of the most complete. Microsoft went to a great deal of effort to try and give developers both the flexibility they need along with the power and security. While this is great for software developers that have been programming for a while, it can be very intimidating for new developers.

As a trainer I have seen many a glazed eye and look of panic when talking about discussing various elements of .NET. The good news is that those glazed eye turn into a look of excitement as the people see both the potential and that it not as intimidating as it first seems.

The goal of this chapter is to lay out the different aspects of programming using .NET in such a way that you can see logically how to use various features for your own purposes. This chapter does the following:

❑   Introduces the .NET Framework.

❑   Explains how .NET assemblies, namespaces, and types work.

❑   Discusses some of the .NET namespaces and types that are useful for your own programming.

❑   Shows how to include .NET namespaces in your programs.

Introduction to .NET Framework

My family just celebrated 10 years of being in our current house that we had custom-built. Like any homeowner-to-be, I was on-site just about every day to make sure that the contractor had all my expertise for the building. Okay, I mainly just got underfoot, but the point is I saw the framework that made up the house.

Much like the core of a well-built house is built from a strong foundation and well-formed frame, the base from which the Microsoft .NET Framework consists of two main elements: Common Language Runtime (CLR) and the .NET Framework Class Library. These two elements handle a lot of work for developers; among other things, the CLR manages memory and is a language-neutral environment.

The .NET Framework Class Library makes for just about unlimited expandability for your application. You can see how these elements fit together in Figure 4-1.

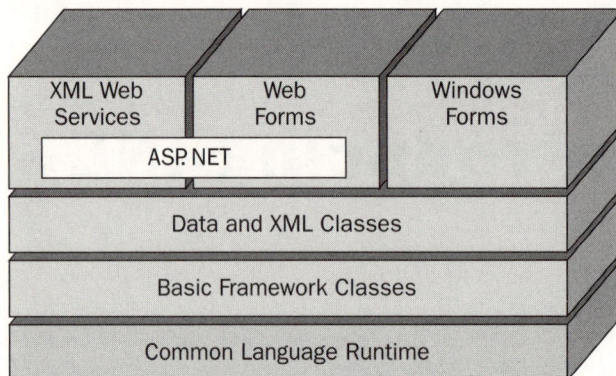

Figure 4-1

C# is used in all of the blocks of the top layer. The various blocks on top all use the same types from the blocks below, with some differences regarding whether or not you are working with the Web. But the great thing is that you don't have to learn all new types when working in one or the other. You can use C#, or whatever language you choose, and use the same types and their properties and methods for the data and Framework classes.

> *Like much of C# Express, the Microsoft .NET Framework manages the majority of the functionality that has been discussed in the chapter thus far. Don't think that you will have to be writing code to get every part of the Framework working; it has been done for you.*

There are a number of reasons for using the .NET Framework for a development platform. Namely, the .NET Framework:

❑ **Guarantees the safe execution of code, including code created by unknown or semi-trusted third parties.** This is where the term *managed code* comes from, because the applications have to meet security standards and are managed just for that very purpose.

❑ **Enables developers to work in a consistent programming environment whether creating applications for desktops or the Internet.** This ensures that although there are techniques that vary between Web and desktop applications, you can use the same languages, such as C#.

❑ **Builds all communication on industry standards to ensure that code based on the .NET Framework can integrate with any other code.** .NET uses XML extensively, as well as other communication protocols such as SOAP (Simplified Object Application Programming), which are both industry standards.

❑ **Minimizes software deployment and versioning conflicts.** Also called DLL hell, these conflicts occurred frequently when you were developing in prior platforms such as Visual Basic and using ActiveX controls. A lot of times when you installed new versions of your applications, controls would conflict and not work.

❑ **Eliminates performance problems of scripted or interpreted environments.** Everything is compiled into a common language that the various parts of the platform are designed to work with.

Common Language Runtime

Common Language Runtime is a runtime engine that takes the various languages such as Visual Basic, .NET, and C# and compiles them into the same common language used when the applications are executed. This means that all the languages can use the same classes provided by the .NET Framework Class Library.

The CLR is extremely convenient and powerful in that it really doesn't matter which language you write in, because you can use the same objects and it all compiles down to the same efficient code.

.NET Framework Class Library

The .NET Framework Class Library is made up of various namespaces. *Namespaces* are actually collections of types, logically organized. This enables you to have multiple versions of types with the same name but in different namespaces, thereby avoiding conflicts.

Just as with a library you have collected in your home of useful books, the class library is a set of types that not only make up the .NET Framework itself, but also are available to developers for their use.

Another big benefit of using the .NET Framework Class Library is to be able to use the classes in your applications consistently no matter whether you are using C# or Visual Basic .NET, Windows, or Web forms. Namespaces can also contain other namespaces in a hierarchical way. By creating sub-namespaces, you can categorize your types for use at different times.

The best way to understand the .NET Framework Class Library is to take a look at some of the namespaces in it. Some of these namespaces are shown in the following table:

Namespace	Description
System	Main system namespace that is broken into many categories.
System.Data	Makes up the classes used for ADO.NET, and overall data manipulation of just about any kind. Sub-namespaces of the System.Data include System.Data.SqlClient and System.Data.OleDB.
System.Drawing	Used for drawing shapes and objects in your applications.
System.Windows.Forms	Namespaces and classes for creating Windows forms applications.

When you create a .NET application, C# Express creates references to different namespaces, based on what kind of project you are creating. An example of references created in a Windows application type .NET project is shown in Figure 4-2.

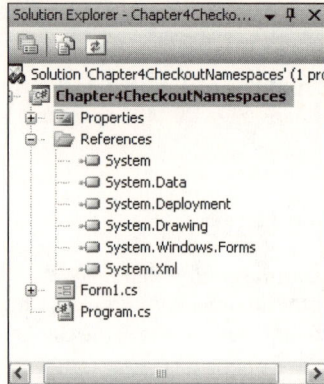

Figure 4-2

To get more comfortable with namespaces and how they work, you need to use them yourself. To do that, you will want to create another Windows project to work with.

Try It Out   Creating the Initial Project

While in C# Express:

1. Choose Project... from the File ⇨ New menu task. The New Project dialog box appears.

2. Highlight Windows Application.

3. In the Name property, type in the name you want to call the project. You can see that Chapter4CheckoutNamespaces was the title given to this project in Figure 4-3.

4. Click OK. C# Express creates the project. The initial Windows form appears.

5. Click the plus sign by the References node in the Solution Explorer; you now see all the references to namespaces that are set by default (see Figure 4-4).

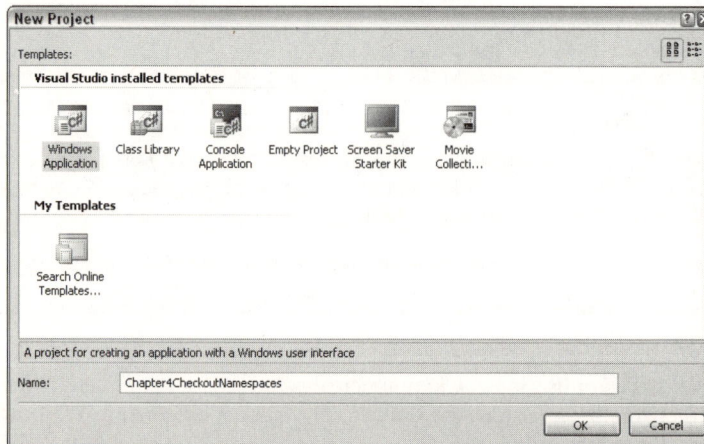

Figure 4-3

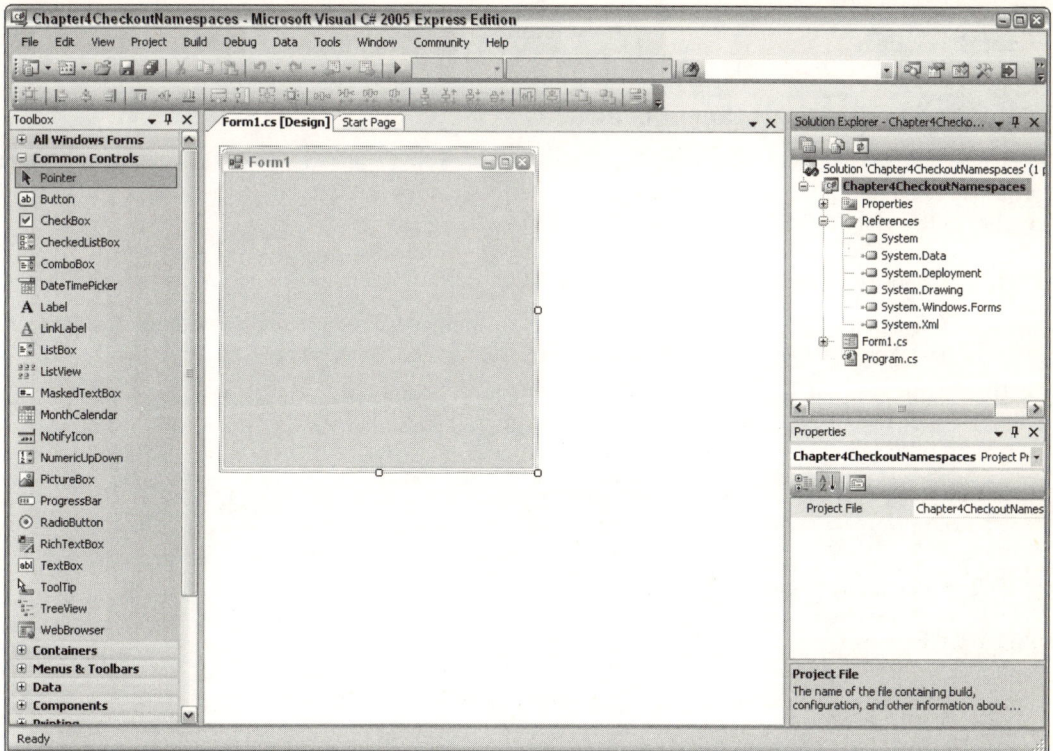

Figure 4-4

While it is great to see the namespaces listed for your project, it is even better if you know what you can do with them.

Working with .NET Namespaces

While some programming environments let you use libraries of code to enhance your programming, few actually use those libraries themselves. Every object that is created within C# Express uses namespaces. Even the form in the form designer has been created using .NET namespaces, but it is maintained by C# Express for you, so you can just drag and drop nicely using the editor. While I could have you open the file that makes up the design portion of the form, it wouldn't really help you get used to working with .NET namespaces.

Object Browser: Tool of the Namespace Trade

One of the tools worthwhile to look at when you are learning about namespaces is the Object Browser. With the Object Browser you can search through and locate the syntax for various classes you want to use. Once you locate the class in the namespace, you can press F1 and get help on it if necessary.

The Object Browser is a great tool when you just want to look through a namespace to get an idea of what is included.

Using the Object Browser

The best way to get comfortable with the Object Browser is to go ahead and use it. For this Try It Out, you will open the Object Browser and search for the `MessageBox` class. So, in the project you created earlier in this chapter:

1.   Choose Object Browser from the View ⇨ Other Windows menu choice, as shown in Figure 4-5.

     Once in the Object Browser, you see all of the namespaces that are referenced in the current project. You even see an entry for the project itself, as shown in Figure 4-6.

2.   In the entry that says <Search>, type in the term `MessageBox`, then press Enter. You will now see a list of classes that have the word MessageBox in them.

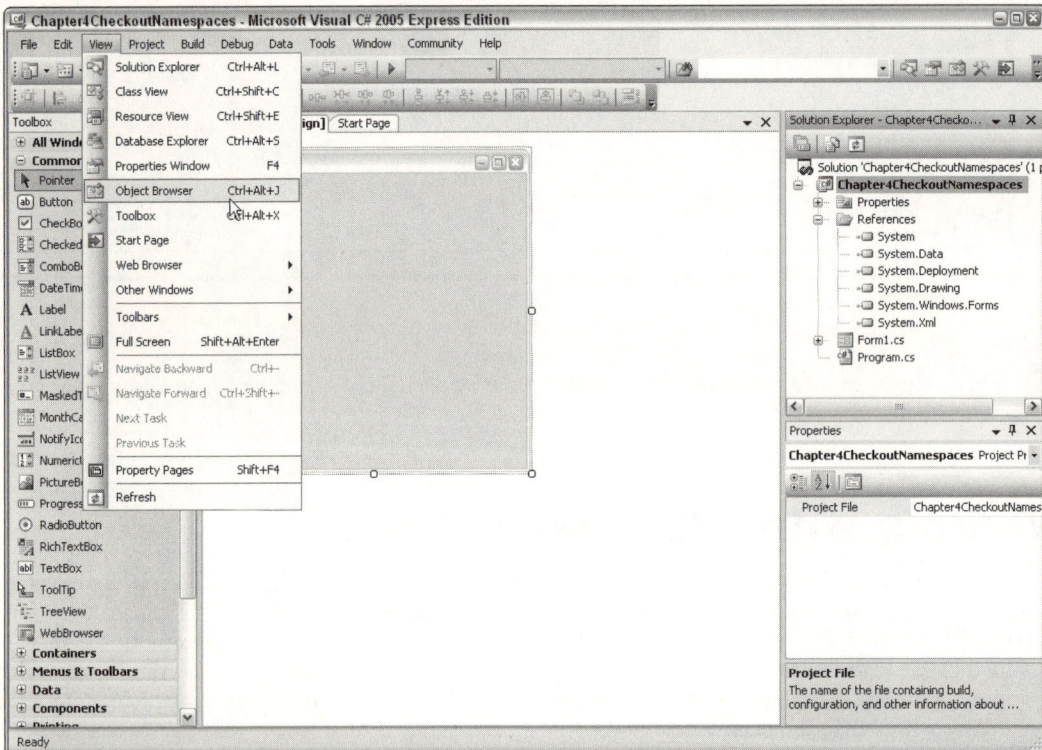

Figure 4-5

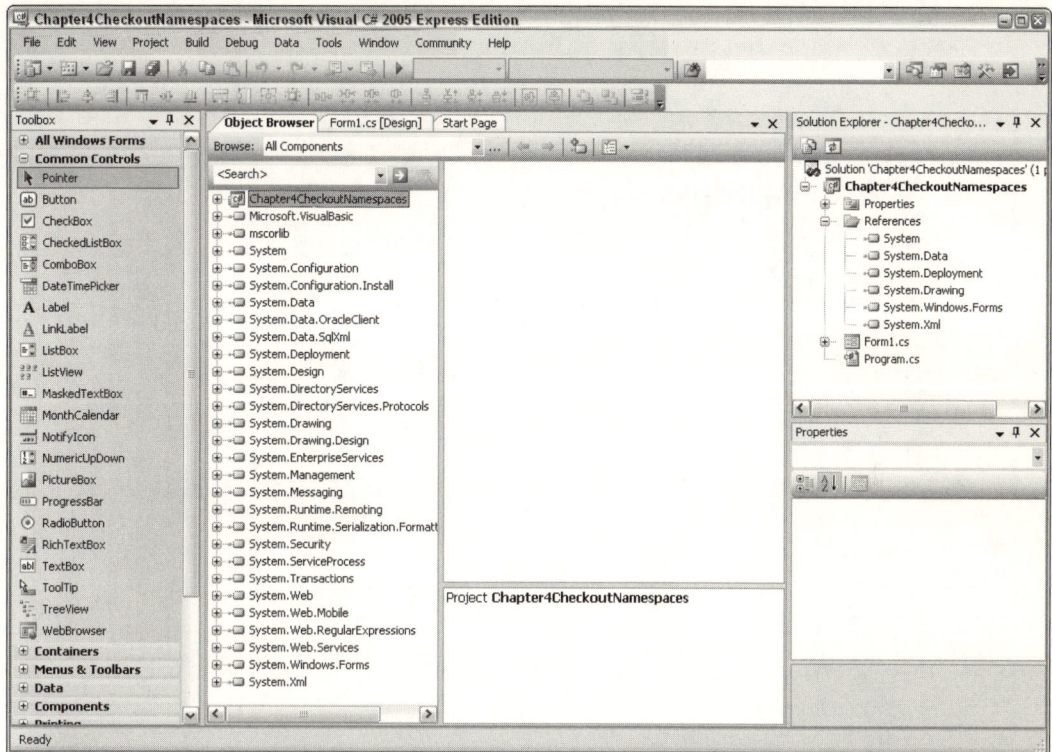

Figure 4-6

3. Highlight the entry that reads System.Windows.Form.MessageBox. All the methods of this class appear, in this case just the Show methods, as shown in Figure 4-7.

4. Highlight any of the entries, and press F1. You will then see the help for that particular method, as shown for the Show method in Figure 4-8.

Many of the methods and properties of classes can have more than one way of being called or set. This is called "overloading." You can create your own classes that use overloading as well.

You can now close both the help screen and the Object Browser by clicking on the red X in the code of each.

There are a number of ways to use the .NET namespaces within your applications. One is by typing the full name of the namespace down to the class or method (action) you want use with the namespace. This is called *using the fully qualified namespace.*

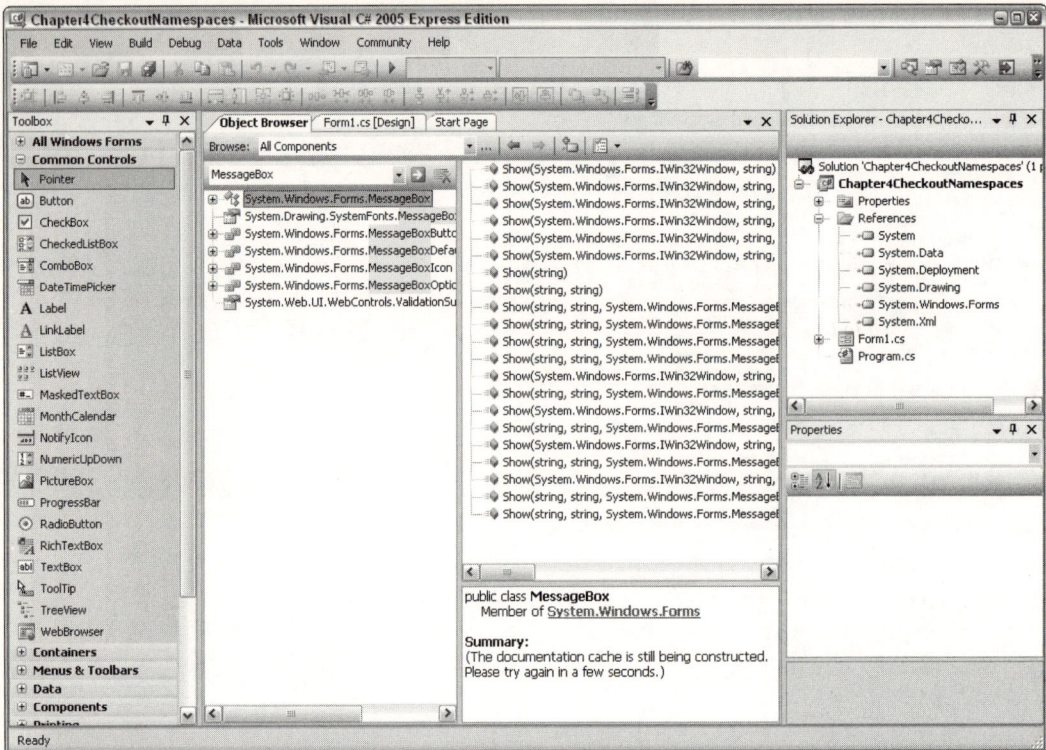

Figure 4-7

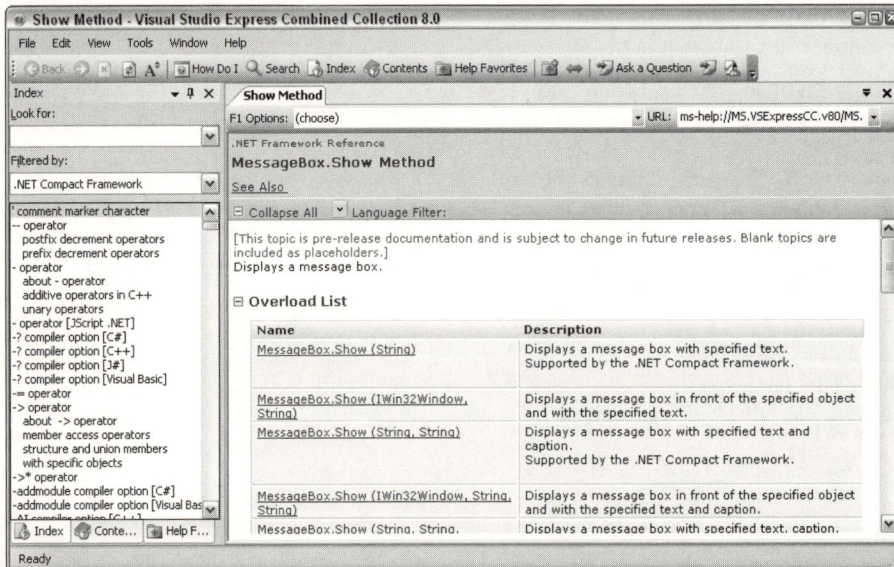

Figure 4-8

Supplying the Fully Qualified Namespace

This is a fancy term for what is really just performing more work than necessary. For example, if you want to use the `MessageBox()` method, which is in the `System` namespace, you would then use the following syntax:

```
System.Windows.Forms.MessageBox.Show("Hey There");
```

One of the nice features of C# Express and other Microsoft editors is that they provide a help feature called IntelliSense. While it is a dumb name, it is a great feature. IntelliSense actually builds your commands as you move down the qualified namespace, and then lets you know the possible arguments that can be passed to the method.

To give you a bit of experience working with fully qualified namespaces and even with using the IntelliSense feature, perform this next Try It Out.

Try It Out   **Calling the MessageBox.Show() Method Using the Fully Qualified Namespace**

Using the project you created in the first Try It Out of this chapter:

1. Double-click on the `Form1.cs`. The code for Form1 appears, as shown in Figure 4-9.

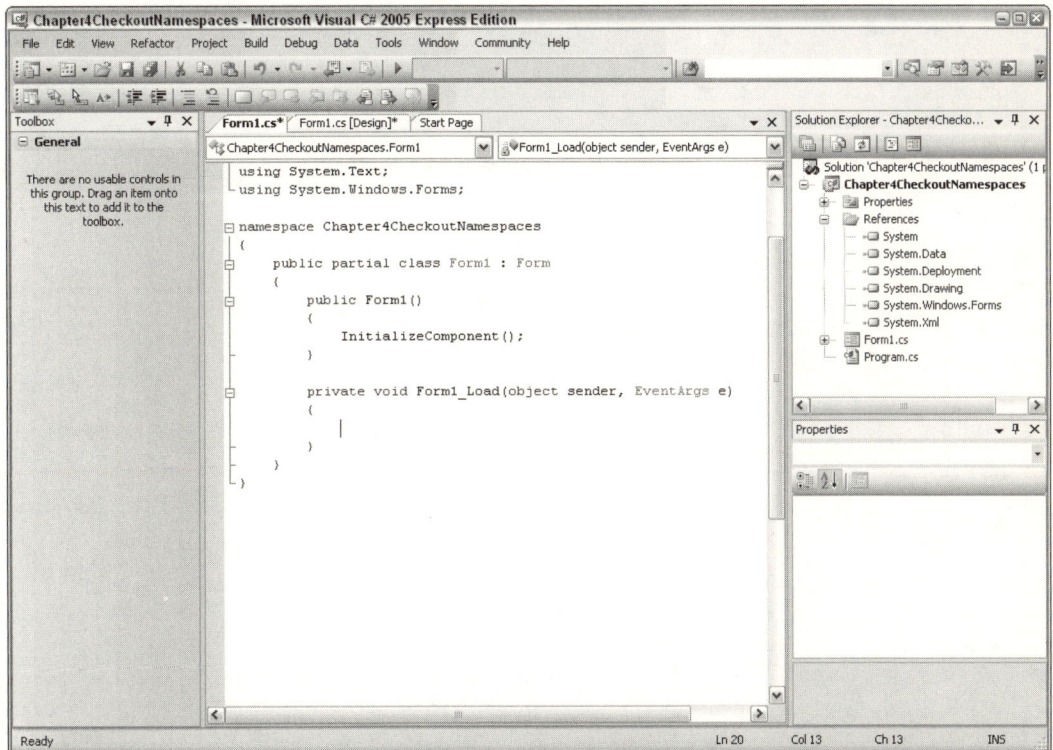

Figure 4-9

2. In between the open and close curly brackets, under the lines that read

```
private void Form1_Load(object sender, EventArgs e)
    {
```

type the following:

```
System.Windows.Forms.messageb
```

As you move through each segment of classes, the editor capitalizes the name and then gives a list for the next segment. You can see this in Figure 4-10.

IntelliSense helps a great deal as you are writing out the statements or are not sure the path or syntax. To go to the next segment, press either the period or parenthesis as you get toward the end of the statement.

If you misspell or don't press the period to complete the segment of the command, it will not get capitalized and will cause problems. Remember that C# is a case-sensitive language. If this happens, either capitalize the command yourself or erase the segment and start over.

3. Complete the rest of the command so that it reads

```
System.Windows.Forms.MessageBox.Show("Hey There");
```

The screen now appears as shown in Figure 4-11.

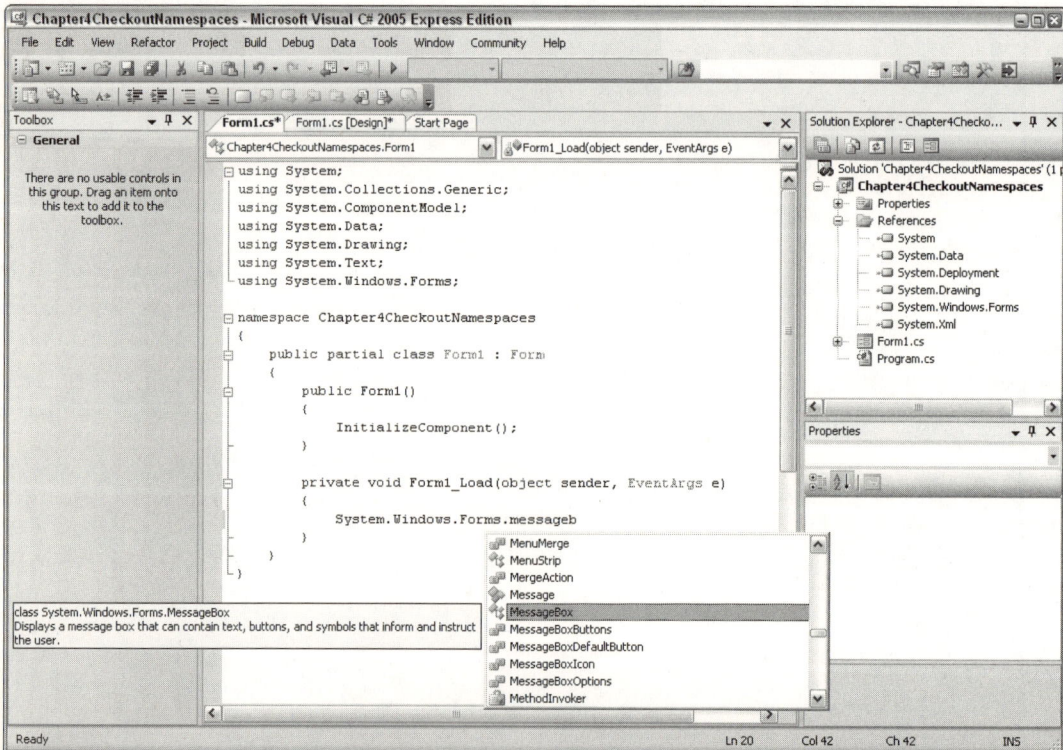

Figure 4-10

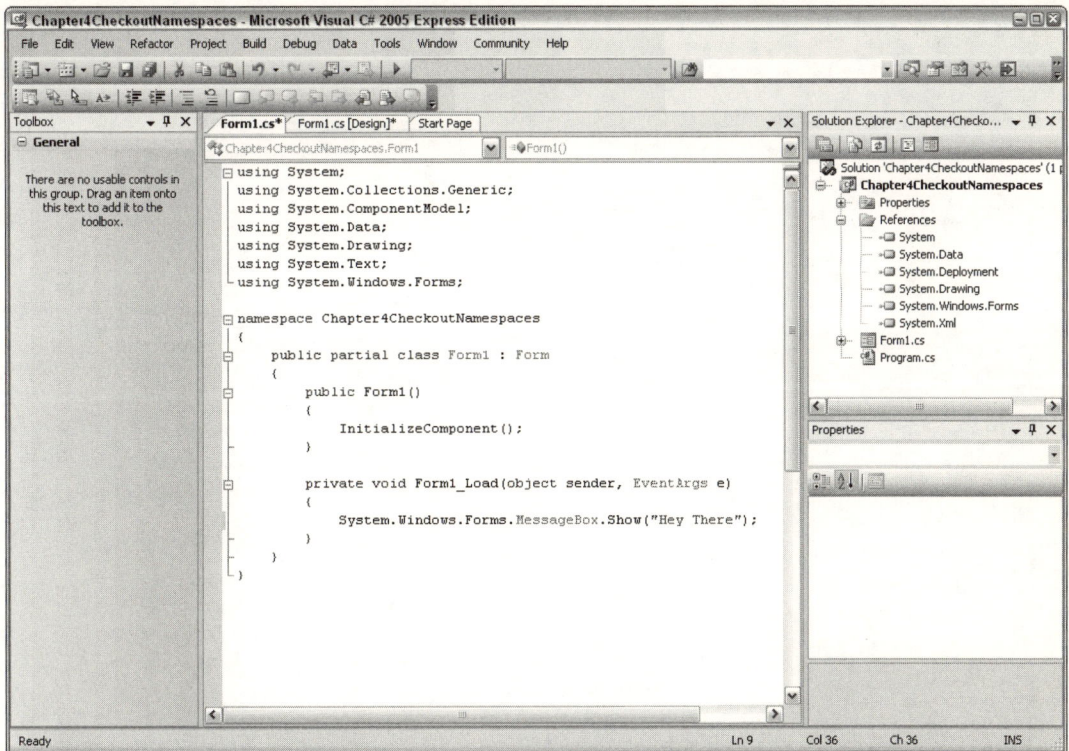

Figure 4-11

Using the fully qualified namespace is good when you have classes or methods that are similarly named. However, it can be somewhat of a hassle to have to keep typing out the full name, even using IntelliSense. .NET provides another way to specify the full path once in the class you are currently working in: with the Using directive.

The program you just created displays a message box as the form is opened. To build and test this application, press F5.

The Using Directive

Instead of opening the form design file, I will show how to use the namespaces by opening the code portion of the form and showing you how .NET "hooks" in the namespaces for you. For example, if you open code for the form1 in your new project, you will see a region, also called code blocks, at the top made up of Using directives By default, you will see a list of namespaces that are included in each Windows form created. You can see this for the current project in Figure 4-12.

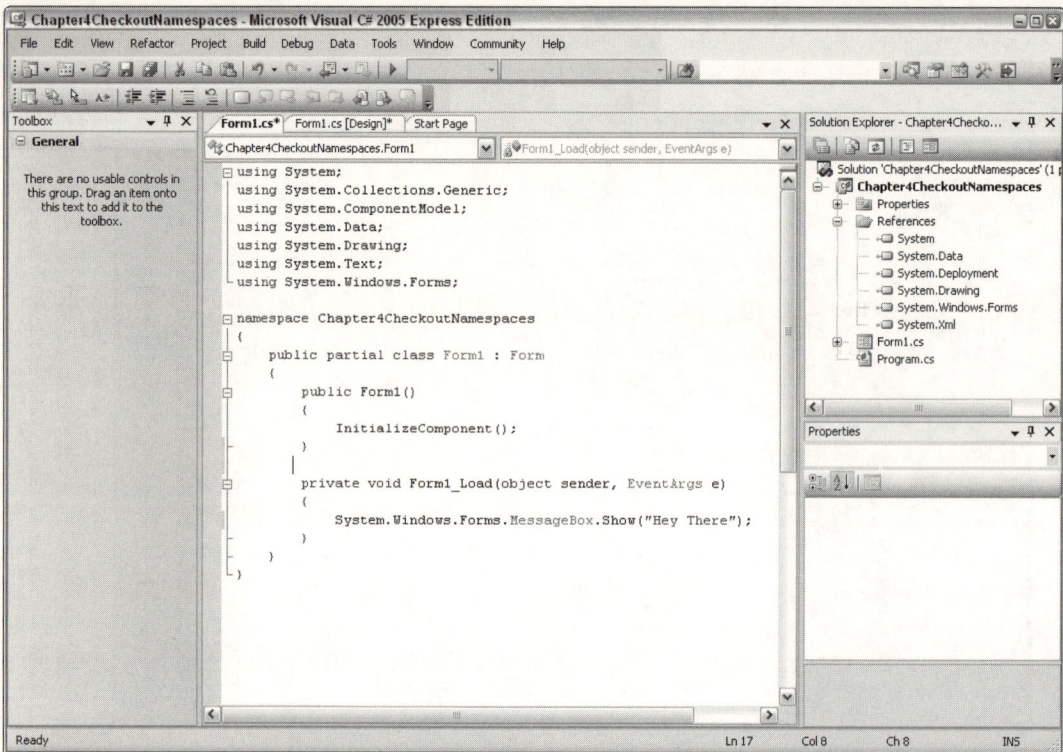

Figure 4-12

By clicking the plus/minus symbols, you are either expanding or collapsing the region. There is quite a bit of code that is created and then placed in regions using both `#region...#endregion` `statements` *and now automatically by the C# Express editor for you based on the code block being created. If you go into some of these regions, be careful, because the majority of the regions are code written by C# Express and should not be changed.*

With the Using directive, you are telling C# that you are planning on using the specified namespace so you don't have to type full syntax out. Remember, the namespaces shown in Figure 4-12 are there by default. As you get more advanced in your writing of code, you will add your own namespaces that you will find useful.

A cool tip if you are going to be using a class from a namespace specified in the Using Directives region is that you can press Ctrl+Space, and a list of available classes and methods is displayed using IntelliSense.

Try It Out   Calling the MessageBox.Show() Method with the Using Directive

Using the project you created in the previous Try It Out, erase the fully qualified `MessageBox.Show` command you created. With the current line in between the curly brackets, again:

1. Press Ctrl+Space. The IntelliSense list appears.

2. Type:

```
Messageb
```

The list then goes to the `MessageBox` class, as shown in Figure 4-13.

3. Finish the statement so it reads

```
MessageBox.Show("Hey There Again");
```

This is shown in Figure 4-14.

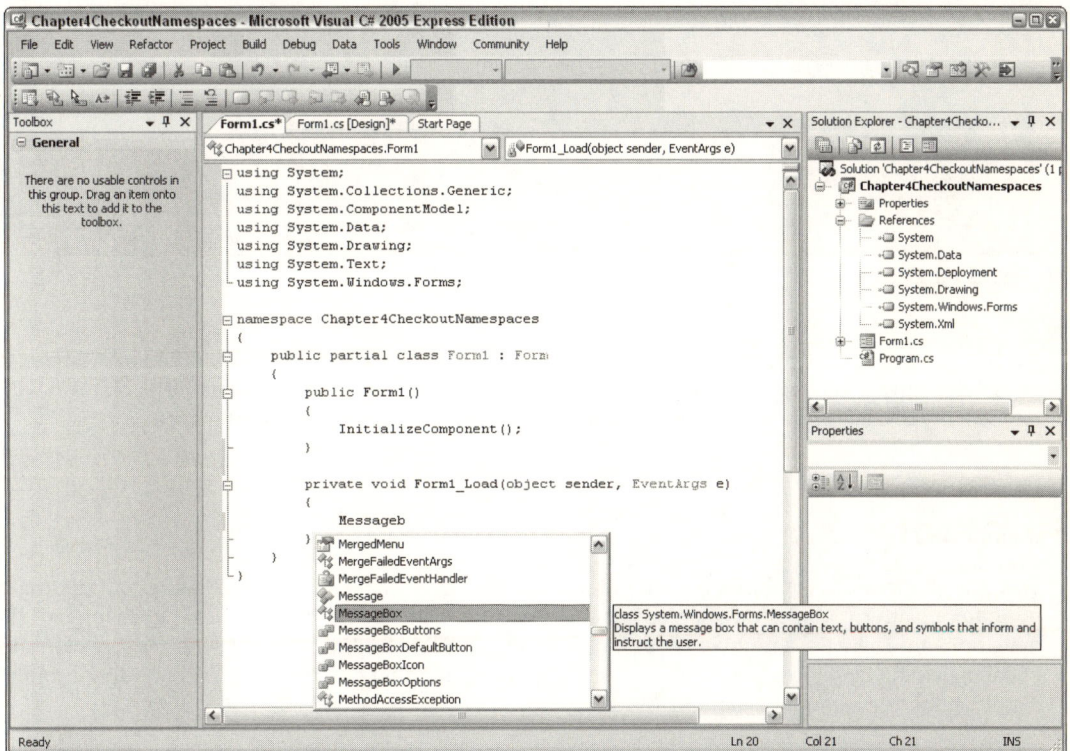

Figure 4-13

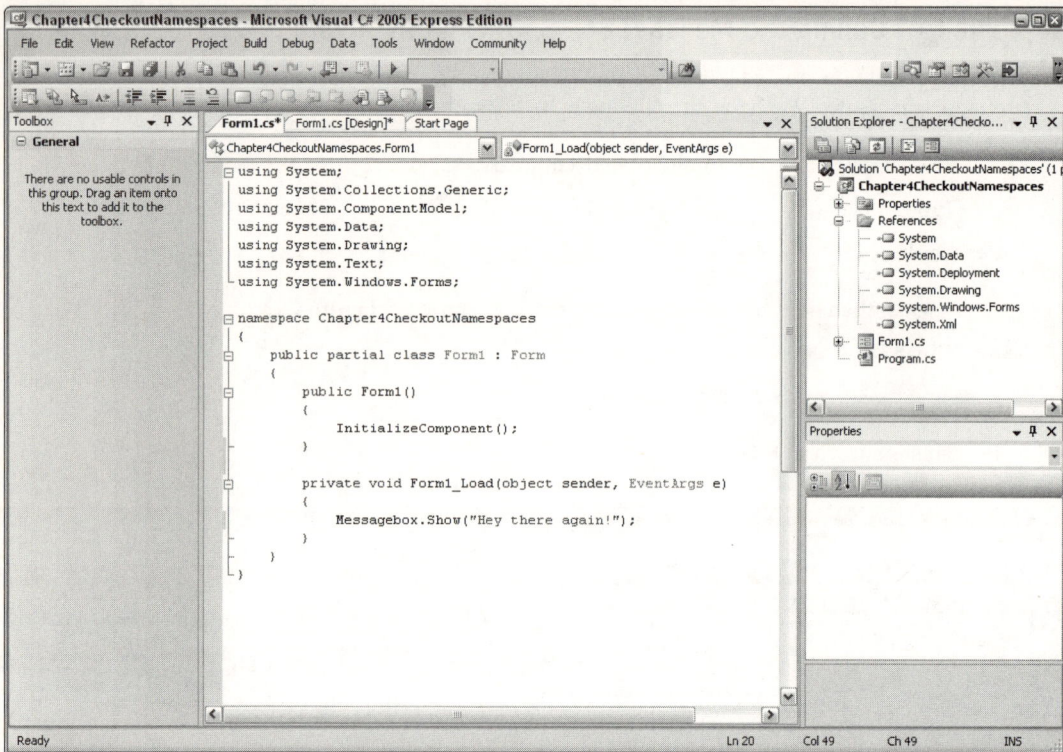

Figure 4-14

And there you go. While it is very convenient to not have to type out the fully qualified namespace, it does help a great deal with those methods that are named the same in different namespaces. You will have plenty of chances to use namespaces as you progress through the rest of the book.

Summary

The .NET Framework combines power and flexibility and also takes some of the hassles out of programming for a platform that can work on different operating systems and even the desktop or Internet (Web) development. There are a number of reasons for using .NET, including guaranteeing the safe execution of code, helping developers to work in a consistent programming environment, and building communication on industry standards, among others.

Namespaces provide flexibility by supplying a number of utilities that not only make up .NET itself but also enable you to put them directly into your code. Tools are supplied for working with namespaces and even let you create your own namespaces to further enhance your applications.

Exercises

1. Name the two main parts of the .NET Framework.

2. What is the category in the Solution Explorer that shows the list of namespaces being used?

3. What is the feature lists parts of namespaces as you are typing the statements in code?

4. You can use _____ _____ to look at the various namespaces, classes, and methods.

5. What are the two ways of using namespaces in code?

5

Getting into C# Types

Just about every programming language uses variables for storing information temporally while the program is running. To provide better control, C# requires you to specify what type of information you plan on storing in the variable. This not only includes standard type of data such as strings (text) and various types of numbers but also various types of objects available in the .NET Class Library. How you use a variable depends on what type of variable it is.

Once variables have been declared, you can assign values and manipulate them using various techniques. They can then be used for testing various conditions, storing values into databases, and displaying them in your application. Just about any application you write will use variables in one of these ways, and many more.

Constants are used for specifying a value once in a procedure or application, and then the constant is used throughout the code. To explain about all variable and constant features, this chapter:

- ❑ Discusses further what variables are and how they are used.
- ❑ Shows how to declare a variable and assign values to it.
- ❑ Demonstrates how to Manipulates information in variables.
- ❑ Shows how to use the C# Express editor to display variables.
- ❑ Shows how to write variables to the console using the `Console.Writeln()` method.

What Are Variables and Constants?

As mentioned in the introduction to the chapter, most programming languages use variables and constants to work with information in memory. There are two types of variables:

❑   Those that are used for storing pieces of information in memory, thus making a copy of the data that is independent of the original data. These types of data are standard types such as strings and numbers.

❑   Those that are really references, or point to existing or new objects created from classes, such as the various .NET library classes discussed in Chapter 4.

Constants are used when you have a value throughout your application or procedure that you are not going to be changing. You will read more about constants later in the chapter in the section titled "Using C# Constants."

Declaring and Assigning C# Variables

Unlike other languages, C# is very strict when you are declaring variables. This means that you need to know and declare your variables as specific types. While there are ways around this, it is a good idea to get used to using the strict or explicit way. An example follows, showing how to declare an integer type variable named `intValue1`:

```
int intValue1;
```

The various C# types will be discussed shortly in the section called "Standard C# Types." For now, just bear with me as I present different types.

Once you have declared your variable, .NET reserves a spot in memory for that variable, but it still has no value. In fact, if you were to create a project with just the declaration of the variable as just shown, and you try to display or use the variable without assigning it a value, you would get an error from C# Express when you attempt to build the project. Take time to perform this Try It Out to create a Windows application for this chapter and to test the situation just presented.

Try It Out   **Creating a Windows Application and Declaring a Variable**

For this first Try It Out, you create a Windows application that is a switchboard for trying out the different examples presented in this chapter. Switchboards are discussed further in Chapter 8, "Working with Forms and Controls," but for now know they are buttons on a form that launch routines that you created. So, after starting up C# Express:

1.   Choose Project... from the File ⇨ New menu.

2.   Select the Windows Application template, and type in the name you want to call the project. For the example, Chapter 5 was used, as shown in Figure 5-1.

3.   Click OK to create the project. The form is displayed by default.

4.   Drag and drop a button control onto the form as shown in Chapter 3, "Quick Start Creating Your First C# Express Windows Project," in the section titled "Adding Controls to the Form."

5.   Set the `Text` property to `Variables`.

6.   Set the `Name` property to `btnVariables`, as shown in Figure 5-2.

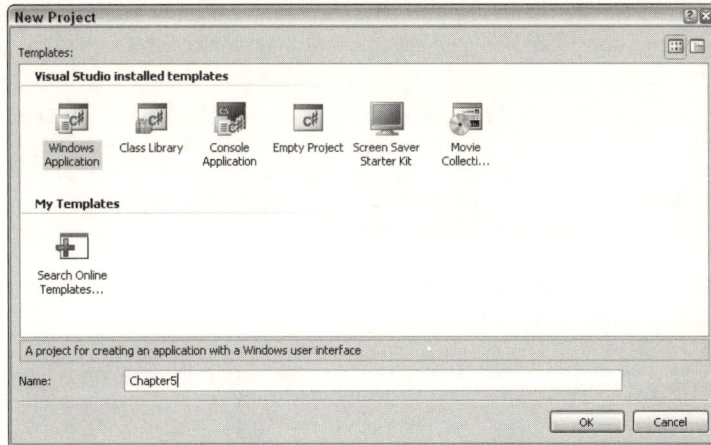

Figure 5-1

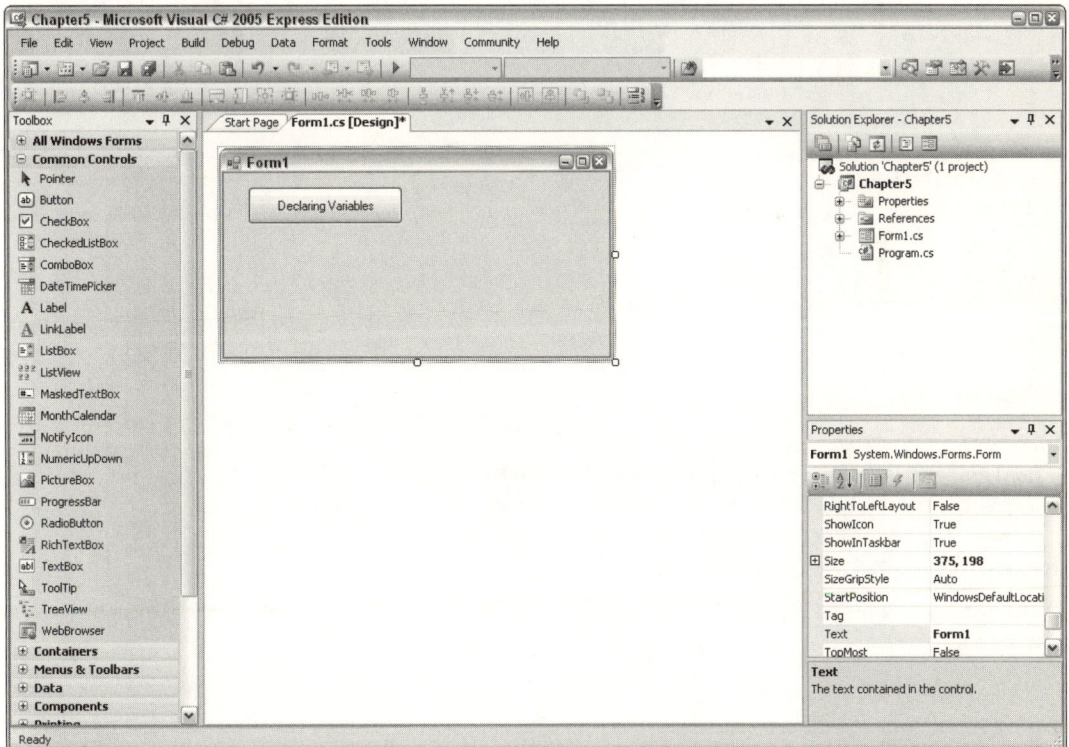

Figure 5-2

7. Double-click the btnVariables button. The code for the form is displayed, and you see Type the
    following lines of code in between the open and close curly brackets of the main procedure:

```
int intValue1;
MessageBox.Show(intValue1.ToString());
```

The ToString() *method of* intValue1 *is used to convert the value passed to the* MessageBox.Show
method to a string value. Converting between C# types is discussed further in the section called
"Converting between Variable Types," later in this chapter.

8. Press F5 to run the application. A build error occurs. C# Express lists them nicely at the bottom
    of the IDE, as shown in Figure 5-3.

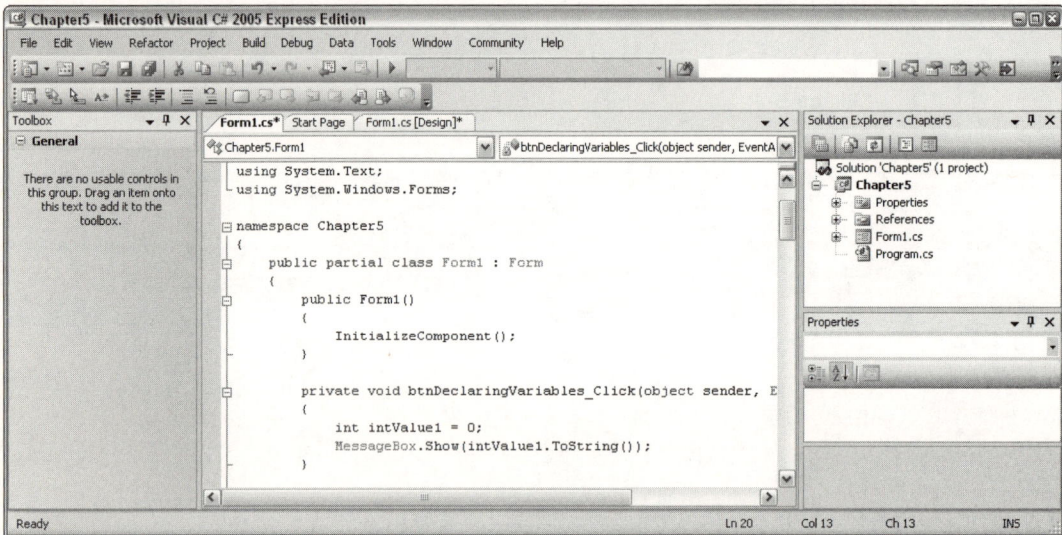

Figure 5-3

I am going to leave you hanging for a moment with the error in place. The next section discusses assignment of variables, which will provide the information you need to correct the error.

Simple Assignment of Variables

The error displayed in Figure 5-3 is what is returned when you use a variable without assigning a value
to it first. To assign a value, use the equal sign as the operator:

```
intValue1 = 3;
```

When assigning values, you can perform operations at the same time such as:

```
intValue1 = 3 + 5;
```

Assigning Variables with the Declaration

You also can also assign a value to the variable at the same time you are declaring. For example:

```
int intValue1 = 3;
int intValue2 = intValue1 * 5;
```

You just need to make sure you declare the variables that you are using in each of the statements. In the last example, you would want to make sure that `intValue1` was declared and the variable's value, 3 in this case, was assigned before using it in the line of code assigning it to `intValue2`.

You also can perform operations using other variables:

```
int intValue1;
int intValue2;

intValue1 = 3;
intValue2 = intValue1 * 5;
```

Besides assigning values to variables in your code, you can take values from text boxes and assign them to a variable. This can take a bit more work, as in more code, and is explained in a section called "Converting between Variable Types," later in this chapter.

To correct the error caused by the first Try It Out, change the declaration statement to:

```
int intValue1 = 0;
```

Try It Out   Assigning Variables

In this Try It Out, you declare and assign a couple of variables, one assigning the variable in the declaration, the other using a separate line of code.

1.   Drag and drop another button onto the form created in the last Try It Out.

2.   Name the button as desired, and specify the `Text` property.

3.   Double-click the button. C# Express creates a routine for the `Click` event, and opens the code file.

4.   Add the following code between the opening and closing curly brackets:

```
int intValue1 = 3;
int intValue2;

intValue2 = intValue1 * 5;

MessageBox.Show(intValue2.ToString());
```

The editor code portion now looks Figure 5-4.

```
      private void btnAssigningVariables_Click(object sender, EventArgs e)
      {
          int intValue1 = 3;
          int intValue2;

          intValue2 = intValue1 * 5;

          MessageBox.Show(intValue2.ToString());
      }

  }
}
```

Figure 5-4

5. Press F5 to build and run the application.

6. Click the button you created for assigning variables. The message box in Figure 5-5 appears.

Figure 5-5

Besides showing how to assign values to variables, the following line of code performs a C# arithmetic operation when assigning values to intValue2:

```
intValue2 = intValue1 * 5;
```

C# Arithmetic Operations

The operations you have the program perform depend on what tasks you are trying to accomplish. Following is a list of operators you can use for arithmetic operations:

Operator	Description
+	Addition
-	Subtraction
*	Multiplication
/	Division
%	Remainder of a division performed, known as the modulus
++	Incrementing the value of a variable by 1
--	Decrementing the variable of a variable by 1

Another thing to keep in mind with operations: Just as with high school algebra, you can use parentheses to perform operations in the specific order you want. This means that the following line of code

```
intValue1 = (3+6) * 5;
```

assigns 40 to `intValue1`. That is, 3 plus 6 equals 8, and 8 multiplied by 5 equals 40.

Standard C# Types

Thus far, you have seen some examples in the chapter of a couple of data types that you can use when declaring variables. The data types discussed have been standard C# types. There are a number of standard C# types you can use that will hold various types of data. Following is a list of some of the more commonly used C# types with the equivalent .NET type.

Type	.NET Data Type	Description
bool	System.Boolean	True/false values
byte	System.Byte	1 or 0 values
char	System.Char	Single characters
decimal	System.Decimal	Decimal values
double	System.Double	Large floating-point number
float	System.Single	Small floating-point number
int	System.Int32	Integer value
long	System.Int64	Large integer value
object	System.Object	Generic object that can hold other types
short	System.Int16	Short integer value
string	System.String	Array of characters

You will be using some of these types throughout the rest of this chapter and the rest of the book.

Working with C# String Types

Strings can be manipulated similarly to numeric values but are handled differently by C#. Strings are actually multiple characters strung together.

The characters strung together are actually called an array. *You can have arrays of various types of variables.*

While you use the + (plus symbol) to concatenate (add) string values together, there are other methods on string type variables. Following are some of the methods you can use with string data types:

Method	Description
Compare	Compares two specified strings.
Contains	Returns a boolean value indicating whether the specified string occurs within this instance.
Copy	Creates a new instance of a string.
IndexOf	Reports the index of the first occurrence of a string, or one or more characters, within this instance.
Insert	Inserts a specified instance of a string at a specified index position in the instance.
IsNullOrEmpty	Indicates whether or not the specified string is null or an empty string.
LastIndexOf	Reports the index position of the last occurrence of a specified character or string within the current instance.
PadLeft	Right-aligns the characters in this instance, padding the left with spaces or a specified character for a specified length.
PadRight	Left-aligns the characters in this string, padding the right with spaces or a specified character for a specified length.
Remove	Deletes a specified number of characters from this instance.
Replace	Replaces all occurrences of a specified character or string in this instance with another specified character or string.
Split	Returns a string array containing the substrings in this instance that are delimited by elements of a specified character or string array.
StartsWith	Determines whether the beginning of an instance of a string matches a specified string.
Substring	Retrieves a substring from this instance.
ToUpper	Returns a copy of a string converted to uppercase.
Trim	Removes all occurrences of a set of specified characters from the beginning and end of a string.
TrimEnd	Removes all occurrences of a set of characters specified in a string from the end of this instance.
TrimStart	Removes all occurrences of a set of characters specified in a string from the beginning of this instance.

Now it's time to put some of your knowledge about strings to use. To accomplish this, perform the following Try It Out.

Try It Out   **Manipulating Strings**

For this Try It Out, you will use two of the methods displayed in the preceding table: `IndexOf` and `Substring`.

1. To start, assign the name "Sam Spade" to a variable called `strWholeName`:

```
string strWholeName = "Sam Spade";
```

2. Next, use the `IndexOf` method to locate the space in between first and last name in the original string:

```
intSpaceLoc = strWholeName.IndexOf(" ");
```

3. Taking the value returned by the `IndexOf` method, use the `Substring` method to return the first name and then the last name:

```
strFirstName = strWholeName.Substring(0, intSpaceLoc);

strLastName = strWholeName.Substring(intSpaceLoc+1);
```

As with other methods and properties, the `Substring` method is overloaded. This means you can call the method passing different arguments. For the first name, you pass the starting point (0) and the length of the string you want to return. For the last name, just the starting point is passed, and the `Substring` method returns the rest of the string. So, to get busy:

4. Drag and drop another button onto the form created for this chapter.

5. Name the button as desired, and specify the `Text` property. For the purposes of this Try It Out, the button was named `btnStringVariables`, and the `Text` property is set to String Variables.

6. Double-click the button. C# Express creates a routine for the `Click` event and opens the code file.

7. Add the following code between the opening and closing curly brackets:

```
string strWholeName = "Sam Spade";
int intSpaceLoc;
string strFirstName;
string strLastName;

// The index of the space in the name
intSpaceLoc = strWholeName.IndexOf(" ");

// Using the location of the space, grab the first and last name
strFirstName = strWholeName.Substring(0, intSpaceLoc);
strLastName = strWholeName.Substring(intSpaceLoc+1);

// Display the first and last name
MessageBox.Show("The first name is: " + strFirstName +
                "\nThe last name is: " + strLastName);
```

Besides the comments, denoted by the double backslash, notice the literal (meaning the actual characters) "\n" added to the `MessageBox.Show` *line of code adds a carriage return line feed into the string displayed.*

After you add the code in Step 4, the editor looks as shown in Figure 5-6.

```
private void btnStringVariables_Click(object sender, EventArgs e)
{
    string strWholeName = "Sam Spade";
    int intSpaceLoc;
    string strFirstName;
    string strLastName;

    // The index of the space in the name
    intSpaceLoc = strWholeName.IndexOf(" ");

    // Using the location of the space grab the first and last name
    strFirstName = strWholeName.Substring(0, intSpaceLoc);
    strLastName = strWholeName.Substring(intSpaceLoc+1);

    // Display the first and last name
    MessageBox.Show("The first name is: " + strFirstName +
                    "\nThe last name is: " + strLastName);
}
```

Figure 5-6

8. Press F5 to build and run your application. If you get errors, double-check your code against Figure 5-6. When running correctly, the message in Figure 5-7 appears.

The first name is: Sam
The last name is: Spade

OK

Figure 5-7

Throughout this chapter, you have been using variables without paying attention to why you are naming them how you are. This next section discusses various ways of naming variables.

Naming C# Variables

One consideration when using variables is how to name them. When they begin developing, some people tend to use the shortest variable names they can. For example, if they are declaring a variable that stores the last name of a person, they would type

```
string ln;
```

This last line of code isn't very easy to read, is it? I don't know about you, but if I came in after the developer who used the last line of code, I would have a hard time working on the developer's code. And even if *I* wrote the code, I would be hard-pressed to remember what the variable was for a month later.

Another naming standard is to type the name of what the developer plans on storing in the variable. For example, for a string variable storing the last name of a person in it, the developer would use the following:

```
string lastname;
```

A number of standards are used for naming variables in C# and other programming languages. A couple of common standards used for .NET development are as follows:

❑ **Camel notation.** Takes the first word and displays it using lowercase and then uses proper case on the second part of the variable name. For example, say you have a variable that stores a person's last name. You would declare and name the variable like this:

```
string lastName;
```

❑ **Hungarian notation.** In this naming standard, you place the type of data you are using for the variable as the prefix for the variable name. The rest of the name is then typed in proper case. This is the version I tend to use, because I like being able to see what type of data I am working with. With this notation, the previous example would look like this:

```
string strLastName;
```

To me, this last notation makes the most sense, and, again, it is the one I use for most of my programming.

When you are working on other people's systems, you will need to use whatever naming standard they use, if they use one at all. Make sure that if they don't have one, you recommend they adopt one.

For additional information of Microsoft's recommendation for naming standards, check out the MSDN article located at `http://msdn.microsoft.com/library/default.asp?url=/library/en-us/cpgenref/html/cpconnamingguidelines.asp`.

Converting between Variable Types

There will be times when you need to take one type of data and convert it to another. A good example is taking a numeric value and displaying it in a message box. To do this, you can use the `ToString()` method, which each object and data type have. This is the most common type of conversion, and it is easily accomplished, as shown here in the line of code from the first Try It Out:

```
MessageBox.Show(intValue2.ToString());
```

However, at times you will want to convert to other C# types besides strings. To accomplish this, you can use a few different methods, two of which are discussed here. Based on which method you use, the data is converted differently. The first method is to convert the expression using the type you want to convert to. For example, if you want to convert a value to an integer, you would use the syntax of `(int)` in the assignment of the expression. But if you type the following:

```
double dblValue = 2.7;
int intValueTotal1;

intValueTotal1 = (int) dblValue;
```

the answer in `intValueTotal1` would be 2. That's right, the value is truncated. If you want to make sure that the value is rounded correctly, you should use the `Covert` class. The `Convert` class has various methods to covert pass values to the specified type. For example:

```
intValueTotal2 = Convert.ToInt32(dblValue);
```

In this case, the value in `intValueTotal2` would be 3, since it would be rounded up.

Try It Out   Converting Values between C# Types

Using the form created earlier in the chapter:

1. Drag and drop another button onto the form.

2. Name the button as desired, and specify the `Caption` property. For the purposes of this Try It Out, the button was named `btnConvertingTypes`, and the `Caption` property is set to `Converting Types`.

3. Double-click the button. C# Express creates a routine for the click event and open the code file.

4. Add the following code between the opening and closing curly brackets:

```
double dblValue = 2.7;
int intValueTotal1;
int intValueTotal2;

// First way of converting by casting the value to convert.
intValueTotal1 = (int) dblValue;

// Second way is to use the Convert classes methods.
intValueTotal2 = Convert.ToInt32(dblValue);
```

The code editor appears, as shown in Figure 5-8.

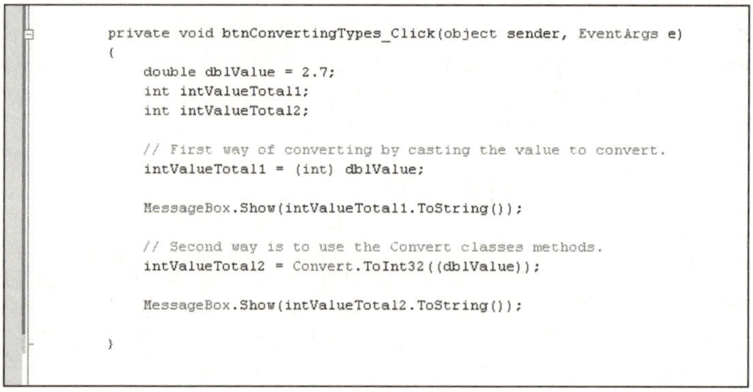

```
private void btnConvertingTypes_Click(object sender, EventArgs e)
{
    double dblValue = 2.7;
    int intValueTotal1;
    int intValueTotal2;

    // First way of converting by casting the value to convert.
    intValueTotal1 = (int) dblValue;

    MessageBox.Show(intValueTotal1.ToString());

    // Second way is to use the Convert classes methods.
    intValueTotal2 = Convert.ToInt32((dblValue));

    MessageBox.Show(intValueTotal2.ToString());

}
```

Figure 5-8

As you type the `Convert` object, you will see all the methods available for the various types to convert to. When the code is run, the first message box displays the value in `intValueTotal1`, and the second the convert value in `intValueTotal2`.

Enumerations

Enumerations are a type of variable that can be used to reflect various values. You have seen enumerations quite a bit in this book, mainly when using a class such as `MessageBox`. When you call the `Show` method of the `MessageBox` class, you can pass an argument to the method. This is also very useful when you are passing an argument to your own procedure and you want to limit the values sent. For example, say you want to create an enumeration called `intMonths`. In this variable, you create enumerators for each month in a year. The declaration for such an enumeration would look like the following:

```
enum Months
    {
        January, February, March,
        April, May, June, July, August,
        September, October, November, December
    };
```

The values are actually integer values representing starting the value 1. When you are using the enumeration in your code, you can type the name of the base name, such as `Months`, and see the list of possible values. You can see this in Figure 5-9.

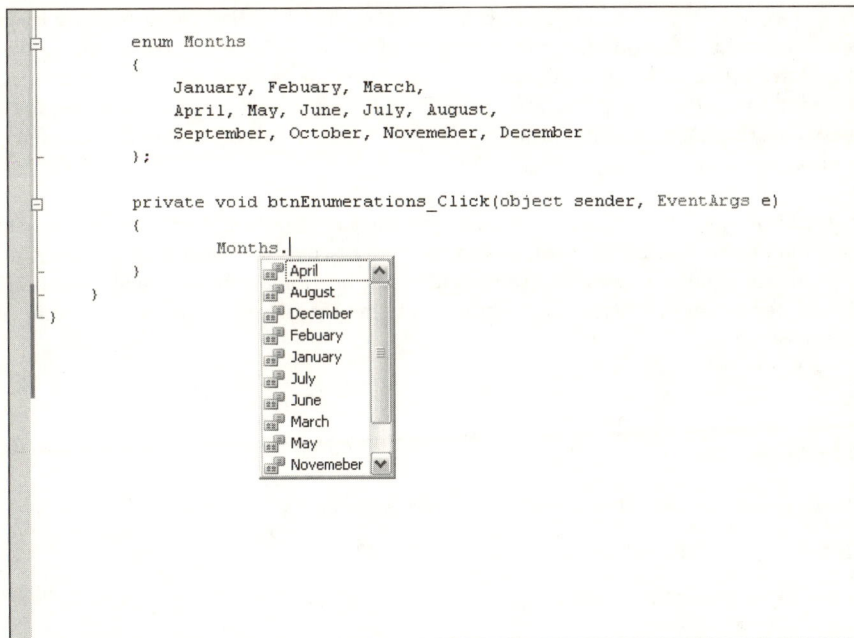

Figure 5-9

Using C# Constants

Constants are different from variables in that you will declare and assign their values once in a module or namespace. They are useful when you use a value that may mean little when viewed as a number but makes perfect sense as a label. For example, if you were creating a recipe where the standard heat for the ingredients is 450°, you could create a constant by using the `const` statement:

```
const string BakeTemp = "450°";

        private void btnConstants_Click(object sender, EventArgs e)
        {
            string strMessage = "The temperature should be at: " + BakeTemp;

            MessageBox.Show(strMessage);

    }
```

Now you could use the `const` throughout the form, and then if you had to change it, you change it at the declaration line. When the code is compiled and built, C# Express takes the label and replaces it with the value throughout the application.

Summary

Wow, this was a busy chapter. You have been shown how, as with other programming languages, C# provides the ability to store and manipulate temporary values in memory. After storing the values and performing the required tasks with the data, you can throw the values away, record them to disk using ADO.NET with XML or other means, or display them on a form. C# requires variables to be strictly typed when declaring them, and if you want to use the values with other types, you must convert them using the classes and methods provided by .NET.

In this chapter, you saw how to declare and assign values to variables. You also read how to use various operators to manipulate variables. Next, constants were discussed, including how to declare and assign values to them and what purposes they serve within applications. You saw how to convert variables between the different standard types. Finally, you saw how to use `const` to make your application easier to read and maintain.

Exercises

1. What is the difference between variables and constants?
2. How do you add a value to an existing variable?
3. Multiply the value in `intValue1` by 10 and assign the answer to a variable called `intAnswer`.
4. What is the command used to convert a C# type of `double` to `int`?
5. Declare the variable named `intMonth` and assign it the value 10 in a single line.

6

Debugging Applications in C# Express

One of the most important things in any programming language and environment is providing the ability to find errors, also called bugs, in your programs. In C# it is no different, since there are different types of errors that can occur in programming C#. When working on locating and fixing the bugs, you are "debugging" your application.

But where does the term "bug" originate? The most common story, though one that is disputed by some, is that in one of the original computers, the Mark I, the programmers were having a hard time with the system when they found out what the problem was. It was, literally, a bug — that is, a moth that was caught inside the system. From there on whenever a problem occurred, the programmers said there was a bug in the system.

C# Express provides various tools to help you debug your applications, including the ability to stop the application, putting it into break mode, which temporarily halts the execution of the program, and use some of its tools. Which tool you use to debug your application depends on the bug. Some tools are used interactively, and some display information that can be used to correct errors within your application. Learning which tools to use can save you hours of time debugging.

In this chapter, you will see examples of the various types of errors and how to debug them within your applications before deploying (releasing for production) them. The chapter includes the following topics:

- ❏ What debugging is
- ❏ An overview of various debugging tools inside C# Express
- ❏ Working with breakpoints and working with data at break time
- ❏ Utilizing watch points
- ❏ Looking at the edit and continue feature
- ❏ Various tools for stepping through code

What is Debugging in C# Express?

Debugging is how you find errors and mistakes in your code. Perhaps you forgot to declare a variable, and then you must fix the resulting errors and mistakes, if possible. If you didn't have the ability to locate errors, you wouldn't be able to create very stable applications—if they ran at all. C# Express includes many tools for debugging your applications that make life much easier. Before jumping into those features, I want to discuss some of the types of errors that can occur in your applications.

Types of Errors That Can Occur in Your Applications

There are actually three types of errors that can occur in your applications:

❑ **Syntax errors.** The most basic type error, a syntax error is an error in the language, like a missing curly bracket (used to begin and end code blocks) or an incorrectly formatted line. It's basically something that the compiler can't understand. These errors will pretty much always be displayed in the Error List window, which is discussed in the next section.

❑ **Semantic/logical errors.** Semantic/logical errors are harder to find, because they won't get read as an error. This is because they aren't a mistake in the language, but rather something that means something other than what you intended, or are caused by data the user entered. You will see these errors when you run your program, but you won't necessarily know what is wrong or where it is in the code.

❑ **Exception errors.** There are some errors that occur during runtime that you can't get rid of. These errors are called *exceptions,* and while they can be trapped and programmed for, because they occur at runtime in the "real world," they will occur regardless of what you do to plan for them. Logical and semantical errors sometimes cause exceptions because the logic fails due to bad data or some other cause. Exceptions and handling them is discussed in Chapter 7.

C# Express Debugging Features: Tools of the Trade

C# Express excels when it comes to providing the tools necessary to help you debug your applications. Depending on which error you are debugging, you will be able to the advantage of the different features included in C# Express. The following sections outline these features.

Using the Error List When Building

The error list is one of the simplest debugging tools, but it is undoubtedly the most important. The error list shows all the errors in the code that prevented the program from running. As mentioned, these are usually syntax errors. The error list also will alert you to various gaps or such in your code. A good example is an integer that you declare but never use; the error list would tell you that. So the error list even helps to clean your code of useless clutter. How cool is that?

When the error list finds an error, it displays several things. The first, of course, is what the error is. It may just be a semicolon you forgot or something similar. The rest of the error list indicates the location of the problem, including its filename, line number, and even the column. While it gives you this data, don't think you still have to hunt for it by yourself. Just double-click the error in the error list and it takes you straight to the problem. It also does the same for warnings.

Try It Out   Creating the Chapter Project and Using the Error List

To start debugging, of course, you need a project to debug. In this project you will add a couple of errors to cause the Error List window to appear.

1. Open C# Express.

2. Click New Project. The New Project dialog box appears.

3. Pick the Windows application.

4. Give the project a name of your choice. The project for this example was named Chapter 6.

5. Drag and drop a `Button` control onto the form. This will be the button to show how to use the Error List window to locate errors in the code.

6. Type `Error List` in the `Text` property of the button.

7. Type `btnErrorList` for the name of the button.

8. Double-click the `btnErrorList` button. The `Click` routine will be created with the following displayed:

```
private void btnErrorList_Click(object sender, EventArgs e)
{

}
```

9. Type the following text in the code block displayed in Step 8.

```
bool blnTest;
blnTest = 0;
if (blnTest = false);
```

10. Now choose Build ⇨ Build Solution. This builds the solution without executing the application. You can then see the Error List window in the left bottom corner of the IDE, as shown in Figure 6-1.

As you can see from the list of errors in the Error List window, you can double-click the errors and correct the bugs. The last error has occurred because you need to have a == when evaluating criteria. You can see the error is highlighted in Figure 6-2.

As you click the other issues in the error list, you will see other bugs that can be fixed. Once you have corrected all the errors in the list, you can rebuild the solution again to test for more errors.

As you rebuild your solution and correct the errors that occur, you will see new errors occurs. This is because some errors can hide other errors.

The next thing to look at is how you go into break mode to work on debugging the application.

You will want to comment-out the lines of code with the errors that you typed in Step 9. To do this, highlight them, and press Ctrl+E, C, or use the toolbar button that looks like the graphic to the right.

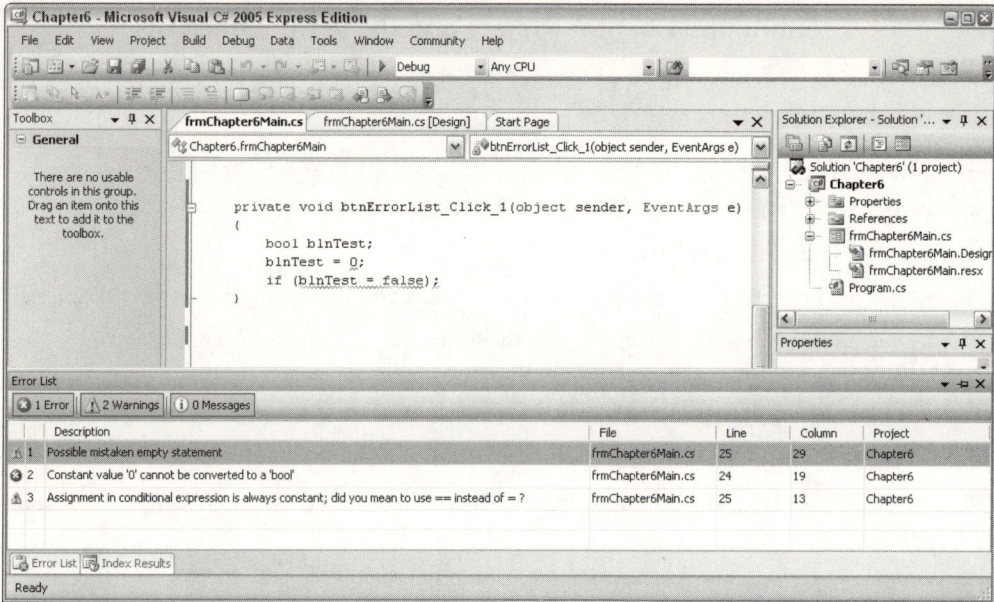

Figure 6-1

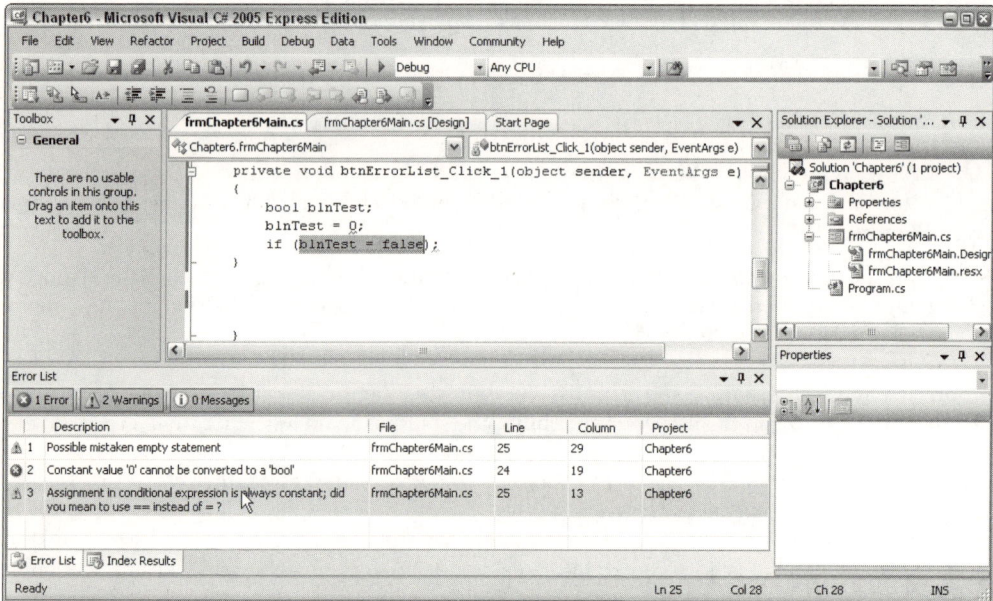

Figure 6-2

Break Mode versus Executing Mode

There will be times when you will need to stop, or pause, code as it is executing. When you are doing it to debug the code and plan on continuing the execution, then the code is placed in break mode. Once in break mode, there are a number of ways you can research various issues with the code and examine various aspects of your application, including examining and manipulating variables. Another task you can accomplish is fixing those semantic and logical errors mentioned before. Remember how they don't show up on the error list? Well, break mode is one of the best ways to find these errors. Break mode enables you to go step-by-step through your program and watch the code working. Several tools are available to you in break mode.

The remainder of this chapter introduces the various tools that you have at your disposal for debugging your applications. You can cause the application to go into break mode several ways. The way that you will probably use the most is by setting breakpoints. These are discussed in the next section in greater detail.

The other way is to move into the editor and choose Debug ⇨ Break All from the menu. When this happens you will then be taken to the editor in break mode, with the line of code the application is breaking on highlighted in green.

Try It Out   Put the Application into Break Mode Using the Menus

Using the application you created in the last Try It Out:

1. Drag and drop another button onto the form.

2. Type btnBreakUsingMenus for the Name property, Breach Using Menus for the Text property.

3. Double-click the button you added. The routine for the Click event will be created as shown here:

```
private void btnBreakUsingMenus_Click(object sender, EventArgs e)
{

}
```

4. Type the following line of code to add a command that will cause the application to pause:

```
MessageBox.Show("Break Me");
```

5. Press F5 to build and execute the application.

6. Click the new button you created.

7. Switch back to the editor.

8. Choose Debug ⇨ Break All from the menu. The code will break and display the last line it was on, in this case the line of code with the MessageBox.Show() method was called. You can see this in Figure 6-3.

9. At this point, you can press F5 to continue executing the application or quit by pressing Shift+F5.

While it is nice to be able to break into the application whenever you need to, it can get kind of hard to break it exactly at the right spot where you want it to break. C# Express provides other ways to break into your application. The main way is by using breakpoints.

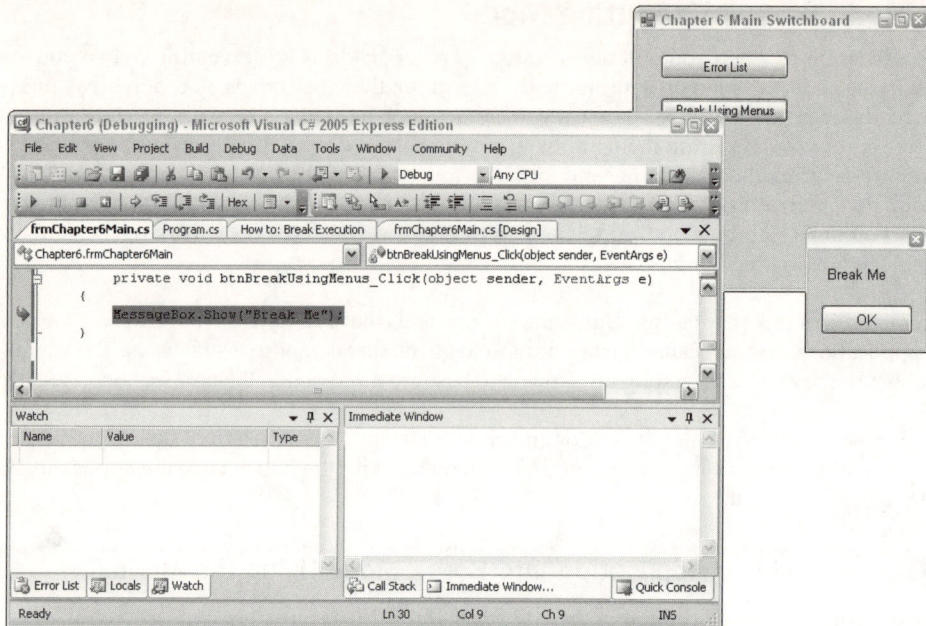

Figure 6-3

Working with Breakpoints

When you add breakpoints in your application, you are specifying which lines of code you want to have the program stop on. The great thing about breakpoints is that you can toggle them on and off as your need them for debugging purposes in just about anyplace in the code. With breakpoints you can:

❑ **Set breakpoints.** While in the code file, either in editing or break mode, you can set breakpoints a number of ways, all of them able to toggle the breakpoints on and off: pressing F9, choosing Debug ➪ Toggle Breakpoint, or clicking the left mouse button in the gray gutter on the left-hand side of the window. No matter how you set the breakpoints, a red circle will appear in the gutter, and the whole line will be highlighted in red.

❑ **Delete Breakpoint.** While you can toggle using the different methods described, you also can right-click the left gutter and choose Delete Breakpoint.

❑ **Disable Breakpoints.** Disabling breakpoints enables you to keep a breakpoint in the program, but not have it run. For example, say you are testing a piece of code a few times and want the code to run through a couple times in between without having to reset the breakpoints,. You can disable a breakpoint by right-clicking the breakpoint in the gutter and choose Disable Breakpoint from the menu. If in the highlighted breakpoint line, you can then choose Breakpoint ➪ Disable Breakpoint.

You can see a couple of breakpoints set in Figure 6-4.

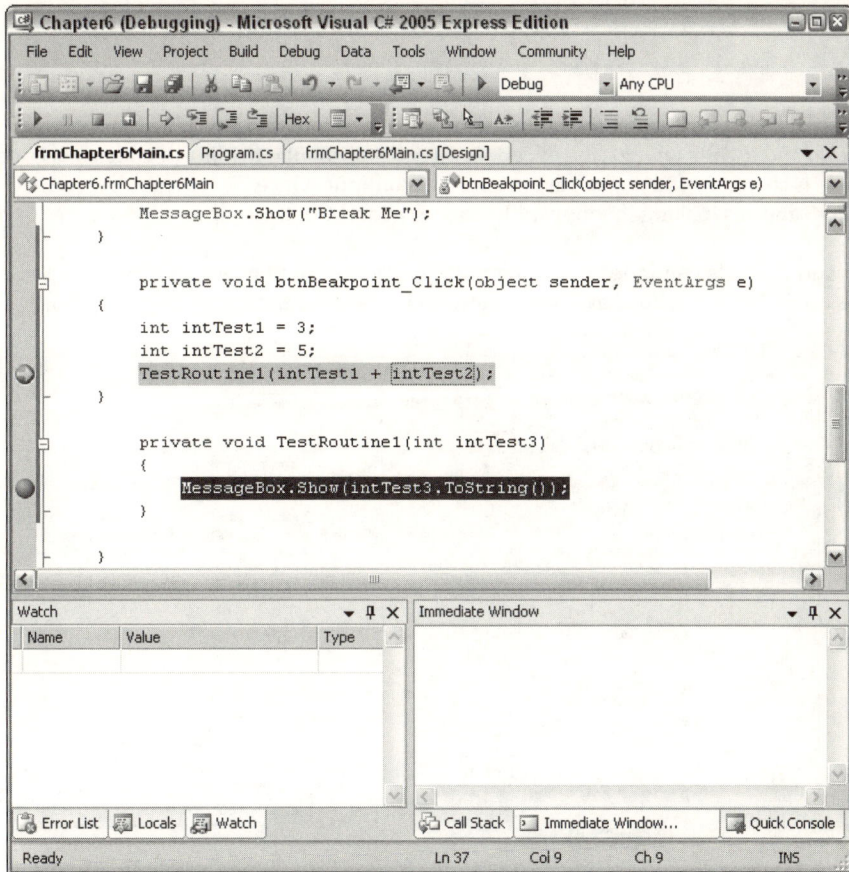

Figure 6-4

Edit and Continue Feature in C# Express

One exciting feature in C# Express is the ability to edit your application in break mode and then continue on with executing your application. This is exciting because in the past whenever you had to edit your program in break mode, Visual Studio would have to reset the application and you would have to rerun it.

In Figure 6-4, you can see that the following code

```
int intTest1 = 3;
int intTest2 = 5;
TestRoutine1(intTest1 + intTest2);
```

was passing 3+5 to `TestRoutine1`. If you decided mid-execution you wanted change it to be

```
TestRoutine1((intTest1 + intTest2)*3);
```

you would do this by setting a breakpoint on the line of code calling `TestRoutine1`. When you execute the program and it halts on that line of code, you can just change the line of code as needed. Once the line of code is changed, you could then press F5 to continue. Once F5 is pressed, a dialog box, as shown in Figure 6-5 appears, asking if you want to have Edit and Continue apply the changes to the code.

Click Yes and the code continues executing with the most current changes. Answer No and the program continues on, but with the code as it was before changes at runtime.

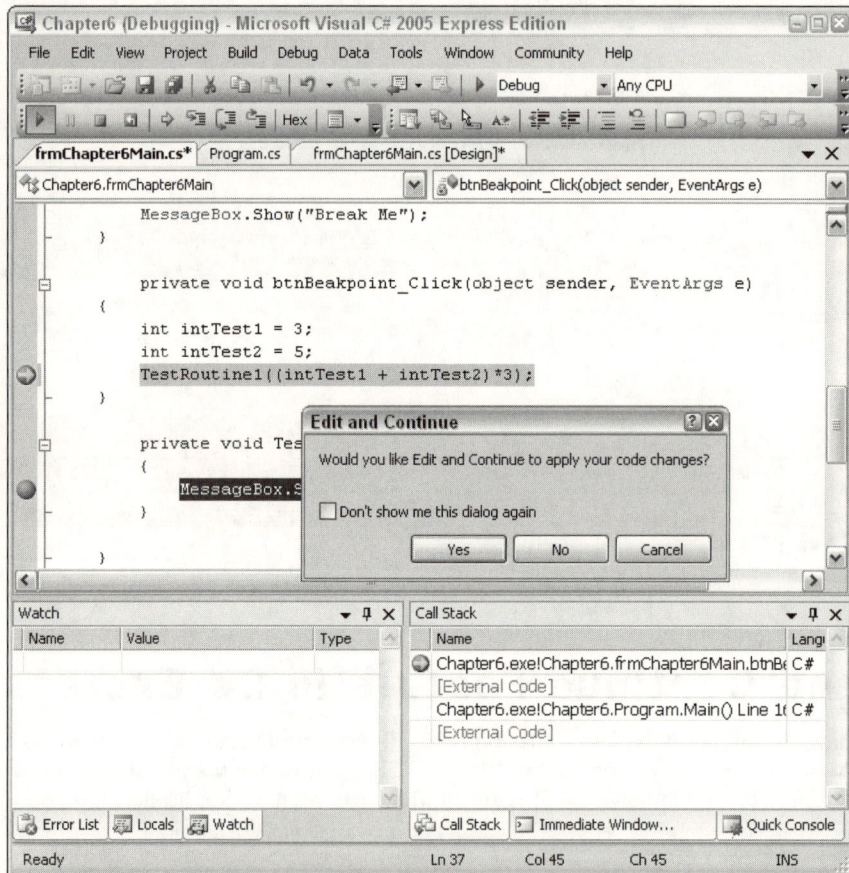

Figure 6-5

You have a lot of options for how you can use Edit and Continue, and the way to see those options is to choose Tools ⇨ Options. Then click the Edit and Continue option under Debugging. When you click these options, the options appear, as shown in Figure 6-6.

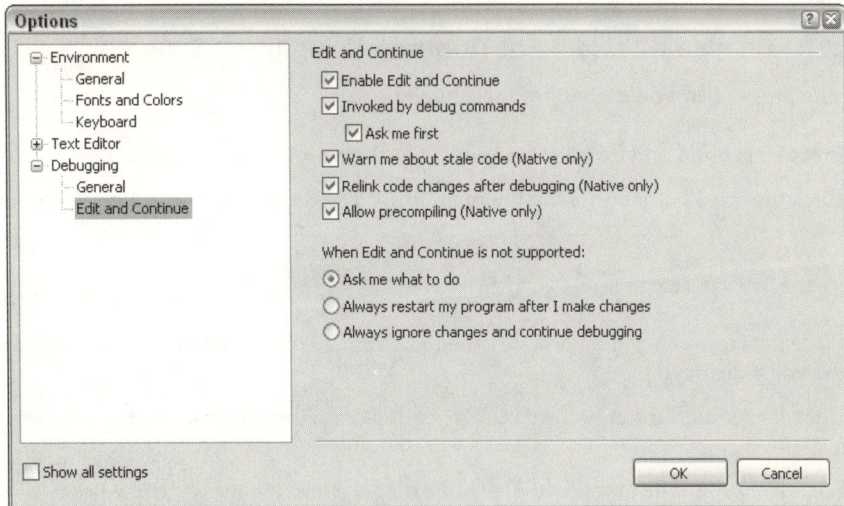

Figure 6-6

Now take some time to look through them and experiment a bit. Then we will discuss displaying and modifying the contents of variables.

Displaying and Modifying Variables when in Break Mode

While in break mode, besides being able to view what part of the code you are in, there are a number of ways that you can view and even modify the variables in your applications. The quickest way to look at variables is to use a feature that is also used for other purposes in the C# Express IDE, called *IntelliSense*.

Using IntelliSense

One of the ways to use IntelliSense is, when in break mode, placing the mouse over a variable. This feature goes along with other IntelliSense features such as displaying classes, properties, and methods as you are typing the name of the objects in code.

Once you have the mouse over the variable, you then see the name and value currently stored in the variable. But IntelliSense doesn't stop there; you can click the value portion of the variable and change it right there. When you change it, C# Express doesn't even call the Edit and Continue feature, but uses the new value. Previously, when you wanted to change values, you had to use the Watch or Immediate windows, both of which are discussed in the next sections.

First, you should try out changing a variable yourself.

Try It Out   Change a Variable at Runtime Using IntelliSense

Utilizing the project that you created for this chapter:

1. Press F5 to build and execute the applications.

2. Click the Breakpoint button on the main form. The code should break on the following line of code:

```
TestRoutine1(intTest1 + intTest2);
```

3. Place the mouse over the variable called `intTest2`. You now see the name of the variable and the value displayed.

4. Click the mouse button in the variable portion of the IntelliSense display, and change the value as desired.

5. Press F5 to continue execution. The value displayed in the message box now uses the new value you placed in `intTest2`.

Additional Ways of Displaying Variables

Besides using IntelliSense, there are a few other ways to display and modify variables as the code is running. The following sections briefly discuss each one and explain how to use them.

Locals Window

When you are running your code, you will have variables that are used locally by your program. In addition to the variables you create, C# generates and uses variables as well. The Locals window displays these variables, including giving you access to the properties and collections for variables that have them. A good example is that when you are in a form, you will be able to see the various form properties, as shown in Figure 6-7.

You can get to the Locals window when the application is running or in break mode via the Debug ⇨ Windows menu item. You also will find the rest of the various tools that I discuss off this menu. If you right-click an entry in the Locals window, you can choose Edit Value to modify a value of one of the local variables.

You also can get to the majority of the debugging tools using the Debug toolbar, located above the editor windows. The toolbar, with the Windows options displayed, is shown in Figure 6-8.

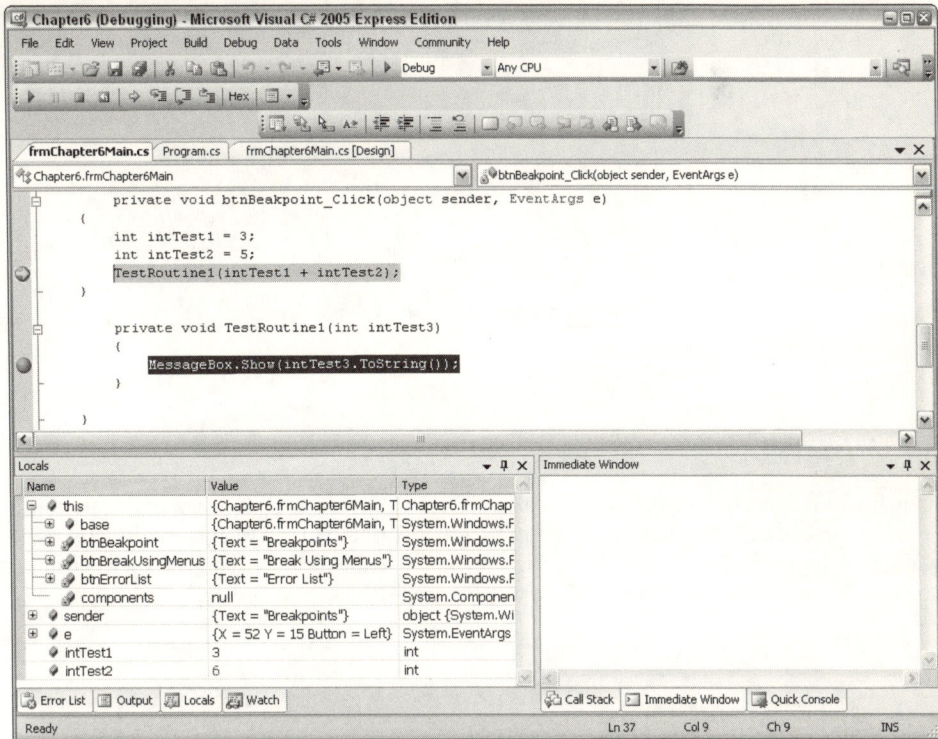

Figure 6-7

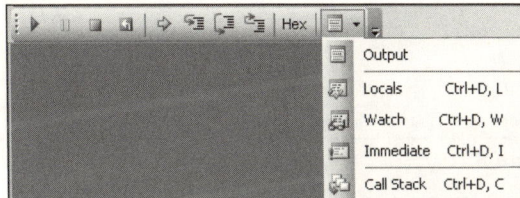

Figure 6-8

Immediate Window

On the right side of the screen in Figure 6-7, you can see the Immediate window. This window provides the ability to display and modify variables as well execute commands. As you get more comfortable with programming and debugging your applications, you will find yourself using this window more. To start with, you can see in Figure 6-9 where `intTest1` is displayed using the `?`, and is set to a new value using the Immediate window.

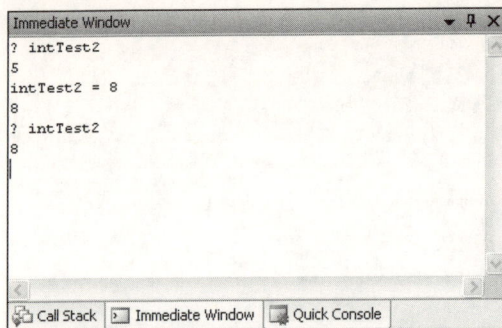

Figure 6-9

Watch Window

The Watch window is useful when you have a variable you want to keep track of throughout your application. When the application is running, you can add a variable to the Watch window by right-clicking the variable in break mode and choosing Add Watch. Once this is done, you can then see and manipulate the variable in the Watch window, shown in Figure 6-10.

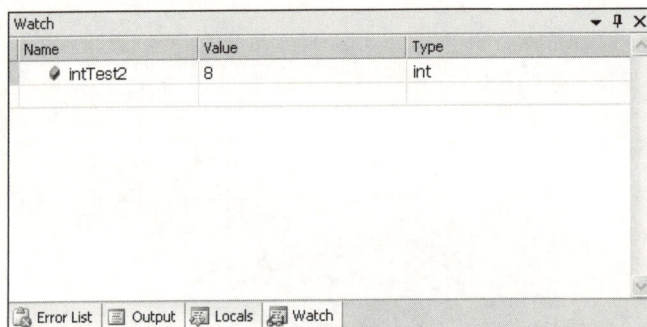

Figure 6-10

Additional Windows

There are some additional windows you can take advantage of such as the Output and Quick Console windows. These windows offer you different ways to debug your applications, where you can send your output to the Output window and perform commands using the Quick Console windows.

Stepping through Code

After breaking in your code, at times you will want to step through your code either line by line or using a little less granular method, but still one that provides more control than using F5. A number of commands offer you control over stepping through code. When in code you can access these commands using either the Debug toolbar or choosing them off the Debug menu:

❑ **Step Into.** This command single-steps you through code, including stepping into routines that are called from other routines. When the routine called is completed, the step goes back up to the next line of code in the calling routine. F11 also is used to invoke the Step Into command.

❑ **Step Over.** Much like the Step Into command except when you are on the call for a routine, it will execute the call (and the routine) but continues on the line of code following the routine.

❑ **Step Out Of.** Just as it sounds, this command steps you out of a routine and sends you back up into the calling routine, once again continuing on the next line of code that called the routine.

The following commands can be found by right-clicking the mouse in the code window during break mode. For these commands, place the cursor where you want the commands executed.

❑ **Run to Cursor.** This command starts executing the program until either a breakpoint is encountered or the line of code is reach that you invoked this command on.

❑ **Set Next Statement.** This command enables you to totally skip lines by jumping to the cursor location.

Other Debugging Tools

A number of additional tools are available for debugging your applications, some of which are a bit more advanced; others just make sense to cover in other chapters. Following are some of these tools:

❑ **Call Stack window.** This window displays the routines that have been called in the current execution of the program. The routines are displayed in reverse order. An example of the call stack is shown in Figure 6-11.

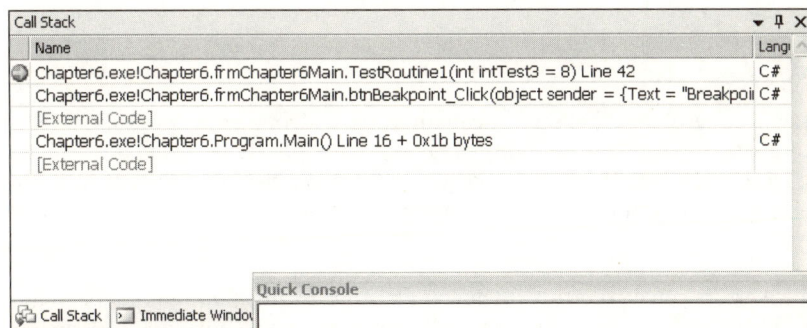

Call Stack	▾ 廿 ✕
Name	Langu
⊙ Chapter6.exe!Chapter6.frmChapter6Main.TestRoutine1(int intTest3 = 8) Line 42	C#
Chapter6.exe!Chapter6.frmChapter6Main.btnBeakpoint_Click(object sender = {Text = "Breakpoi	C#
[External Code]	
Chapter6.exe!Chapter6.Program.Main() Line 16 + 0x1b bytes	C#
[External Code]	
Quick Console	
🔁 Call Stack ⊡ Immediate Window	

Figure 6-11

As you click the routines displayed, you are taken to those routines, and the last line executed is displayed in green.

❑ **Breaking on Exceptions.** This option enables you to specify which errors (exceptions) you want to have your system break on. Exceptions are runtime errors that you can't necessarily debug and remove from your applications. However, you can "catch" the errors and handle them. Sometimes you will purposely want your exceptions to break your applications when you are debugging them, so you can figure out how to handle them. You can get to the Exception feature by choosing Debugging ⇨ Exceptions. When chosen, you will then see the Exceptions dialog box displayed in Figure 6-12.

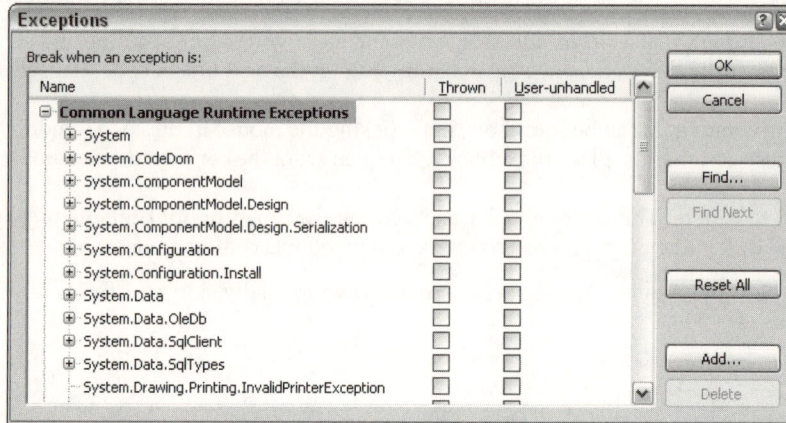

Figure 6-12

Exceptions are discussed in Chapter 7.

❑ **Data Visualizers.** A new feature in C# Express, Data Visualizers let you visualize your data when in debugging mode. This is very cool because it enables you to work though data as you would other variables in your application.

Summary

In this chapter, you have seen that there are many ways to debug your applications. Some of the syntactical errors are caught when you are trying to build your applications, using the Error List by double-clicking the error, and having the editor take you to the exact piece of code that is causing the errors. As you are fixing errors, you will notice that sometimes when you fix one error, you uncover a number of others.

There are some errors you can correct when you walk line by line through the code and examine the data. C# Express provides many tools to make the job easier using breakpoints, Watch windows, and the new Edit and Continue feature. Breakpoints give you the ability to stop the execution of your application just about anywhere in your code. You can even disable a breakpoint while leaving it in the code for later use.

By debugging your application thoroughly and adding exceptions, as described in Chapter 7, you can make your applications pretty darned bulletproof. This chapter showed you how to use the various tools in C# Express to debug your applications. As mentioned, don't sweat it if you are a little confused or nervous with some other tools presented in this chapter. It is a big tool chest, but just like in real life, you start with the easy tools like a hammer or screwdriver, get comfortable with those, then move onto the jigsaws and routers (whatever those are).

Exercises

1. Name the two different types of errors you can debug.

2. What are some of the ways to work with breakpoints?

3. Name two of the windows that are used for displaying values in break mode.

4. What is the technology that enables you to hover the mouse over variables and see their values in break mode?

5. What are the three commands for stepping through code?

7

Selections, Iterations, and Catching Exceptions

In living your day-to-day life, you have to make decisions. I remember when I graduated from high school I didn't really want to make any decisions, but alas, such is life. It can also be said that when programming your applications, regardless of what language you are using, you will have to make decisions in the code. In both code and life, once decisions are made, you will take one action or another. In coding, this decision making is called *selection*, also known as *branching*. When you need to make decisions and branch, C# provides a number of statements, such as `if . . . else` and `switch`, that can help you compare variables and objects in your code and execute blocks of code based on decisions made.

Another necessary feature of the programming language is to perform loops, also referred to as *iterations*. Examples of iterations are when you want to have your code loop through the days of a given month and perform an action for each day, or just do a count up to 10. You need to be able to tell your application to perform a code block for a specified number of times. C# provides a number of statements for accomplish iterations depending on what the task is.

Lastly, no matter how well you build your code, issues are going to occur. These issues, called *exceptions* in the .NET realm, can cause serious problems if not handled correctly. How you handle these exceptions affects the overall user experience in working with your applications (and also could spare you from getting beat up by IT people).

In discussing the topics just mentioned, this chapter will cover:

- ❑ Calling routines from one another
- ❑ Working with `if . . . else` statements to handle simple conditional selection
- ❑ Using `switch` statements for more complex selections
- ❑ Working with `for` statements to accomplish iterations
- ❑ Learning how to use `try . . catch . . finally` to catch exceptions that can occur

Performing Selections in Your Applications

While not every routine you create in C# will require you to make decisions and select either a single line or blocks of code, it happens quite frequently. It would be very limiting if C# didn't offer commands that take the need to branch in your code into consideration. The majority of programming languages offer some kind of branching statements as far back as some of the original machine languages.

C# has two main statements to facilitate selection in C#: `if . . . else` for simple branching and `switch . . . case` for more complex selections. Before jumping into the statements, I want to discuss the project used for these examples and have you create it.

Creating the Chapter 7 Project

To show this and the other examples in this chapter, you will create a form that can be used to display results from all the examples. The form is shown in Figure 7-1.

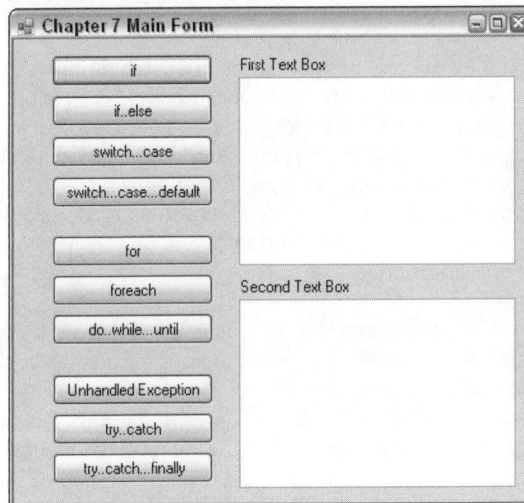

Figure 7-1

As you can see from the number of buttons displayed here, there is a lot of work to do. So get started already!

Try It Out   **Create the Sample Form**

To help you understand how to use the various statements discussed in this chapter, besides the buttons used for executing the examples that most of the forms in the book use, you will add two `Label` and two `TextBox` controls. You will use the first text box to input values, and when you click each of the buttons, the code will display values in the second text box.

1. Open C# Express.

2. Click New Project.

3. Choose Windows Application for the template to use.

4. Name the project, and click OK. The project is created and the default form displayed.

I will leave it up to you to specify the properties of the form and command buttons as you see fit, since the purpose of this chapter is to focus on statements, and you have had a lot of experience creating simple forms.

5. Add the two `Label` controls and specify the `Text` property in the Properties window to display "First Text Box" and "Second Text Box".

6. Add the two `TextBox` controls below each `Label` control added. Make sure that the `Name` properties of the two controls are `textBox1` and `textBox2`, which should be the default setting.

7. Set the `Multiline` property of each `TextBox` control to `True`, as shown in Figure 7-2 for `textBox1`. The figure also shows how the four controls described in these steps could look.

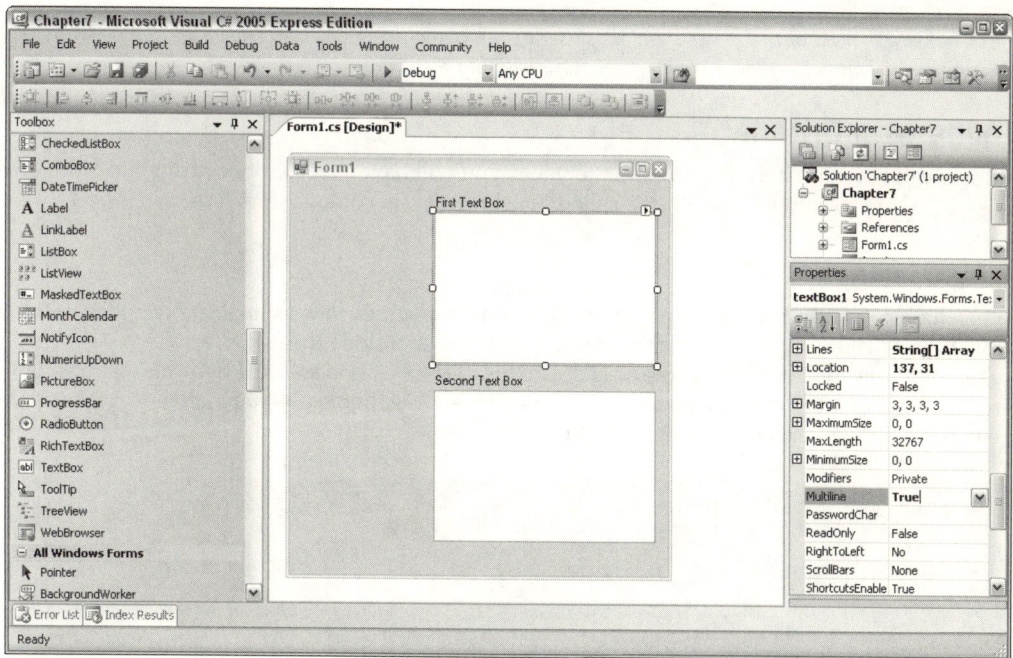

Figure 7-2

Okay, now you're ready to get into the various statements I wanted to discuss in this chapter.

Simple Selection Using if...else Statements

When you have a quick decision to make in your code, if . . . else statements are the ones to use. The syntax for these statements is as follows:

```
if (criteria true value)
     statement(s) to perform if true
else
     statement(s) to perform if false
```

As I mentioned, you are making decisions in code and selecting a path (code) that you want to take, just like in real life.

One nice thing about the `if` statement is if you only want to execute a line of code if something is true, you don't even have to use the `else` portion of the statements. This is shown in the following:

```
if (this.textBox1.Text == "Display")
     this.textBox2.Text = "I am displaying";
```

This way, you perform the action only if the criteria in the `if` statement is met, in this case:

```
this.textBox1.Text == "Display"
```

You need to make sure you surround the criteria with parentheses (). Also, remember that by using the == you are performing a comparison, not assigning the value.

Working with Criteria

When dealing with criteria in various statements, you will have to remember your good old high school algebra. Actually, you will use what is called *boolean algebra* in comparisons.

Utilizing Operators

When looking at criteria, whenever you need to compare values such as the text box value with the literal string `"Display"`, you will use an *operator*. Operators provide the means for C# to perform boolean evaluations, meaning returning true or false. In this case == is used so see if two values are equal. There are a number of other operators that you can use, depending on the criteria you are trying to evaluate. Here is a table of some of the other operator possibilities:

Symbol	Description
==	Equal
>=	Greater than or equal to
>	Greater than
!=	Not equal to
<=	Less than or equal to
<	Less than

There are additional operators, but these are the most common and will get you started nicely. You will use operators with more than just selection-type statements. You will use them for iteration statements as well.

For another example of using one of the other operators, if you wanted to look at a variable called `intAge` and make sure that code was only executed if the age was 18 or older, the selection line of code would look as follows:

```
if (intAge >= 18)
```

I think you get the idea. One last topic to discuss with regard to criteria is the use of complex criteria.

Complex Criteria

When you need to compare more than one value on a line, you will use additional operators that performs AND and OR logic. Below are some of those operators.

Symbol	Description
&&	Logical AND
||	Logical Or

Suppose you need to look not only at those who are 18 and over but also (AND) check that the value in `strState` is equal to `"WA"`. The selection line of code would be

```
if ((intAge >= 18) && (strState == "WA"))
```

Notice the use of parentheses; just as in algebra, you can control which operators get evaluated based on how you have the parentheses positioned. Those operators inside parentheses are evaluated first.

Using Code Blocks with Selection

Instead of single lines of code as shown previously, you can use code blocks surrounded by {}. Say in addition to updating the second `TextBox` control, you want to display a message box. This would be accomplished with the following lines of code:

```
if (this.textBox1.Text == "Display")
{
    this.textBox2.Text = "I am displaying";
    MessageBox.Show("Displaying here too");
}
```

Time to go ahead and use the `if` statement.

Try It Out   **Use an if Statement to Select a Block of Code**

Using the form you created in the first Try It Out:

1. Drag and drop a `Button` control onto the form.
2. Name it as desired. For this example, the `Button` control was named `btnIf`.

3.   Double-click the `btnIf` button. The `btnIf_Click` routine is created as shown here:

```
private void btnIf_Click(object sender, EventArgs e)
{

}
```

4.   With the cursor between the curly brackets, type the following lines of code:

```
if (this.textBox1.Text == "Display")
{
    this.textBox2.Text = "I am displaying";
    MessageBox.Show("Displaying here too");
}
```

So the complete `btnIf_Click` event code looks as follows:

```
private void btnIf_Click(object sender, EventArgs e)
{
    if (this.textBox1.Text == "Display")
    {
        this.textBox2.Text = "I am displaying";
        MessageBox.Show("Displaying here too");
    }
}
```

5.   Press F5 to build and execute the application.

6.   Type **Display** into the first text box.

7.   Click the `Button` control you added. The form (minus some of the buttons) and message box shown in Figure 7-3 appears.

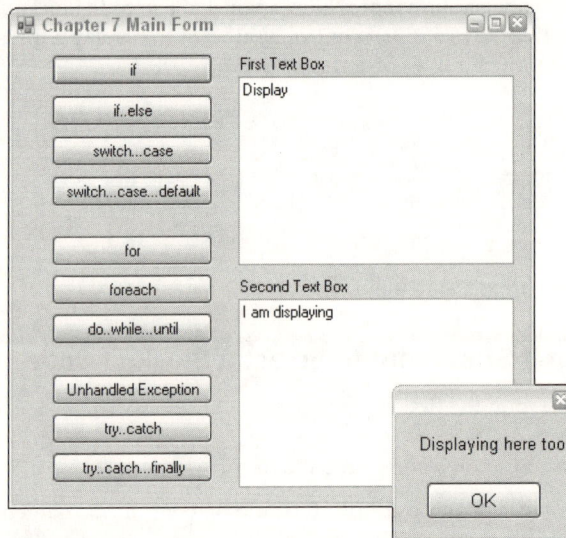

Figure 7-3

While this is great when you only want to perform actions when a value is true, you can also use an `else` statement to perform an alternate line or block of code.

Adding the else Statement

As mentioned, adding an `else` statement onto an `if` statements gives you the ability to perform more than one set of commands. To accomplish this, you place the `else` statement after the last statement executed for the `if` statement:

```
if (this.textBox1.Text == "Display")
    this.textBox2.Text = "I am displaying";
else
    this.textBox2.Text = "I am not displaying";
```

So you can see how easy it is to handle this type of situation.

Additional Ways to Use the if . . . else

In addition to using the `else` statements, there are a couple of other ways to control the selection of code:

❏ **Using** `if . . . else if . . . else`. To make it even more complete, you can add `if` statements onto the `else` statements for even more control. The syntax for this would be as follows:

```
if (<criteria true value>)
    statement(s) to perform if true
else if (<criteria2 true value>)
    statement(s) to perform if second criteria is true
else
    statement(s) to perform if false
```

❏ **Nesting** `if...else` **statements.** By nesting `if . . . else` statements, you can perform additional statements and control the flow of the code as necessary:

```
if (<criteria true value>)
  if (<criteria 2 true value>)
    statement(s) to perform if true
else
    statement(s) to perform if false
```

Try It Out	Use if . . else Statements to Select Code

Using the form you created for the chapter:

1. Drag and drop another `Button` control onto the form.

2. Name it as desired. For this example, the `Button` control was named `btnIfElse`.

3. Double-click the `btnIfElse` button. The `btnIfElse_Click` routine is created as shown here:

```
private void btnIfElse_Click(object sender, EventArgs e)
{

}
```

4. Type the following code between the curly brackets:

```
if (this.textBox1.Text == "Display")
    this.textBox2.Text = "I am displaying";
else
    this.textBox2.Text = "I am not displaying";
```

The final block of code now looks like the following:

```
private void btnIfElse_Click(object sender, EventArgs e)
{
    if (this.textBox1.Text == "Display")
        this.textBox2.Text = "I am displaying";
    else
        this.textBox2.Text = "I am not displaying";
}
```

5. Press F5 to build and execute the application.

6. Click the new button without typing anything into the first text box. "I am not displaying" appears in the second text box, since the Text property in the first text box is not set to "Display." You can see this in Figure 7-4.

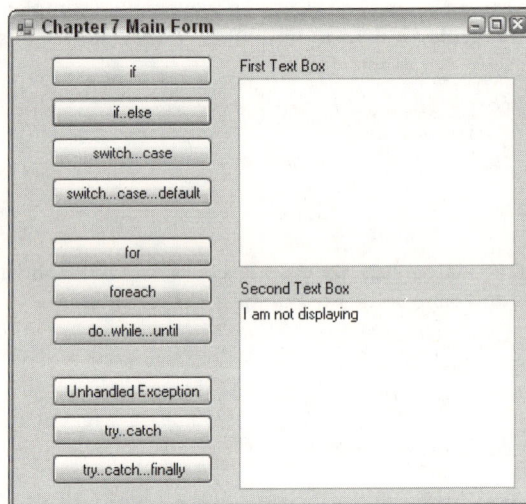

Figure 7-4

While you can use as many if . . . else if . . . else statements together as necessary, it gets pretty messy very quickly when trying to read that type of code. To help with this issue, you can use the switch statement.

Working with switch . . . case Statements

When you need to act on more than a couple of values for a given criteria, using the switch . . . case statement is the way to go. To work with it, you will actually be able to look at the value as more than just a boolean statement, although you can do just that. This means that instead of just looking at whether the criteria value is true, you can supply an expression and act on what exactly the value of the expression is.

Starting with switch...case

The partial syntax for switch...case is as follows:

```
switch (expression)
{
    case constant-expression:
        statement
        jump-statement
}
```

I say *partial* because there is another part that will discussed in the next section. Taking the text box used on the form for the chapter, you will test to see if numbers have been stored in the Text property. After using the switch . . . case statement, the code looks to see if the value are equal to the text values of "1", "2" . . ., and so on. You can see the partial code:

```
switch (this.textBox1.Text)
{
    case "1":
        this.textBox2.Text = "Monday";
        break;

    case "2":
        this.textBox2.Text = "Tuesday";
        break;
        . . .
}
```

Note the lines of code that read:

```
break;
```

This is called the jump statement. Jump statements are used when you are done performing the specified tasks for each case code block. For now you will only be using the break statement. It causes the program to "break" out of the switch statement and continue on the line of code directly after the end of the switch code block. This statement is required if you are not using the jump statement.

Test a TextBox control Value Using switch...case

Using the form you created for the chapter:

1. Drag and drop another Button control onto the form.

2. Name it as desired. For this example the Button control was named btnSwitchCase.

3. Double-click the btnSwitchCase button. The btnSwitchCase_Click routine is created as shown here:

```
private void btnSwitchCase_Click(object sender, EventArgs e)
{

}
```

4. Type the following code between the beginning and ending curly brackets:

```
switch (this.textBox1.Text)
{
    case "1":
        this.textBox2.Text = "Monday";
        break;

    case "2":
        this.textBox2.Text = "Tuesday";
        break;

    case "3":
        this.textBox2.Text = "Wednesday";
        break;

    case "4":
        this.textBox2.Text = "Thursday";
        break;

    case "5":
        this.textBox2.Text = "Friday";
        break;
}
```

5. Press F5 to build and test the application.

6. Type **1** into the first text box.

7. Click the new button you added to the form. The second text box should display "Monday".

8. Type **3** into the first text box. Note that you will type numbers, not the actual label for the day.

9. Once again click the new button. The second text box displays "Wednesday," as shown in Figure 7-5.

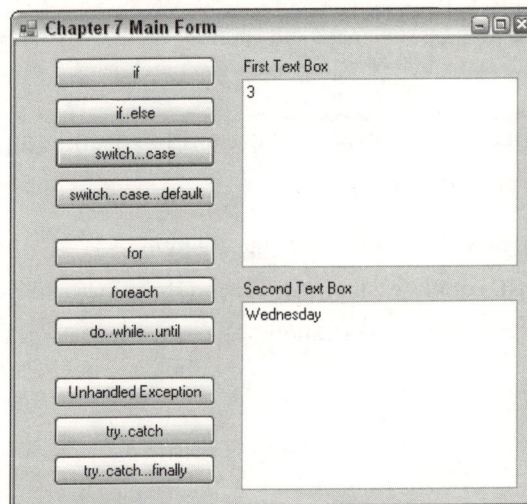

Figure 7-5

One place where the `switch . . . case` statements come up short as discussed thus far is that if you type in anything but those five days, nothing gets placed in the second text box. To handle this, there is another statement included in the `switch . . . case` statements called `default`.

Add the default Statement

The complete syntax for the `switch . . . case` statements can be seen here:

```
switch (expression)
{
    case constant-expression:
        statement
        jump-statement
    [default:
        statement
        jump-statement]
}
```

The code block created for the default statement is performed if none of the other case statements are fulfilled. So in the case of the code created to look at days in a week, if none fall into the first five days, the following default statement and code block are executed:

```
default:
    this.textBox2.Text = "Weekend";
    break;
```

Now, of course, this isn't going to take care of all values, because the user can type in any other number or letter and in this instance gets the default code block, but it is a good example for the default.

Try It Out   **Use if...else Statements to Select Code**

Using the form you created for the chapter:

1. Drag and drop another `Button` control onto the form.

2. Name it as desired. For this example the `Button` control was named `btnSwitchCaseDefault`.

3. Double-click the `btnSwitchCaseDefault` button. The `btnSwitchCaseDefault_Click` routine is created as shown here:

```
private void btnSwitchCaseDefault_Click(object sender, EventArgs e)
{

}
```

4. Type the following lines of code:

```
switch (this.textBox1.Text)
{
    case "1":
        this.textBox2.Text = "Monday";
        break;

    case "2":
```

```
            this.textBox2.Text = "Tuesday";
            break;

      case "3":
            this.textBox2.Text = "Wednesday";
            break;

      case "4":
            this.textBox2.Text = "Thursday";
            break;

      case "5":
            this.textBox2.Text = "Friday";
            break;

      default:
            this.textBox2.Text = "Weekend";
            break;
   }
```

As all good developers do, you could cut and paste the majority of the code above from the last Try It Out to save time and steps.

5. Press F5 to build and run the application.

6. Type **6** in the first text box.

7. Click the new button you added in Step 1. The word "Weekend" is displayed in the second text box, as shown in Figure 7-6.

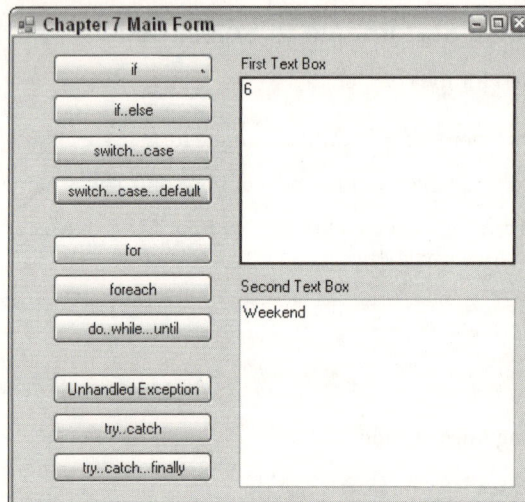

Figure 7-6

As you are developing your applications, after a while you will know when you need to use one selection-type statement over another. Sometimes you will start out with one, and as you work with the routine more, you change it to another because it is more appropriate.

Performing Iterations

In addition to selecting which code needs to be executed, it is inevitable that a situation will arise where you will need to perform iterations (loops) in your code. Following are some examples where you may perform iterations:

❑ **Perform actions against individual records in a database table.** You will get a chance to do this in Chapter 13, "Working with ADO.NET."

❑ **Work through the days of the given month.** This is given as an example in Chapter 14, "Getting More Experience with Controls."

❑ **Display the date of a specified day of each month for the next 12 months.** You will get a chance to do this in this chapter throughout the sections.

Depending on what tasks you are performing, there are a number of different types of iteration statements you put to use. In the next section you learn how to use each and when you should use one over the other.

Working with for Statements

When you are iterating a set number of times, and know that number ahead of time, then the `for` statement is a good one to use. With this statement you specify the number you want to start at and the maximum value to execute the up to. The syntax for the `for` statement is as follows:

```
for ([initializers]; [expression]; [iterators])
```

❑ `initializers` — A typed variable that is used to iterate the number of times you are going to execute.

❑ `expression` — A boolean expression used to terminate the iterations when `expression` is `false`.

❑ `iterators` — Taking the variable that is initialized, this segment of the statement performs an iteration against it. Examples of iterations are `++`, which takes the value and adds 1 to it, and `--`, which subtracts 1.

Following is an example of the `for` statement used for this example:

```
for (int i = 1; i < 6; i++)
```

Where the expression in this case is `I < 6`*, you could also use a variable such as* `I < intMax` *if needed.*

The code inside this iteration statement will occur 5 times `int i = 1`, specifying the starting value, and `i < 6` specifying the maximum). In this case the code that will be executed inside the iteration statement is as follows:

```
this.textBox1.Text +=
        DateTime.Today.AddMonths(i).ToShortDateString() + Environment.NewLine;
```

In this command the variable i is used with the AddMonths() method of the DateTime.Today property, displaying the ShortDate format (mm/dd/yy). As my excellent technical editor pointed out, this will change based on the region you are in. The Environment.NewLine is included so that each date is displayed on a separate line in textBox1.

Try It Out   **Use the for Statement**

Using the form you created for the chapter:

1.   Drag and drop another Button control onto the form.

2.   Name it as desired. For this example the Button control was named btnFor.

3.   Double-click the btnFor button. The btnFor_Click routine is created as shown here:

```
private void btnFor_Click(object sender, EventArgs e)
{

}
```

4.   Type the following lines of code:

```
for (int i = 1; i < 6; i++)
    this.textBox1.Text +=
        DateTime.Today.AddMonths(i).ToShortDateString() + Environment.NewLine;
```

5.   Press F5 to build and test the application.

6.   Click the new button you added in Step 1. The next five months are displayed with the same day as today, as shown in Figure 7-7.

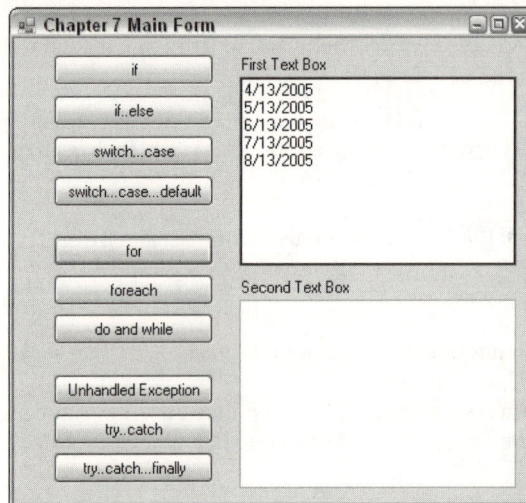

Figure 7-7

If you need to loop through objects or in collections such as controls on a form, you can iterate through them by using the variable that is created for the index of the array or collection. But a more efficient way to accomplish the task is the use the `foreach` statement.

Handling Objects with foreach Statement

When you want to iterate through a collection (or array), you will use the following syntax:

```
foreach (type identifier in expression)
    statement(s)
```

where the `type` will be an individual item in the collection specified by `expression`. The identifier will be the name you give the individual that will be used in the statement or statements inside the iteration. In the example in this section you, will iterate through the `Controls` on the current form.

```
foreach (Control ctlCurr in this.Controls)
```

Inside this loop you change the `ForeColor` property of each of the controls to red, using the following statement:

```
ctlCurr.ForeColor = Color.Red;
```

Try It Out   Use the foreach Statement

Using the form you created for the chapter:

1.   Drag and drop another `Button` control onto the form.

2.   Name it as desired. For this example the `Button` control was named `btnForEach`.

3.   Double-click the `btnForEach` button. The `btnForEach_Click` routine is created as shown here:

```
private void btnForEach_Click(object sender, EventArgs e)
{

}
```

4.   Type the following lines of code.

```
foreach (Control ctlCurr in this.Controls)
    ctlCurr.ForeColor = Color.Red;
```

5.   Press F5 to build and test the application.

6.   Click the new button you added in Step 1. The fore color of all the controls on the form will be changed to red. I won't bother displaying the form since you can't really see it in black and white.

As you can see from this example, C# makes it fairly easy to work your way through collections. To read more about the `foreach` statement, see Chapter 14, "Getting More Experience with Controls."

Using do and while Statements

The last iteration statements to discuss are the do and while statements. As with the other statements, which one you use will depend on what you are trying to accomplish. The syntax for the do statement is as follows:

```
do
{
    statement(s)
}
while (expression);
```

With the do statement, the code will execute until the expression in the while portion of the statement is false. Here is the do statement used in the example for this section, along with the statements used within it:

```
do
{
    this.textBox2.Text +=
            DateTime.Today.AddMonths(intCurr).ToShortDateString() +
            Environment.NewLine;
    intCurr++;
}
while (intCurr < 5);
```

You can use the intCurr++ syntax inside the expression used with the while portion of the do statement do (intCurr++). If you did, then you wouldn't need it inside the code block.

An alternative to the do statement is the while statement. The syntax for that can be seen here:

```
while (expression)
{
    statement(s)
}
```

Here is the while statement used in the example:

```
while (intCurr < 5)
{
    this.textBox2.Text +=
            DateTime.Today.AddMonths(intCurr).ToShortDateString() +
            Environment.NewLine;
    intCurr++;
};
```

You will notice that the difference between the two is where the expression is evaluated. Because the do statement evaluates the expression at the bottom of the code block, it will always execute for at least one iteration, even if the expression is false to begin with.

Try It Out   **Use the do and while Statements**

Using the form you created for the chapter:

1.   Drag and drop another `Button` control onto the form.

2.   Name it as desired. For this example the `Button` control was named `btnDoAndWhile`.

3.   Double-click the `btnDoAndWhile` button. The `btnDoAndWhile_Click` routine is created as shown here:

```
private void btnDoAndWhile_Click(object sender, EventArgs e)
{

}
```

4.   Type the following lines of code:

```
int intCurr = Convert.ToInt32(this.textBox1.Text);
        textBox2.Text = "Using do" + Environment.NewLine;

        do
        {
            this.textBox2.Text +=
                DateTime.Today.AddMonths(intCurr).ToShortDateString() +
                Environment.NewLine;
            intCurr++;
        }
        while (intCurr < 5);

        intCurr = Convert.ToInt32(this.textBox1.Text);
        textBox2.Text += "Using while" + Environment.NewLine;

        while (intCurr < 5)
        {
            this.textBox2.Text +=
DateTime.Today.AddMonths(intCurr).ToShortDateString() +
Environment.NewLine;
            intCurr++;
        };
```

The only code different from in the examples shown in the section earlier is the inclusion of the two following lines of code, used twice:

```
intCurr = Convert.ToInt32(this.textBox1.Text);
textBox2.Text += "Using statement type" + Environment.NewLine;
```

These are used to initialize the variable `intCurr` the first time with the value from `textBox1`, and then display a header in `textBox2`.

5.   Press F5 to build and test the application.

6.   Type **1** for the value in the first text box.

7.   Click the new button you added in Step 1. You will then see the display in Figure 7-8.

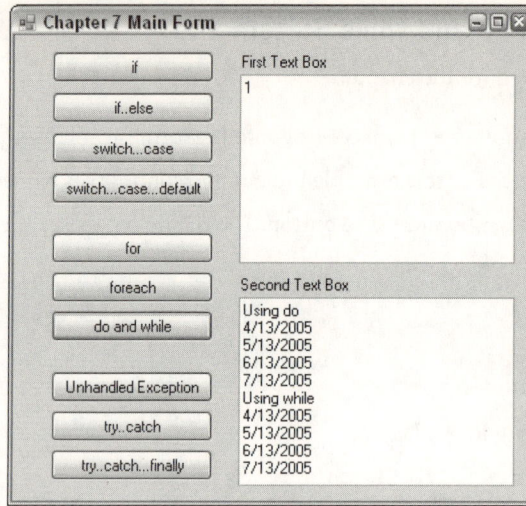

Figure 7-8

As you can see in Figure 7-8 there isn't much difference when using the two statements with an expression that is true more than the first time through the loop. However, when you use an expression that evaluates to false the first time, you can see the difference.

8. Type **6**; then click the button added in Step 1. Since 6 comes back false the first time (`intCurr < 5`), then the `while` statement never gets executed. You can see this in Figure 7-9.

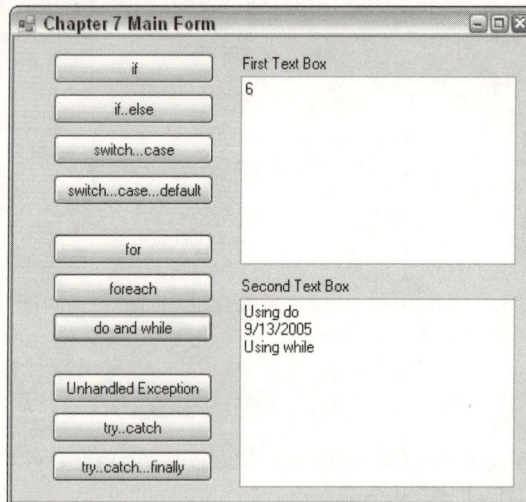

Figure 7-9

Hopefully you can see the difference between the two. As with selection-type statements, you will gain confidence and see where you will use one type of iteration statement over the other.

Catching Exceptions in Your Code

When you are writing code you will have errors that occur at runtime. Even if you write the most perfect code in the world, there will be issues that happen because of outside influences. An important feature of the code is to be able to handle the errors when they do occur, and keep the application running. As mentioned, these errors in .NET are called *exceptions*. Exceptions can occur for a variety of reasons, and in fact there are even classes created in .NET to help you trap and handle the exceptions.

If left unhandled, your application will give a rude error message and dump you out to Windows. If running in the Release mode into the code if in Debug, which is the default mode for running. Before seeing how to trap the exceptions mentioned in the last paragraph, I want you to see what it looks like to have an exception to occur unhandled.

Try It Out   **Create a Routine with an Unhandled Exception**

Using the form you created for the chapter:

1. Drag and drop another `Button` control onto the form.

2. Name it as desired. For this example the `Button` control was named `btnUnhandledException`.

3. Double-click the `btnUnhandledException` button. The `btnUnhandledException_Click` routine is created as shown here:

```
private void btnUnhandledException_Click(object sender, EventArgs e)
{

}
```

4. Type the following lines of code:

```
int intCurr = Convert.ToInt32(this.textBox1.Text);
textBox2.Text = Convert.ToString(intCurr + 3);
```

This code can break if a nonnumeric value is entered in `textBox1`. This includes no value. You can see the complete routine here:

```
private void btnUnhandledException_Click(object sender, EventArgs e)
{
    int intCurr = Convert.ToInt32(this.textBox1.Text);
    textBox2.Text = Convert.ToString(intCurr + 3);
}
```

5. Press F5 to build and execute the application.

6. Click the new button you added in Step 1 without putting any value in `textBox1`. The error is displayed in Figure 7-10.

While the rest of the chapter discusses the various ways to catch exceptions, I generally let the exceptions occur while I am writing the code, until I am ready to release it. The reason is that you can see some of the exceptions that can occur and possibly program for them.

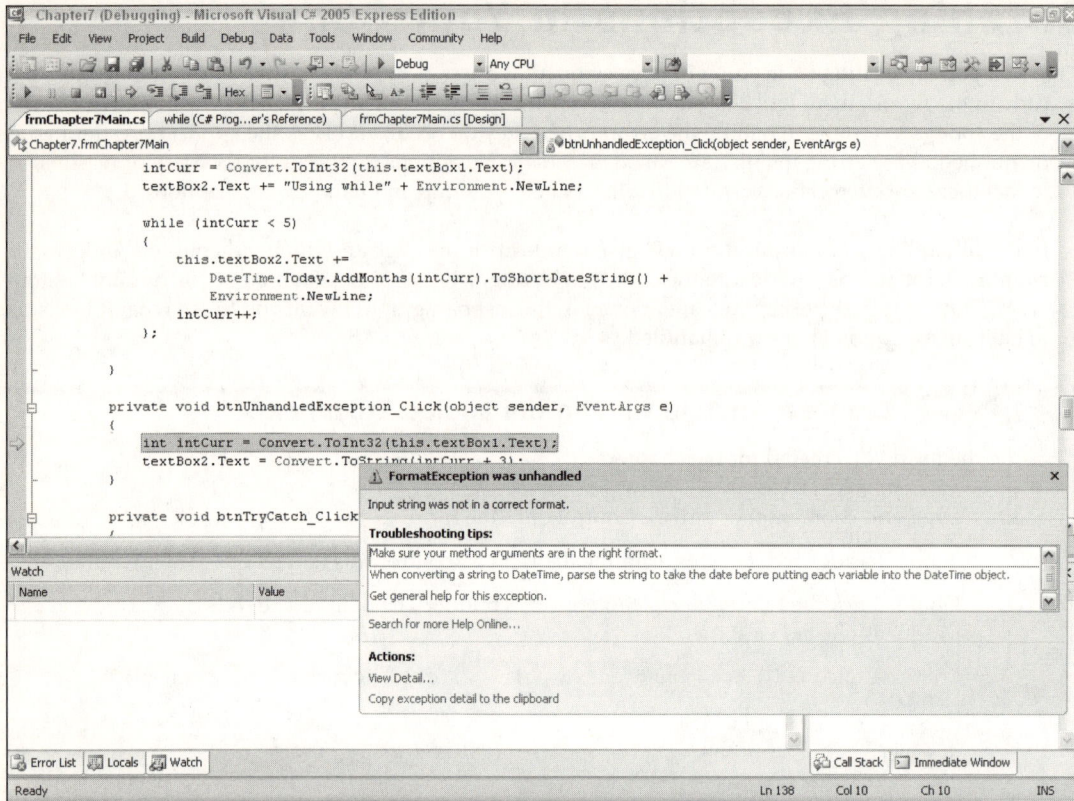

Figure 7-10

Starting Off Easy with try...catch Statements

To catch exceptions you will start with the `try . . . catch` statements, the syntax of which can be seen here:

```
try
{
}
Catch[(exceptiontype variable)]
{
}
```

For now, don't worry about the (`exceptiontype variable`) portion of the syntax. When you just want to catch and handle any exception that occurs, you can use the `try . . . catch` statements alone. As an example, taking the two lines of code from the last section, you can wrap the code with the try code block and then handle resulting exceptions with the catch code block. Here is how it looks:

```
try
{
    int intCurr = Convert.ToInt32(this.textBox1.Text);
```

```
            textBox2.Text = Convert.ToString(intCurr + 3);
    }
    catch
    {
            textBox2.Text = "Exception Occurred";
    }
```

In this code a literal string is placed into the `Text`property of `textBox2` to let the user know an error has occurred. Sometimes that is the way you handle exceptions, by simple displaying a message that informs the user that an exception has occurred.

Try It Out   **Use the try...catch statements**

Using the form you created for the chapter:

1. Drag and drop another `Button` control onto the form.

2. Name it as desired. For this example the `Button` control was named `btnTryCatch`.

3. Double-click the `btnTryCatch` button. The `btnTryCatch_Click` routine is created as shown here:

```
private void btnTryCatch_Click(object sender, EventArgs e)
{

}
```

4. Type the following lines of code:

```
try
{
    int intCurr = Convert.ToInt32(this.textBox1.Text);
    textBox2.Text = Convert.ToString(intCurr + 3);
}
catch
{
    textBox2.Text = "Exception Occurred";
}
```

This code can break if a nonnumeric value is entered in `textBox1`. This includes no value. You can see the complete routine here:

```
private void btnTryCatch_Click(object sender, EventArgs e)
{
    try
    {
        int intCurr = Convert.ToInt32(this.textBox1.Text);
        textBox2.Text = Convert.ToString(intCurr + 3);
    }
    catch
    {
         textBox2.Text = "Exception Occurred";
    }
}
```

5. Press F5 to build and execute the application.

6. Click the new button you added in Step 1. Because you did not add any value in textBox1, the error occurs and the line of code in the catch statement is displayed, as shown in Figure 7-11.

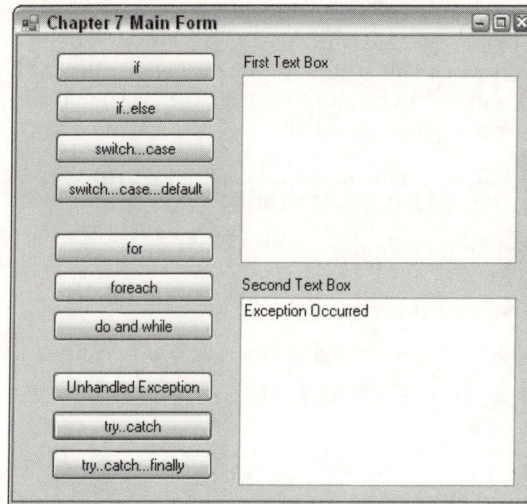

Figure 7-11

Using the finally Statement

Sometimes you want to have certain lines of code to execute regardless of whether the code caused an exception or not. The syntax for this will look as follows:

```
try
{
}
catch
{
}
finally
{
}
```

The finally block will occur whether the try block throws an exception or not. The finally block is a great place to put any cleanup code that you want to have run. Here is the code used for the current example:

```
private void btnTryCatchFinally_Click(object sender, EventArgs e)
{
    try
    {
        int intCurr = Convert.ToInt32(this.textBox1.Text);
```

```
            textBox2.Text = Convert.ToString(intCurr + 3);
        }
        catch
        {
            textBox2.Text = "Exception Occurred";
        }
        finally
        {
            textBox2.Text += Environment.NewLine + "Completed";
        }

    }
```

In this example the same two lines of code are run to cause the exception to occur. The `catch` statement stores the string literal into `textBox2`. Lastly, the `finally` statement code block adds a `NewLine` statement and adds it to a string literal `"Completed"`. So regardless of what you put in the `TextBox`, this code will place the word "Completed" after the value in the `TextBox`.

Try It Out   ## Use the try...catch...finally Statements

Using the form you created for the chapter:

1. Drag and drop another `Button` control onto the form.

2. Name it as desired. For this example the `Button` control was named `btnTryCatchFinally`.

3. Double-click the `btnTryCatchFinally` button. The `btnTryCatchFinally_Click` routine is created as shown here:

```
private void btnTryCatchFinally_Click(object sender, EventArgs e)
{

}
```

4. Type the following lines of code:

```
try
{
    int intCurr = Convert.ToInt32(this.textBox1.Text);
    textBox2.Text = Convert.ToString(intCurr + 3);
}
catch
{
    textBox2.Text = "Exception Occurred";
}
finally
{
    textBox2.Text += Environment.NewLine + "Completed";

}
```

The final block of code looks like this:

```
private void btnTryCatchFinally_Click(object sender, EventArgs e)
{
    try
    {
        int intCurr = Convert.ToInt32(this.textBox1.Text);
        textBox2.Text = Convert.ToString(intCurr + 3);
    }
    catch
    {
        textBox2.Text = "Exception Occurred";
    }
    finally
    {
        textBox2.Text += Environment.NewLine + "Completed";
    }

}
```

5. Press F5 to build and execute the application.

6. Type **1** in the first text box.

7. Click the new button you added in Step 1. Since a legitimate entry was made in `textBox1`, no error occurs, and the "Completed" message is displayed (see Figure 7-12).

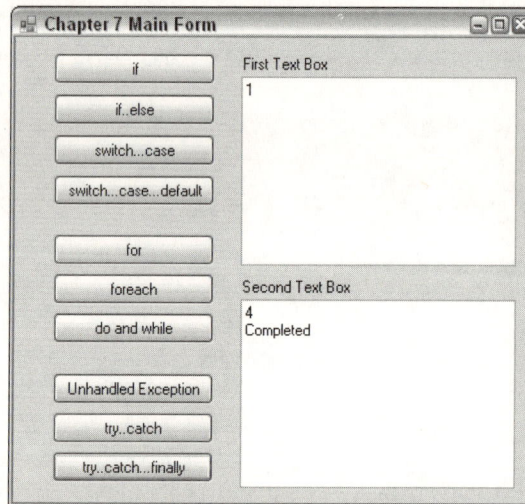

Figure 7-12

8. Now delete the entry in `textBox1`.

9. Click the new button you added in Step 1. Now you will see the message that an exception occurred, and also still see the "Completed" message provided by the `finally` statement (see Figure 7-13).

There is definitely more you can do to the `try . . . catch` code blocks, especially when you add in code to track specific errors.

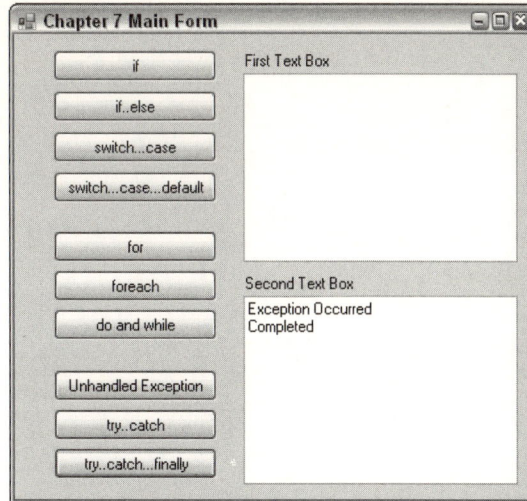

Figure 7-13

Summary

If all you could do in a programming language is just write single lines of code that execute one by one without making any decisions or selecting blocks of code on those decisions, you may not be able to accomplish some tasks. Either that or it would either take a lot more code to accomplish it. The same could be especially said when you have the occasion to make iterations such as working through the days of the month. You would need to write the same piece of code, maybe changing one or two lines, for each day of the month. At the risk of sounding technical, it would be a pain, to say the least.

C# provides statements such as `if . . . else` and `switch . . . case` for selecting code, and `for` statements as well as others to help with iterating through code. Which of the statements just mentioned you use will depend on what task you are trying to handle in the code. This chapter discussed how to use these statements. It also discussed how to trap errors, called exceptions, that can occur at runtime. Lastly, the chapter talked about what you can do with the exceptions that occur.

Exercises

1. When would you use an `if . . . else` statement versus a `switch . . . case` statement?

2. What category of statements does the `if . . . else` statement fall into?

3. What is the different between the `for` and `foreach` statements?

4. Which statement, `do` or `while`, does the code execute at least one code block if the expression starts as false?

5. If the developer wants to have a code block occur whether an exception occurs or not, which statement does the developer use with the `try` statement?

Part II

Creating Applications with C# Express

8

Working with Forms and Controls

Forms and controls are central to creating professional Windows applications. The more you know about those forms and controls, the more you can take advantage of them. There are standards that are used for creating Windows applications. Utilizing those standards ensures that users can count on having a similar experience when working in various Window applications, even though they may be created by different developers.

The great thing is that today the available controls are designed in such a way as to make it easier to follow these standards, and harder to break them. Often, things work just as you'd expect them to and fit in with the look and feel of other Windows apps with the minimum of effort (such as the default behavior of a form—even with no controls on it).

Besides following standards to create professional applications, developers can utilize properties, methods, and events to control information being entered and displayed on those forms and in the controls. There are various controls that are used for various tasks depending on what you are trying to accomplish with the forms. This chapter will discuss the following:

- ❑ Some of the Windows standards used for creating interfaces
- ❑ How to use properties, methods, and events to work with forms
- ❑ How to utilize toolbars and menus on your forms
- ❑ Useful controls available for use on forms
- ❑ How to work with properties, methods, and events of those controls

Creating User Interfaces Using Windows Standards

Learning the basics of how to create forms and utilize controls in C# Express is essential to creating applications. If you don't create applications that are laid out logically and consistently, users will just get frustrated and not want to use those applications.

Windows interface standards could fill a whole book, but I want to give you some suggestions on some standards that can make your interfaces more attractive and usable. To do this, I will cover the following areas: using form standards, adding menus and toolbars, and using the right control for the right purpose. I will start with a type of form that is simple to create and convenient to use.

Use of Switchboards

When creating switchboards, you will place buttons on forms to display possible tasks. Some of the chapters, including this one, use switchboard to help organize the tasks, and display those tasks in logical orders. This helps create a consistent interface for your application. Figure 8-1 displays the switchboard created for this chapter.

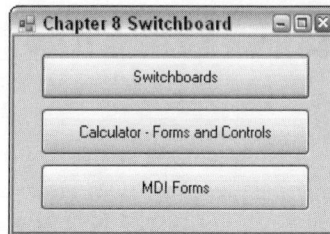

Figure 8-1

Switchboard can take on many forms. The ones used by the chapters of this book are probably the simplest. Multiple switchboards also can be used to display sub-menu-type tasks. For example, you may have a main switchboard that reflects all the choices for a application on the form's buttons, with one of the buttons having a caption of "Reports." This button then opens another switchboard when clicked. The two switchboards are displayed in Figure 8-2.

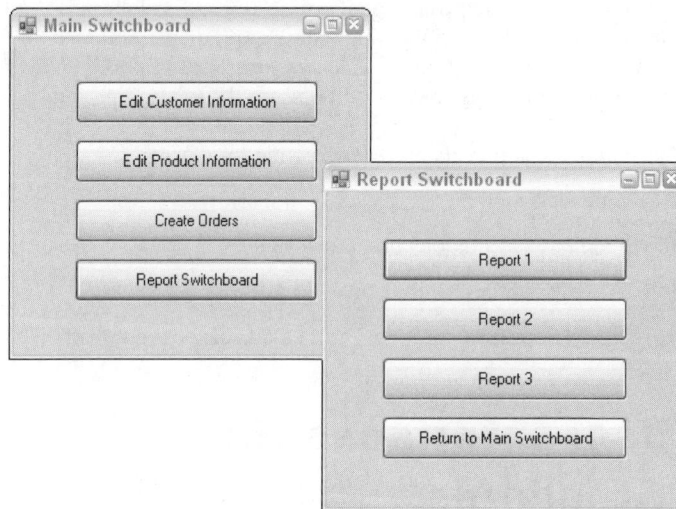

Figure 8-2

Form Application Types and Standards

Before jumping into the various form standards that can be used, I want to discuss two types of form application standards that affect how your overall application works with forms.

Form Application Types

There are two main types of application styles that you can use to display your forms: single-document interface (SDI) and multiple-document interface (MDI). By default, the single-document interface is what is created when you create a Windows application project using C# Express. Single-document interface means just that, a single document (form) is displayed separately. You can see that in Figure 8-2 where each of the switchboards is treated as a separate window.

With MDI forms, you will have a main window, and then all windows (forms) are then opened within that main window. An example of using MDI forms is shown in Figure 8-3.

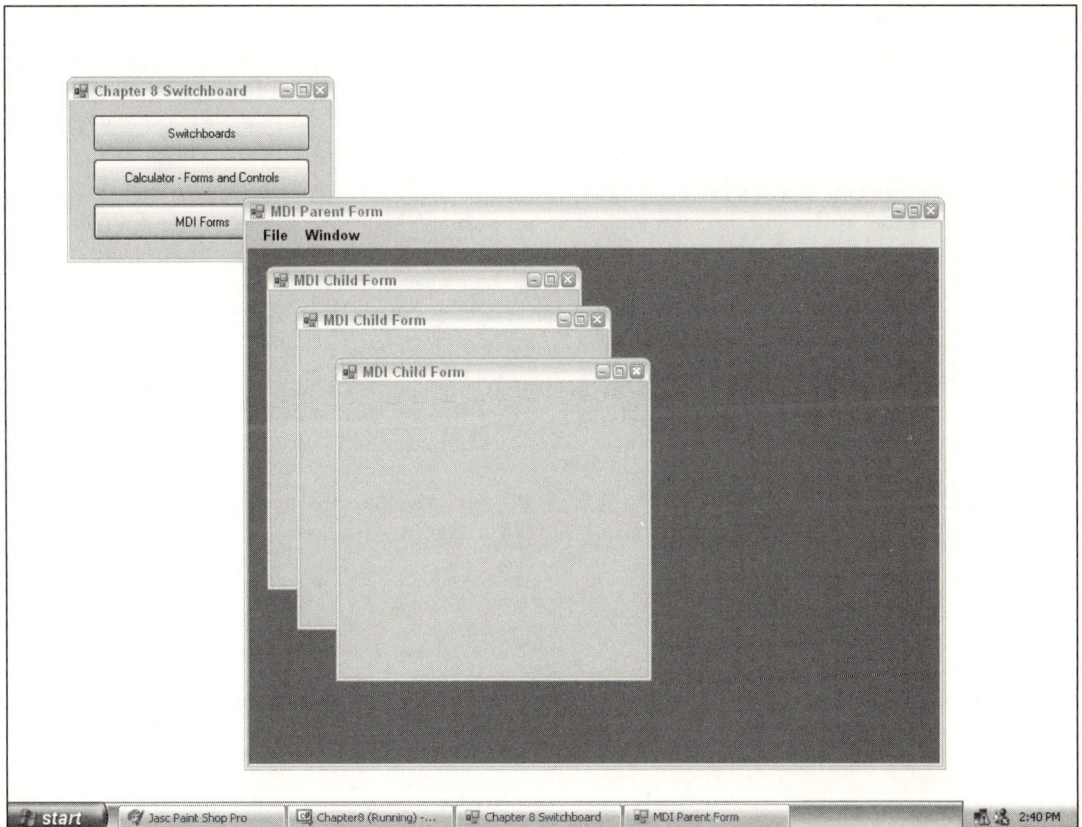

Figure 8-3

Notice that even though there are two additional (child) forms opened inside the MDI parent or main form, you only see the parent form in the Windows task below the bottom of the screen. These child forms also are limited to moving inside the main parent form. You will learn how to create MDI forms later in this chapter in the section titled "Working with MDI Forms."

Some Form Standards

Besides which type of application you decide to use, there are certain form standards that can be adhered to that make the users' experience with your forms more enjoyable and, even more important, easier to use. While you can create your own style of forms that you think would be interesting and useful for the user, there are some things you can do to give the user a more consistent interface:

- ❑ **Be conservative with colors.** Instead of having a different color for every form you create, use a consistent color combination, and keep it conservative. If you use the standard colors that forms are by default, then users can use the Windows theme to change the colors themselves, instead of having them dictated to them. I have literally seen color combinations that change so dynamically that they practically send users into seizures.

- ❑ **Display buttons in standard locations.** When you are using buttons for closing your forms, locate them in the same locations on your forms, instead of making the user guess where you are going to put the buttons because you change them on the forms. If you decide to put the buttons for tasks in the upper right corner, do it on all the forms in your application.

- ❑ **Use menus and toolbars consistently.** Be consistent in your use of menus and toolbars. Generally these two will reflect the same tasks: menus with text to display commands and toolbars to display commands graphically. If you use either one or both of these controls on one of your forms, then use them on all. Also, using the same base menu choices such as File, Edit, View, and Window, that are used in other major Windows applications helps to give a standard feel to the application.

- ❑ **Use the right control for the right purpose.** When using the many various controls available to you in creating forms, you want to make sure you use the right control for the task you are trying to accomplish, down to taking a single piece of information from the user.

Now that you know the basics of creating standard forms, it is time now to go into more detail on how to create effective forms and some of the cool things you can do with them.

Looking at Forms

As discussed throughout the book thus far, when creating Windows applications, keep in mind that they are generally based around forms. To create useful forms, you need to know how to take advantage of them, and to do that, you need to know about how to work with form properties.

Form Properties

As with properties of other types of objects, properties of forms can be used to control how a form looks and behaves. You can see the property sheet for the main switchboard created for Chapter 8 in Figure 8-4.

Figure 8-4

Form and control properties are broken up into the following categories:

Category	Description
Accessibility	Used to control how screen looks and the size of the controls based on which type of accessibility you need, such as for the visually impaired.
Appearance	Controls the default settings for various display settings such as height, width, background color, and starting position for the form.
Behavior	Determines how a form behaves depending on that you are trying to accomplish. Properties in this category include `Visible`, which allows you to hide a form without closing it, so that even if the form isn't visible, you still have access to all the controls on that form.

Table continued on following page

Category	Description
Data	For forms the main property of use in this category is the `Tag` property, which allows developers to store text for their own use. This category is used more on controls, when you can bind the control to data. Data binding is discussed further in Chapter 11, "Using SQL Server Express Features within C# Express."
Design	Used for properties that have to do with how the form is treated in design mode. Also includes localization, controls that determine which language pack is used, and the name of the form.
Focus	The only property in this category is `CauseValidation`, which when set to `True`, causes the validation event to be raised when controls are changed on the form.
Layout	Various properties that control the layout of the form, including start position and the state of the form, such as minimized, maximized, or normal.
Misc	Contains some miscellaneous properties including two that let you specify which control is used when the Enter key is pressed (`AcceptButton`) and the Esc is pressed (`CancelButton`).
Window Style	Using the properties in this category, you can control what the actual window looks like and how it behaves based on which features you specify to use, such as help button and control box.

There are so many properties that it would be hard to cover all of them in one chapter. The fact is that you won't even have to use the majority of the properties, since they are set to use default values that cover most the types of forms you will use.

A Side Step — Creating Switchboards

Even before jumping into the various forms features in the next sections, you need to create the chapter switchboard. You will then use two `Form` properties: `Name`, used to specify the name of the form, and `Text`, used to display text in the title bar of the form.

Try It Out   **Creating the Chapter Switchboard Form**

For this Try It Out, you create the chapter's switchboard form, which will be used for other examples.

1. Create a new Windows Forms project using C# Express as you have throughout the book. In this case, call it `Chapter8`.

2. With the form highlighted, in the Properties sheet, change the `Name` property of the form to be something more meaningful for you. In the sample for the chapter, this form is called `frmChapter8Main.cs`.

Changing the `Name` property doesn't change the filename. Changing the filename does change the `Name` property, though.

3. Type **Chapter 8 Switchboard** in the Text property of the form, found in the Properties sheet.

4. Open the Toolbox if it is not already open by choosing View ⇨ Toolbox.

5. Drag and drop three Button controls on the form, laying them on the form as shown in Figure 8-1. Button controls can be found in the Toolbox under the Common Control category.

6. Click the first button added.

7. Locate the Name property in the Properties sheet.

8. Type **btnSwitchboard** for the Name property of the top button.

9. Click the middle button, and type **btnCalculator** for the Name property.

10. Click the bottom button, and type **btnMDIForms**. MDI forms are discussed later in the chapter in the section called "Working with MDI Forms."

11. Click the first button again, and locate the Text property in the Properties pane.

12. Type **Switchboards** for the Text property of btnSwitchboards.

13. Type **Calculator - Forms and Controls** for the Text property of btnCalculator.

14. Type **MDI Forms** for the Text property of btnMDIForms. The form should then look somewhat as it does in Figure 8-5.

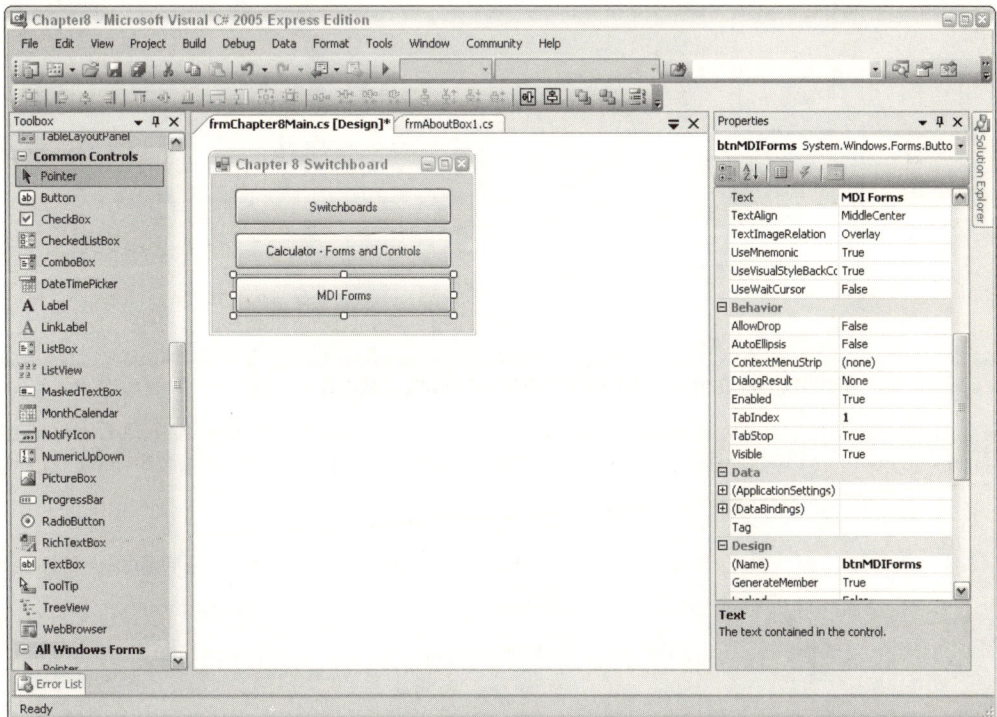

Figure 8-5

Now, even though you have created a form, the switchboard doesn't open another form. You need to create the next form and then write code in the `Click` event code of the buttons you want to program. The next Try It Out walks you through creating a second switchboard form, then writing the code to open the form.

To accomplish this, you create a reference variable used to point to the new form; then you use the `Show` method of the form to open the form for the user. The following code accomplishes this task:

```
frmSwitchboardMain frm = new frmSwitchboardMain();
frm.Show();
```

You are familiar with declaring variables from the last chapter. This time you are declaring one to be the type of the new form you will create in the next Try It Out, adding the preceding code in the `Click` event code for `btnSwitchboards`. When you add a form or other type of object to a project, you will be able to see the object added to the list of types to declare. You can see this in Figure 8-6. When `frmSwitchboardMain` has been added to the project, it can be referred to in code, as shown using the IntelliSense feature.

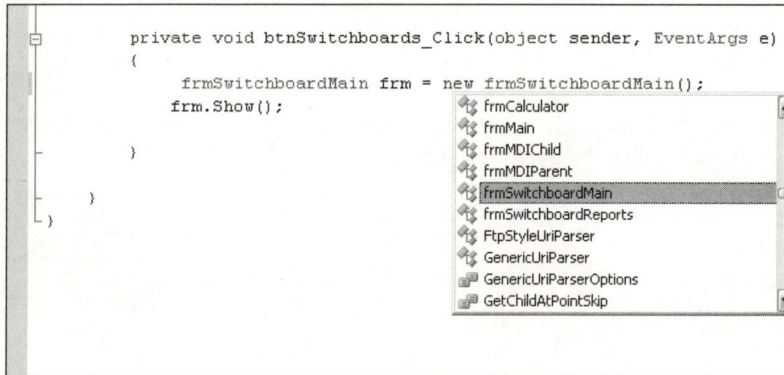

```
        private void btnSwitchboards_Click(object sender, EventArgs e)
        {
            frmSwitchboardMain frm = new frmSwitchboardMain();
            frm.Show();                      frmCalculator
                                             frmMain
                                             frmMDIChild
        }                                    frmMDIParent
                                             frmSwitchboardMain
    }                                        frmSwitchboardReports
}                                            FtpStyleUriParser
                                             GenericUriParser
                                             GenericUriParserOptions
                                             GetChildAtPointSkip
```

Figure 8-6

Try It Out   **Creating and Calling Another Switchboard Form**

To start off this Try It Out, you create a form that is a second switchboard. You then add code to the main chapter switchboard to open the new form. So, using the chapter project created in the last Try It Out:

1. Right-click the C# project file, located in the Solution Explorer.

2. Choose Add ➪ New Item . . . from the right-click menu. You can see this choice in Figure 8-7.

   The Add New Item dialog box opens, letting you choose from various item templates.

3. Highlight the Windows Form template, and type the name **frmSwitchboardMain.cs** in the name of the form.

4. Click Add. The form is now added to the project and displayed in the designer.

5. Type the text **Main Switchboard** into the `Text` property of the form, using the Properties sheet.

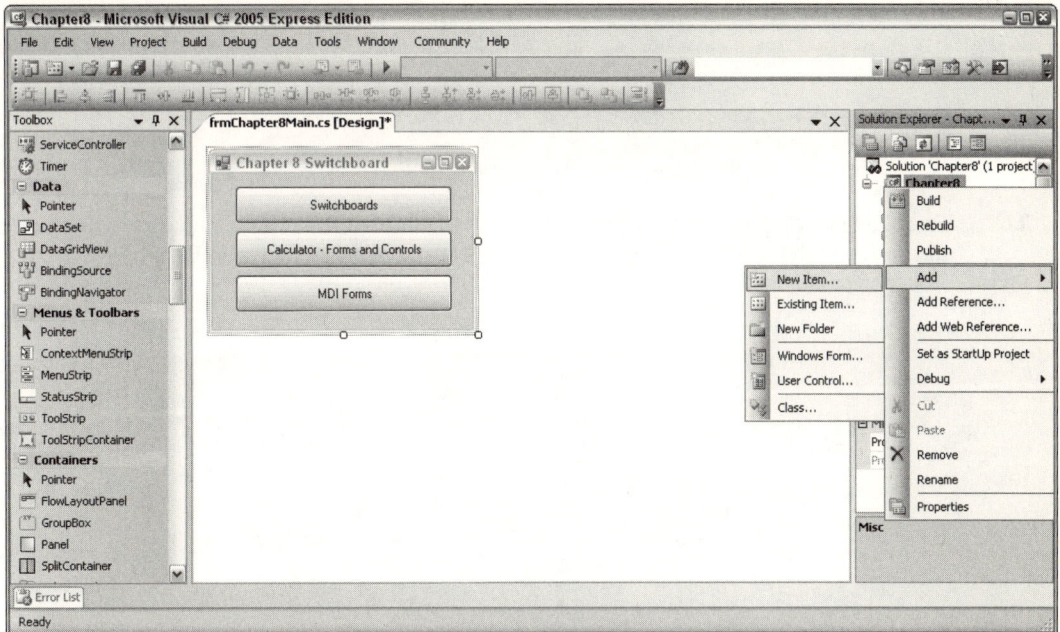

Figure 8-7

6.   Using the same steps outlined in the last Try It Out, drag and drop a few buttons onto the new form; then type in text for the Text property of each button. You can see the four buttons added to the sample form and Text properties assigned to them in Figure 8-8.

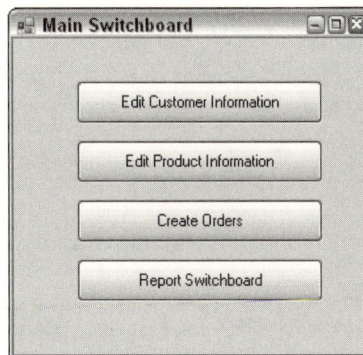

Figure 8-8

7.   Click the Save toolbar button to save your work; then click the frmChapter8Main.cs tab in the main editor page, or double-click the file in the Solution Explorer. The form will then be displayed in the main editor page.

8.   Double-click the btnSwitchboards button. The code for the form appears in the main editor page with the opening and closing curly brackets displayed for the click routine.

9. Type the following lines of code between the opening and closing curly brackets:

```
private void btnReportSwitchboard_Click(object sender, EventArgs e)
{
    frmSwitchboardReports frm = new frmSwitchboardReports();
    frm.Show();
}
```

10. Press F5 to test the application. The Chapter 8 switchboard first opens, and then when you click the button with label Switchboards, the second form opens, as shown in Figure 8-9.

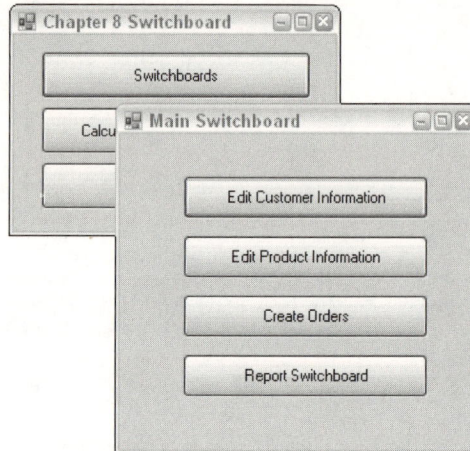

Figure 8-9

This example works fine, but it does contain one fairly major issue. You can click repeatedly on the Switchboards button and open multiple subforms. Two ways around this are to either use ShowDialog() *for a modal window instead of* Show() *or hold a reference to the form and check to see if it exists before calling* Show()*. This last solution takes a bit more explaining, so you might want to just stick to the* ShowDialog() *method.*

Using Form Properties

Just to give you an idea of what you can do with Windows forms, look at the two calculators in Figure 8-10.

You would be hard-pressed to tell which one is the real calculator provided by Windows XP and which is the one created using C# Express. You will get started creating the calculator in this chapter, by creating and setting some properties on the form, and then adding controls in the next few sections. (By the way, the calculator on the left is the one created using C# Express.)

As just mentioned, this chapter walks you through getting started on creating the calculator, but it won't focus on any of the code. That will be covered in Chapter 14, "Getting More Experience with Controls."

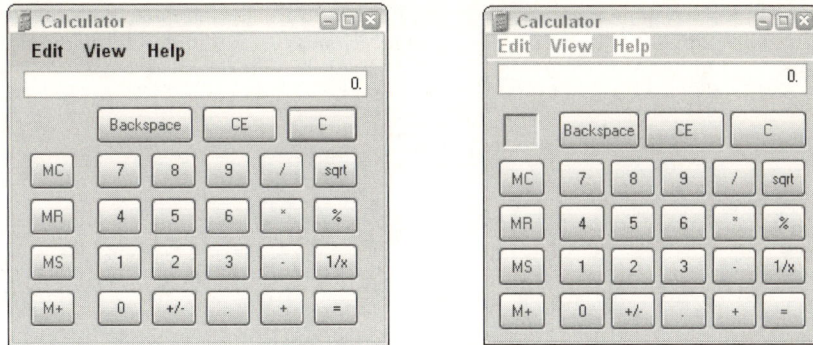

Figure 8-10

Here are some of the form properties that will be used:

Property	Description
Icon	Specifies an icon file to use with the individual form — in this case Calculator.ico, which is located in the folder for this sample chapter.
StartLocation	Set to WindowCenter, this property specifies where to open the form being created.
Text	Sets the text that is displayed in the title bar of the form — in this case "Calculator."

Another form property, called MainMenuStrip, is set automatically for you when you place a MenuStrip control on the form. This is discussed later in this chapter in the section titled "The MenuStrip Control." Other properties such as the Height and Width of the form are set using the designer. Everything else will be left using the default values as set by C# Express.

Try It Out   Setting Form Properties for the Calculator

For this Try It Out, you create a form and specify the properties displayed in the last table, as well as size the form created to match the size of the Microsoft Calendar. You then add the code to the project switchboard to open the form.

1.   Choose Accessories ⇨ Calendar from the Start ⇨ Program Files menu in Windows. Leave the Microsoft Calendar application open to use as an example for creating your calculator.

2.   Returning to C# Express, right-click the C# project file, located in the Solution Explorer.

3.   Choose Add ⇨ New Item . . . from the right-click menu.

4.   Choose Windows Form for the item template to use.

5.   Type **frmCalculator** for the name of the form, then click Add. The form is created.

6. Using the sizing handle on the lower right corner of the form, resize the form to match the Microsoft Calendar application by clicking the handle, holding down the mouse, and drag it to the desired location, as shown in Figure 8-11.

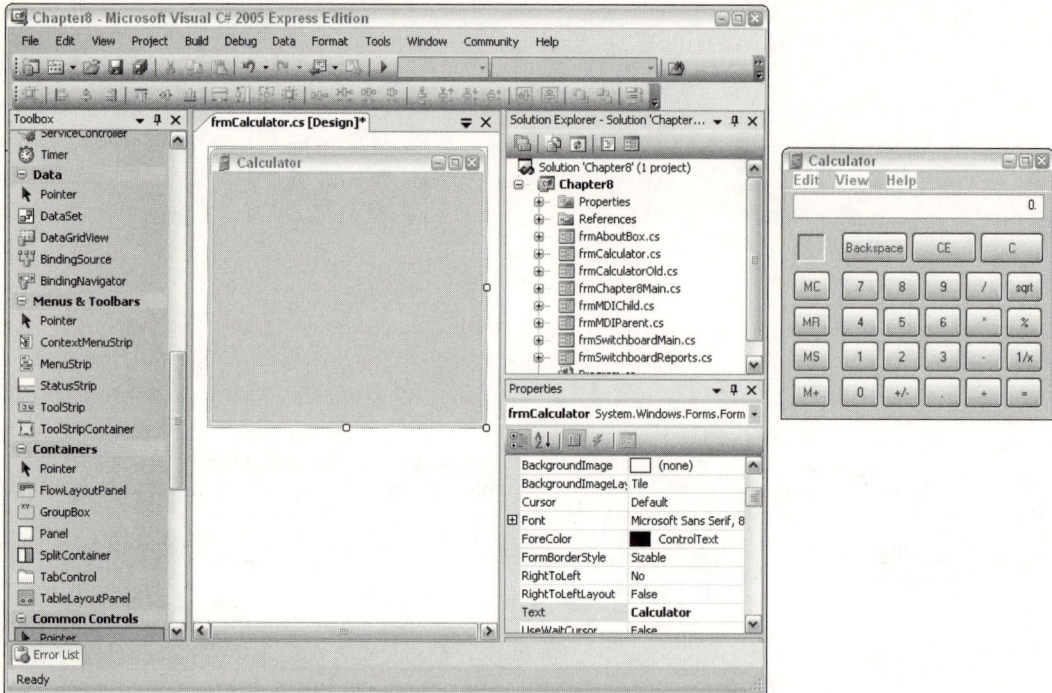

Figure 8-11

7. Type **Calculator** for the Text property, located in the Forms properties.

8. Set the form's `StartPosition` property to be `CenterScreen`.

9. Place the cursor in the `Icon` property of the form.

10. Click the build button (...) next to the `Icon` property, and locate `Calculator.ico` on your sample disk in this chapter's sample folder.

Note that none of the last four steps are required to create the calculator; they simply make it more like the original application, and give it a more professional look and feel.

11. Save the form, and switch to the `frmChapter8Main.cs` form.

12. Double-click the `btnCalculator` button. The code page opens, creating a new event routine for the `btnCalculator Click` event.

13. Type the following code in between the curly brackets:

```
frmCalculator frm = new frmCalculator();
frm.Show();
```

This code will open the `frmCalculator` when you click the `btnCalculator` button.

14. Press F5 to test the form. Clicking the `btnCalculator` button, you will then see the form as it looks in Figure 8-12.

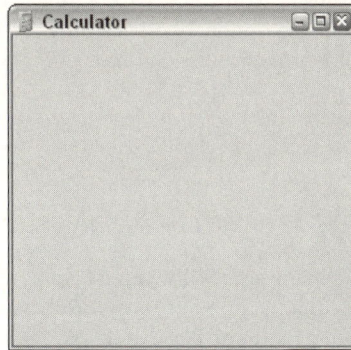

Figure 8-12

At this point the calculator is pretty boring, but it is a great start. The next section goes through some controls that you will be using on your calculator form, as well as forms in general.

Controls Overview

You can set all the properties you want on a form, but if you don't have any controls to go onto the form, it will remain boring, as just mentioned. There are over 80 Windows Forms controls that can be used, so going through each is a little unreal. You have already used a couple of the more common controls such as the `TextBox` and `Button` controls throughout the book thus far. You will use those two again, as well as the `MenuStrip` control, in this chapter. In the following chapter, you will see how to take advantage of some additional controls to create various dialog boxes you can use in your applications.

Controls supplied by C# Express can have different purposes. Some can be used in the place of others. Some controls are used

❑ **Strictly for display.** The `Label` control displays information that is entered into its `Text` property.

❑ **For both entry and display of information.** The `TextBox` control is one of these controls. You can use it to display information on a form, or to allow the user to enter data.

❑ **To perform tasks.** The `Button`, `MenuStrip`, and `TaskStrip` controls cause events to occur that you can program tasks to perform. For example, on the `Button` control, the `Click` event can be programmed.

As with forms, controls have properties you can set to have them react the way you desire, depending on the need.

You can rearrange the display of the categories in the toolbox, because of this the categories in your Visual Studio may be arranged differently than those in this book. However, the tools listed in the categories should be the same.

Control Properties

Much like form properties, you click the control with the property you want to set and modify that property. The categories of properties for controls are the same as those used for forms. Each control will have various properties, depending on that control's purpose. There will be some properties such as `Height` and `Width` that are on a number of the controls.

> *As various controls are used in the samples, some of the properties will be discussed at that point. Topics and controls also will be discussed as the calculator is created.*

The MenuStrip Control

After creating the form for the calculator, you will want to put a `MenuStrip` control onto the form. The `MenuStrip` control is used to place menus on your forms. You can find the `MenuStrip` control in the toolbox under the category Menus & Toolbars. Besides the `MenuStrip` control the following controls can be found:

❑   `ContextMenuStrip`. Used to create a right-click menu, also called *context help menu*.

❑   `StatusStrip`. Broken up into individual panels, this control enables you to display various information at the bottom of a form.

❑   `ToolStrip`. Creates toolbars on forms.

❑   `ToolStrip` containers. When placed on a form, this control can contain other strip controls such as `MenuStrip`, `StatusStrip`, and `ToolStrip` controls.

Depending on the task you want to accomplish, you will choose which control to use.

With the `MenuStrip` control, you click the control in the toolbox and drop the control onto the desired form. The control will appear as a strip across the top of the form with the text "Type Here" displayed. In addition, you will see the component displayed in the bottom of the form.

As you type the text in the place labeled "Type here," the `MenuStrip` control displays two more menu option choices to use, one to the right and one below. You can see this in Figure 8-13 where the top menu choice Edit is entered into the `MenuStrip` control placed on the calculator form.

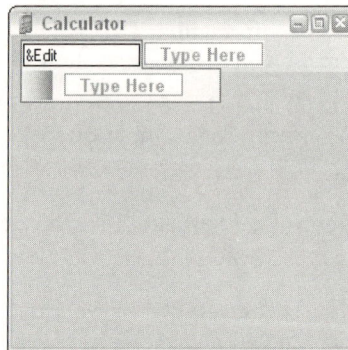

Figure 8-13

To add additional menu choices, the next item over or down is filled in. To add code to one of the menu choices, you double-click the choice and an event handler method will be created. By adding the & before the letter of your choice, you can use Alt + *the letter* to perform the action.

Try It Out   **Adding the MenuStrip Control to the Calculator Form**

In this Try It Out, you add a `MenuStrip` control to the calculator. First though, you will add an About form to display information about the current application, in this case the calculator. Lastly, you add code to open the new form from the About Box choice on the menu. So, using the project created for this chapter:

1. Right-click the C# project file, located in the Solution Explorer.

2. Choose Add ➪ New Item . . . from the right-click menu.

3. Choose About Box for the item template to use.

4. Type **frmAboutBox** for the name of the form, as shown in Figure 8-14.

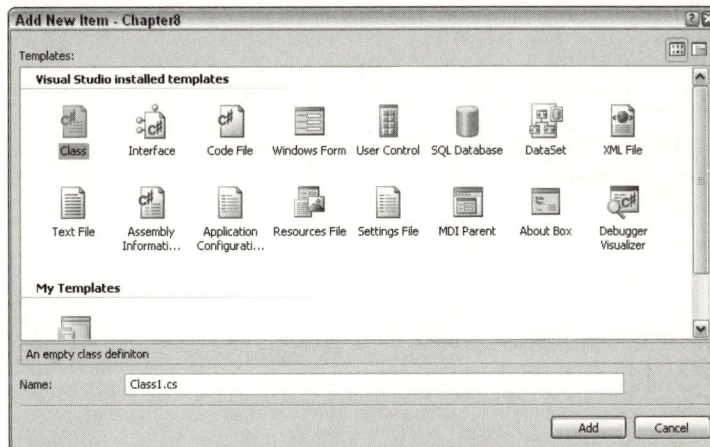

Figure 8-14

5. Click Add. The new About Box form is now added to the project. You can see the form in Figure 8-15.

   You can take this time to fill out the information desired in the about box form, but for this example you just need to add code to close the About box.

6. Double-click the OK button. The code file opens and the routine for the `okButton Click` event is displayed.

7. Add the following line of code between the open and closing curly brackets of the `okButton_Click` routine:

```
this.Close();
```

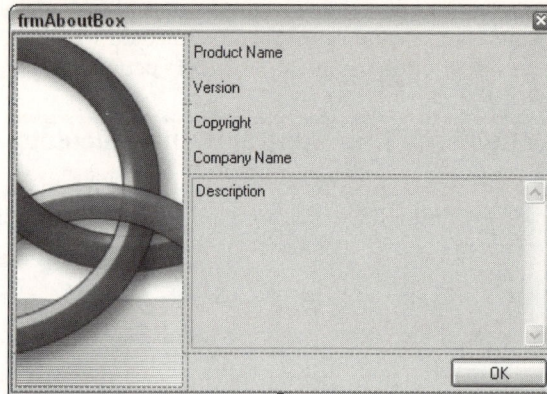

Figure 8-15

This is all it takes to close a form using the `Close` method of the current form you are in. Now it is time to go back to the `frmCalculator` and add the `MenuStrip` control to the form.

8. Switch back to the `frmCalculator` form.

9. Add a `MenuStrip` control on the form from the toolbox.

10. Type in **&Edit** for the first top menu choice, **&View** for the second top menu choice, and **&Help** for the third top menu choice (see Figure 8-16).

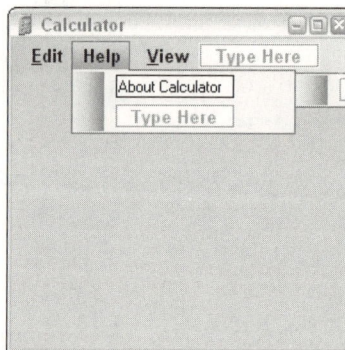

Figure 8-16

11. Type **About Calculator** in the choice under the Help feature.

12. Double-click the About Calculator menu choice. The code file appears.

13. Add the following code to display the about box form:

```
private void aboutCalculatorToolStripMenuItem_Click(object sender,
                EventArgs e)
{
    frmAboutBox frm = new frmAboutBox();
    frm.ShowDialog();
}
```

The menu is now complete for our purposes. You have dealt with TextBox and Button controls throughout the book. For the calculator, you will be using one TextBox and a number of Button controls. Other than changing the fore color of some of the buttons, you will mainly be dealing with moving and resizing the controls.

Moving, Aligning, and Resizing Controls

You have had some experience moving and resizing controls in this chapter already, but I wanted to go through it one more time and show some of the tools provided for moving and resizing controls when dropping controls.

When manipulating the controls one at a time, the C# Express editor does an awesome job of giving you guides to moving and resizing your controls. When you are moving or resizing a control by other controls, blue guide bars appear to guide you as you move or size the control based on the bars. You can see an example of this in Figure 8-17.

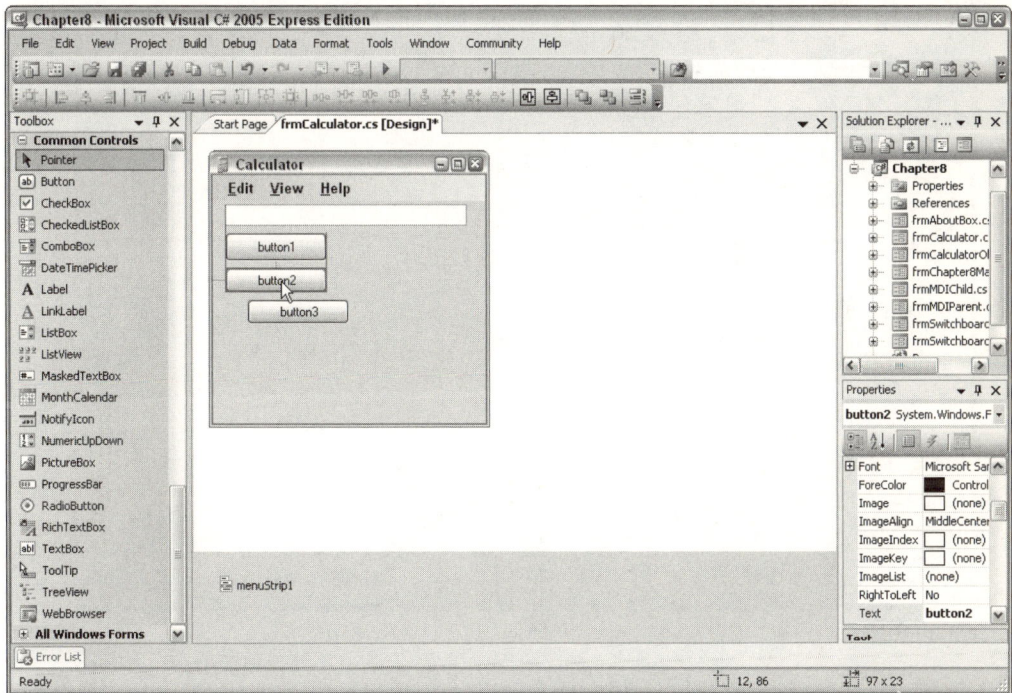

Figure 8-17

Besides using the resize handles to manipulate the size of the controls, you can use another method where multiple controls can be moved, aligned, and resized all at the same time.

When performing one of the tasks just mentioned, you will highlight all the fields you want to manipulate. You can do this one of two ways:

Chapter 8

❑ **Lasso method.** Place the cursor just to the outside of one of the four corners of the controls you want to work with, and then, holding the left mouse button, drag the cursor to the opposite corner of the set of controls.

❑ **Clicking the controls individually.** Click each of the controls while holding down the Shift or Ctrl key.

You can set various common properties on multiple controls at the same time. To accomplish this, you can set the property as it is displayed in the Properties sheet.

Regardless of which method you use, you will want to click the control that you want the other control position, size, or alignment the controls to be based on. You can see this done in Figure 8-18 where the controls selected are highlighted differently than the other controls.

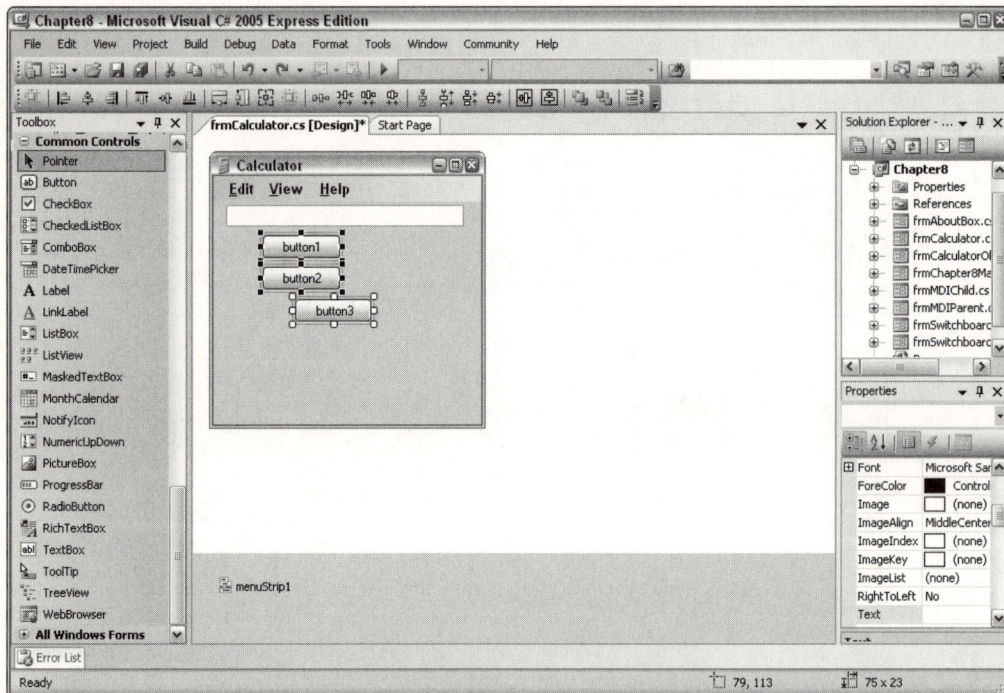

Figure 8-18

Once you have chosen the controls you want to manipulate, the Layout toolbar appears, shown in Figure 8-19.

Figure 8-19

The Layout toolbar is broken up into major categories, which also are displayed on the Format command. Those categories are Align, Make Same Size, Horizontal Spacing, and Vertical Spacing. Each of these categories has different options that you can choose based on your needs. For example, you will use the Align category to line up the buttons displayed on the calendar control.

Try It Out   Adding and Organizing TextBox and Buttons for the Calculator

Using the form you created in the last couple of Try It Outs:

1. Open `frmCalculator`.

2. Locate and add a `TextBox` control from the toolbox.

3. Set the Name property of the new text box to `txtValue`.

4. Drag and drop four button controls used as the memory buttons. They will look much like the buttons did in Figure 8-18, only with four buttons instead of three.

5. Highlight the four controls either by using the Lasso method mentioned or by holding the Shift key and clicking each of the controls.

6. Choose Red for the fore color of all four controls highlighted.

7. Using the options on the Layout Toolbar, align and size the controls as desired to match the original Calendar application. You can see what the four controls should look like in Figure 8-20.

8. Type the values for the `Text` property of each of the button controls: **MC, MR, MS,** and **M+**.

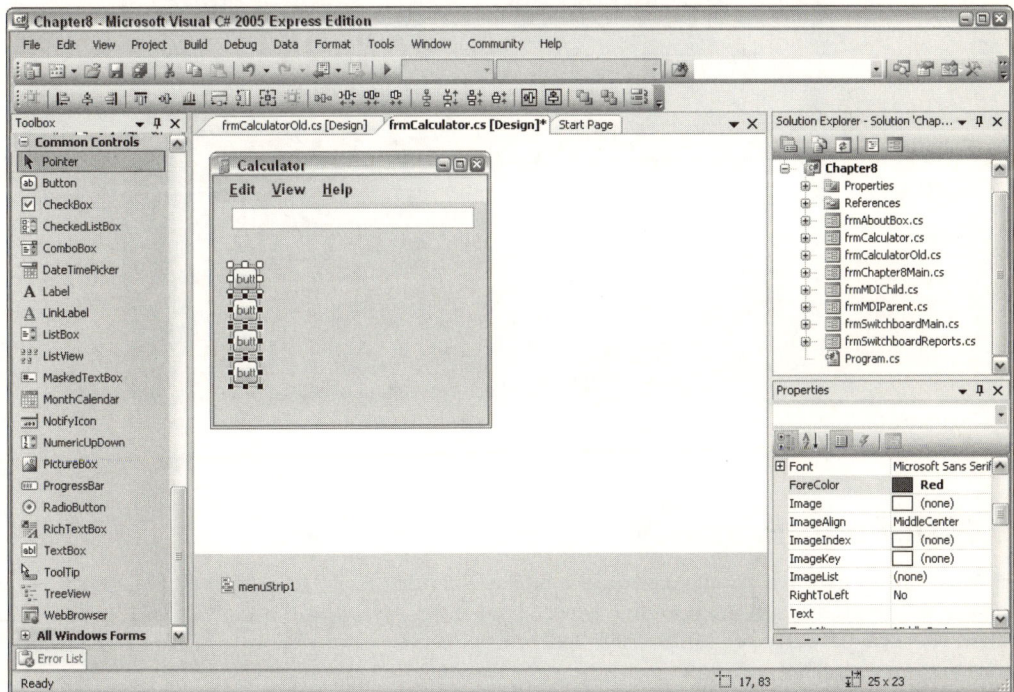

Figure 8-20

That's all there is to it. Taking the steps outlined here, you can look at the Calculator application and lay out the rest of the buttons.

Working with MDI Forms

As previously mentioned in the section called "Form Application Types," earlier in this chapter, it takes longer to explain the concept behind the full name of multiple-document interface, or MDI, than it does to discuss the steps for using it.

C# Express has gone to a lot of effort to make the use of MDI as painless as possible. They have made the majority of the setup for using MDI forms to be accomplished by setting properties. For the example discussed earlier in the book, only one line of code had to be used, and one property on the parent form needs to be set.

As a refresher, take a look at the MDI forms in Figure 8-21

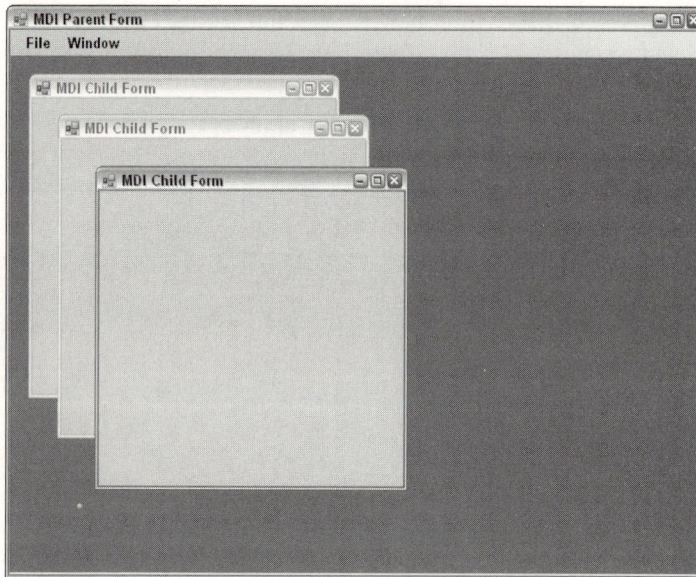

Figure 8-21

The MDI Form Property

MDI has one form that is specified as the parent, and all other forms (child forms) will be opened within the parent form. This is an interface that is used sometimes by applications and is fairly easy to accomplish. The form property you will set is called IsMDIContainer and is located in the Window Style category of form properties.

The MDI Line of Code

Once you have set the `IsMDIContainer` property in the parent form, then all forms opened in the application can be assigned that form as the parent. To accomplish this, after declaring the form reference variable and before using the `Show` method of the form, you will set the `MdiParent` property to be the current form (parent form) using the `this` object, which is a reference (or points) to the current form. The code just discussed in its entirety looks as follows:

```
frmMDIChild frm = new frmMDIChild();
        frm.MdiParent = this;

        frm.Show();
```

Just as with other forms, you can open the child form using code behind a button, or in this case, a menu item. Under the File item in Figure 8-22, there is a command to open a child form. The preceding code is used.

The Optional MDI Menu Property

Last, before getting to the Try It Out, there is another property you can set on the menu that takes advantage of the fact the form the menu is on is an MDI container. The property, `MDIListWindowsItem`, is set to the name of the menu choice that you want to list the opened child windows on. This is normally set to open with the caption of Windows on the main menu of the form.

You can see how the list is displayed in Figure 8-22.

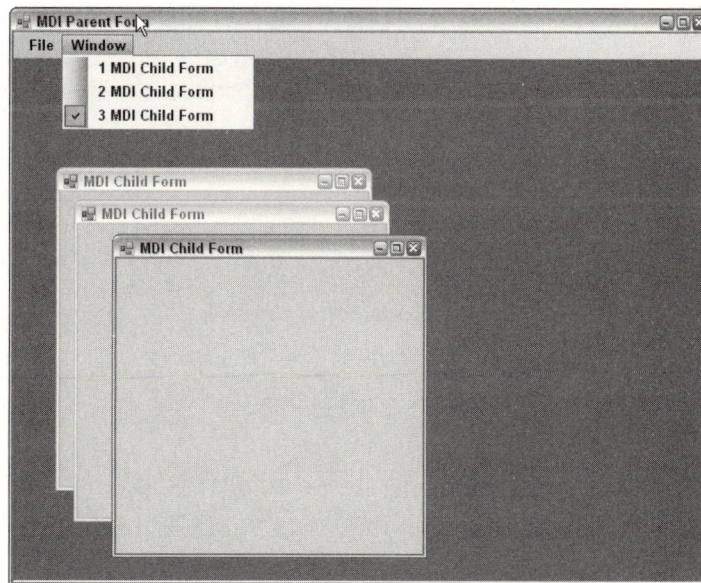

Figure 8-22

You will notice that forms displayed in Figure 8-22 are the same form open again and again. Normally you would have the code open different forms depending on the task you are accomplishing with the application you are creating. You could also open the same form but with different controls on them.

To create the MDI forms, you will add two forms to the chapter application:

1. Right-click the C# project file, located in the Solution Explorer.

2. Choose Add ⇨ New Item . . . from the right-click menu.

3. Choose Windows Form for the item template to use.

4. Type **frmMDIChild** for the name of the form, and click Add.

5. Set the Text of the form to be "MDI Child Form." The form is created as shown in Figure 8-23.

Figure 8-23

6. Choose Add ⇨ New Item . . . from the right-click menu.

7. Choose Windows Form for the item template to use.

8. Type **frmMDIParent** for the name of the form, and click Add.

9. Set the Text of the form to be "MDI Parent Form." The form is created as shown in Figure 8-23.

10. Drag and drop a `MenuStrip` control onto the form.

11. Type **&File** where it currently says Type Here.

12. Type **&Window** in the place to the right where it says Type Here.

13. Click back on the File menu choice.

14. Type **Open Child Form** in the place below that says Type Here. You can see what the form looks like in Figure 8-24.

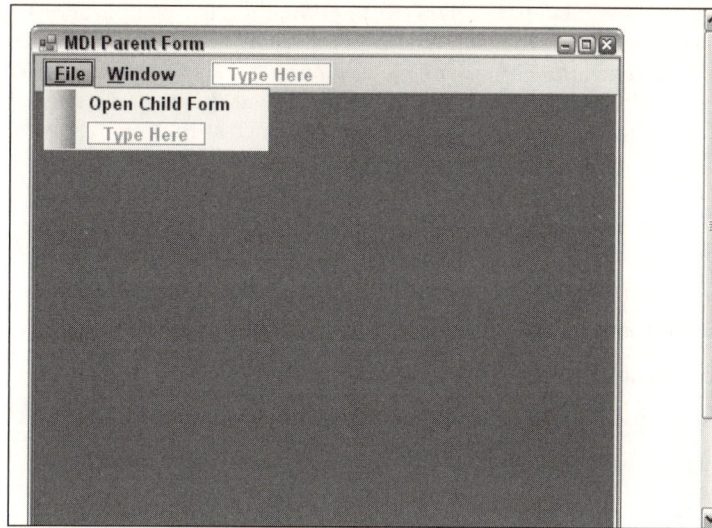

Figure 8-24

15. Double-click the menu item that now reads "Open Child Form." The code file is opened for the form.

16. In between the curly brackets, type the following lines of code:

```
frmMDIChild frm = new frmMDIChild();
frm.MdiParent = this;
frm.Show();
```

17. Click the MenuStrip control you added to the form.

18. Set the `MdiWindowListItem` property of the `TabStrip` control to be `windowToolStrip`.

19. Click the frmChapter8Main; then double-click the button with the text "MDI Forms."

20. Type the following lines of code in between the curly brackets:

```
frmMDIParent frm = new frmMDIParent();
frm.Show();
```

21. Press F5 to run the application. You will now see the forms open within the parent MDI form.

Summary

Forms and controls play a big part in creating your applications. Jumping in to use them is the best way to understand them. Once you have created a few forms, placed controls on them, and modified the properties of both the forms and controls, you are on your way to knowing how to create Windows Forms applications. But besides knowing the mechanics, there are certain standards you want to make sure that you utilize so that the users have a consistent and efficient experience.

There are a couple of different options when creating Windows Form applications: MDI and SDI. Which one you choose will depend on what you what you are trying to accomplish with the application. However, forms are only as powerful as the controls used on them. This chapter showed you how to use various controls, resize and move those controls, as well as set various properties needed to take advantage of the controls. You saw that by adding common controls such as the `TextBox`, `Menu`, and `Button`, you can reproduce the look of even as common an application as the Microsoft Calculator.

Exercises

1. What do MDI and SDI stand for?

2. What are switchboards used for?

3. What is the difference between a `ToolStrip` and `ToolStripContainer` control?

4. How do you add code to the `Click` event on a `MenuStrip` control?

9

Adding Dialog Boxes
and Rich Text to
Your Application

In Chapter 8, you saw how to design and create a calculator much like the actual Microsoft calculator included in Windows. The purpose was to get you comfortable with working with forms and controls, as well as setting properties for both. You will be using those skills in this chapter and throughout the book. When using the `TextBox` control discussed thus far in the book, you can put regular text in it, and even multiple lines of text. However, if you want to do anything more with the text like use fonts or colors, you need to use a more advanced control such as the `RichTextBox` control. Rich text is a format used by Word documents to include font and colors, paragraphs, bullets, and even load and save the text to rich text files.

To take advantage of the `RichTextBox` control, you want to be able to specify the file to open and save which fonts and colors to use, and more. C# Express and .NET provide controls to accomplish this using dialog controls. In this chapter, you create an application that utilizes rich text. Topics include the following:

❑   An overview of some of the features of `RichTextBox` control

❑   Working with the `RichTextBox` control on a form

❑   Introduction to some of the useful dialog controls

❑   How to use the dialog controls with the `RichTextBox` control

Introducing the Application

As mentioned in the introduction to the chapter, the `RichBoxControl` is used on forms to work with rich text in your applications. This coupled with the use of dialog controls open wide the possibilities of what you can do with your applications, with very little programming. As a matter of fact, I went crazy just getting the sample application built for this chapter. I didn't want to stop adding features. The application is show in Figure 9-1.

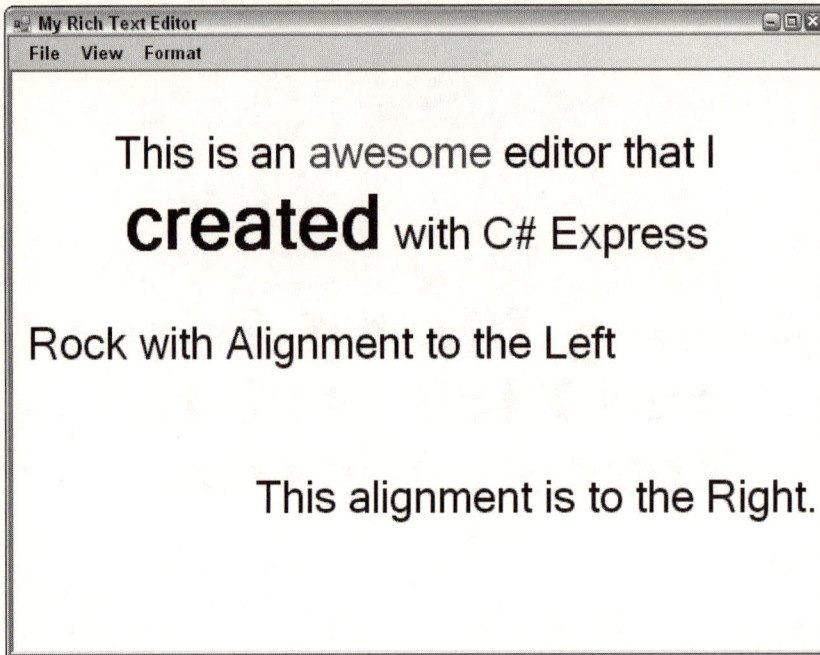

Figure 9-1

You can see the following features displayed in Figure 9-1, some of which use dialog boxes:

❑ **Load and save files.** Using the Open and Save File dialog boxes, you can open this file, called `Chapter6.rtf`, make changes, and save it again. You can see the Open File dialog box in Figure 9-2.

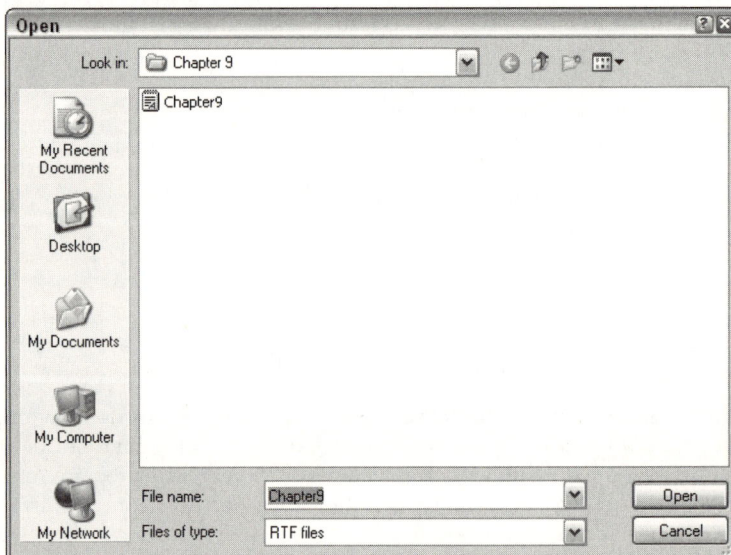

Figure 9-2

❑ **Various colors.** You can set the color of text to basic or custom colors. The color dialog box can be seen in Figure 9-3.

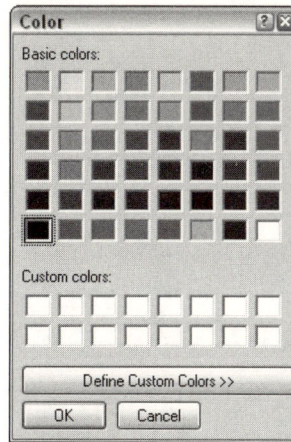

Figure 9-3

❑ **Different font sizes used.** You can choose all the Windows fonts and their styles such as size, underlining, bold, and italic. The dialog box can be seen in Figure 9-4.

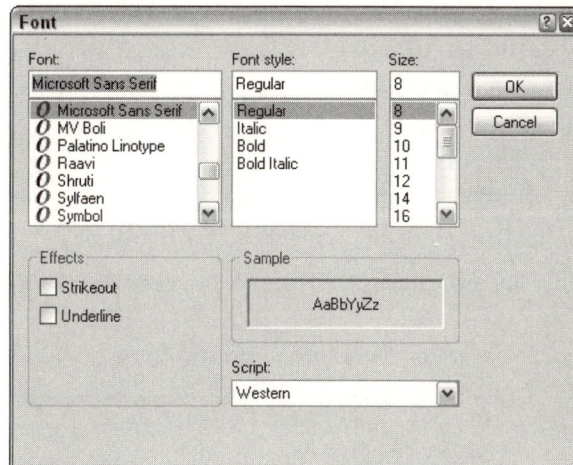

Figure 9-4

❑ **Three types of alignment.** The choices included left, center, and right alignment.

❑ **Zoom feature.** You can zoom in and out, and program what increments you want to zoom out by.

The last two features don't utilize dialog boxes. All the features just listed are found on the menu that was added, displaying File, Edit, and View on the main menu. The menu options are broken up as follows:

Menu	Feature	Control Used
File	Open	OpenFileDialog
	Save	SaveFileDialog
	Exit	None
View	Zoom In	RichTextBox
	Zoom Out	RichTextBox
Format	Colors	ColorDialog
	Fonts	FontDialog
	Alignment	RichTextBox

One of the most exciting features is the fact that with each of the options outlined in the preceding table, you can get away with writing as little as two lines of code—although in the case of the SaveFileDialog, additional lines of code are discussed to show you how to enhance the application. Now let's get started by creating the initial form and laying out the menu structure discussed in the preceding table.

Try It Out   Creating the Form

To get started, you will create a Windows Form application and then add a menu onto the form:

1. Create a Windows form.

2. Rename the form frmRichTextEditor.

3. Type **My Rich Text Editor** into the Text property of the form.

4. Resize the form using the resizing handles to be large enough to display a decent amount of text.

5. Drag and drop a MenuStrip control onto the form.

6. Fill out the menu with the specified options. You can see the base form with the File menu options displayed in Figure 9-5.

    Remember that you can specify accelerator keys by placing an & in front of the letter you want to use. Also, if you want to add a separator in the menu, click the arrow displayed by the text Type Here, and choose a separator.

    The Alignment menu item has an additional three items: Left, Center, and Right.

That's all you need to do for now. You will be adding code for each of the options as they are discussed in the rest of the chapter.

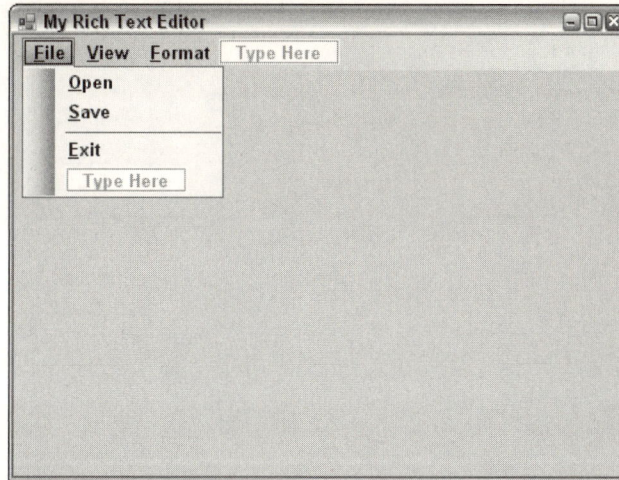

Figure 9-5

Working with the RichTextBox Control

There have been `RichTextBox` controls for previous programming environments, and if you have used the Windows Common Controls, used prior to .NET, then you may have used a `RichText` control that has similar features. The way to take advantage of the `RichTextControl`, located in the toolbox above the `TextBox` control, is to drag and drop the control onto the form, and then utilize its properties, methods, and events, just like other controls you use.

In addition to learning the control features, you will learn how to take advantage of the `Dock` property found on many of the Windows Forms controls. In fact, let's discuss those now.

Docking the RichTextBox Control

When you place a control on a form, and resize the form at runtime, the form usually stays the same size. Sometimes this is fine, but then sometimes, as shown in Figure 9-6, the form can look strange.

The form can look utterly wrong where the form is larger but the control stays small. It would be convenient to the user to have it grow with the form. To accomplish this, you can specify where you want the control docked. Set the `Dock` property of the `RichTextBox` control. When setting the `Dock` property, you can specify which edge of the form you want to have the control docked to. You can specify to fill the form by clicking in the middle of the design prompt, as shown in Figure 9-7.

Then, when you open the form, the control will hug all the edges, and the menu, on the form.

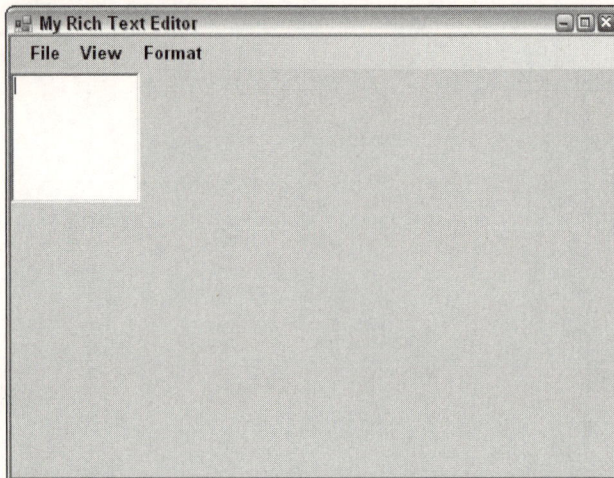

Figure 9-6

Figure 9-7

Try It Out   Adding the RichTextBox Control and Setting the Dock Property

Using the form created in the last Try It Out:

1. Drag and drop a `RichTextBox` control onto the form from the toolbox. Make a note of the name of the control created. By default, if no other `RichTextBox` control has been used on the form, it will be called `richTextBox1`.

2. Open the Properties window by choosing View ⇨ Properties Window.

3. Click the drop-down arrow next to the `Dock` property.

4. Click the center block, as was shown in Figure 9-7. The control now fills the form. It's time now to test the form.

5. Press F5. The form opens, displaying the menu and the `RichTextControl`.

6. Type some text into the `RichTextBox` control on the form.

7. Resize the control by clicking the edge and using the resize handles on the form. You will notice the control expanding and contracting with the form.

Note that you can also use Cut, Copy, and Paste by default with the `RichText` control. It's time now to move on and look at other properties of the `RichTextBox` control.

Some Other RichTextBox Control Properties

As with the majority of the controls you have access to with C# Express, there are far more properties methods and events than there is space for in a section of this chapter. However, in the following table, you will see some interesting properties used in this example, as well some others. Some of them can be accessed both at design and runtime and some only at runtime.

Name	Description
AcceptsTab	Specifies whether or not you can use tabs within the `RichTextBox` control or just have the focus move to another control.
AutoWordSelection	As you move the cursor in the `RichTextControl`, this property is used to specify whether words are highlighted or not.
BulletIndent	Specifies number of spaces indented when utilizing bullets in the text.
Margins	Set the margins for the text including right, left, top, and bottom.
SelectionAlignment	Used for setting the alignment of a paragraph at runtime. Choices here are from the enumerator `HorizontalAlignment`, specifically: `HorizontalAlignment.Left`, `HorizontalAlignment.Center`, and `HorizontalAlignment.Right`.
SelectionBullets	Toggles bullets on and off for selected text. Set at runtime.
WordWrap	Turns on and off word wrap when reaching the end of the line.
ZoomFactor	By specifying values, you can zoom in and out on text.

There are a number of other selection type properties in addition to the two mentioned in the prior table. Many of the properties mentioned here help to give you some of the features found in Word itself, without any programming.

For an example of how to use some of the properties mentioned in the preceding table, you will use `SelectAlignment` and `ZoomFactor` to add a couple of features.

Try It Out   Adding Alignment and Zoom Features to Your Rich Text Editor

Using the form you have been working with in this chapter:

1. Double-click the File ➪ Exit menu item of the `MenuStrip` control.

2. Type the following line of code to the routine:

```
Application.Exit();
```

3. Add the three Alignment menu choices if you haven't already, as shown in Figure 9-8.

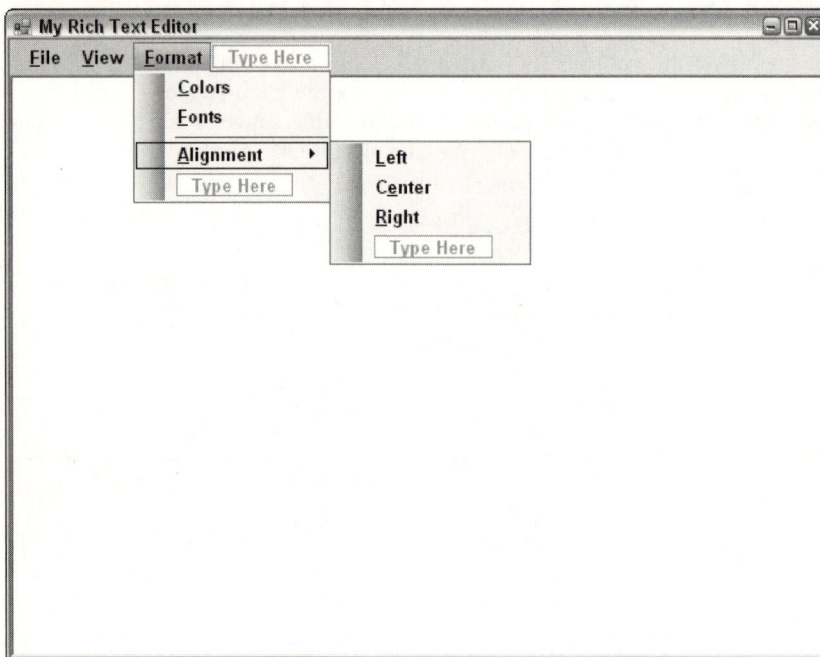

Figure 9-8

4. Double-click the `leftToolStripMenuItem` control. C# Express creates the `Click` event routine.

5. Type the following line of code in between the start and end curly brackets of the routine:

```
richTextBox1.SelectionAlignment = HorizontalAlignment.Left;
```

The routine now looks as it does here:

```
private void leftToolStripMenuItem_Click(object sender, EventArgs e)
{
    richTextBox1.SelectionAlignment = HorizontalAlignment.Left;
}
```

6. Repeat Steps 2 and 3 for the Center and Right alignment menu choices, using the different members of the enumeration.

7. Double-click the Zoom In menu choice.

8. Double-click the `zoomInToolStripMenuItem` control. C# Express creates the `Click` event routine.

9. Type the following line of code in between the start and end curly brackets of the routine:

```
richTextBox1.ZoomFactor += 2f;
```

This increments the `ZoomFactor` property by two. The `f` beside the 2 is another way to specify casting the value as a `Float` value.

10. Double-click the `zoomOutToolStripMenuItem` control. C# Express creates the `Click` event routine.

11. Type the following line of code in between the start and end curly brackets of the routine:

```
if (richTextBox1.ZoomFactor > 1)
    richTextBox1.ZoomFactor -= 2f;
```

This decrements the `ZoomFactor` property by two. The reason for the `if` statement is to make sure you don't decrement the value below 1.

The code for all five choices can be seen in Figure 9-9.

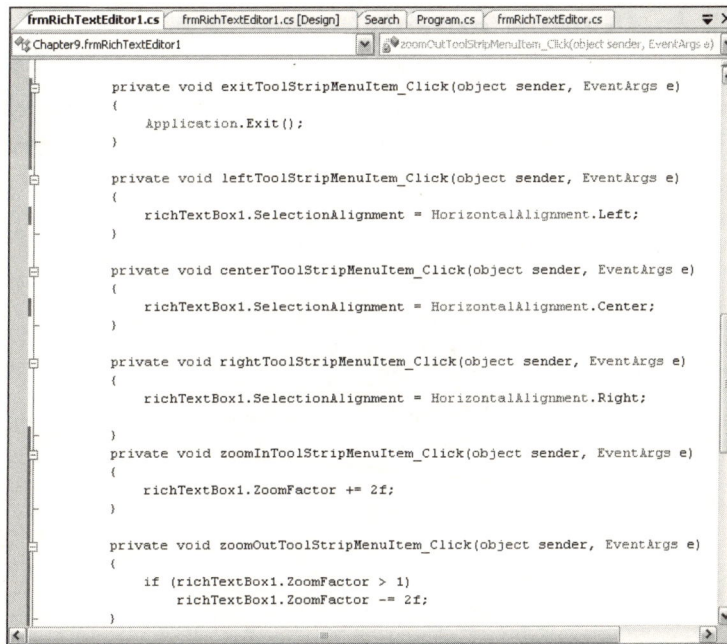

Figure 9-9

12. Press F5 to test the application. You can then choose the different alignment and zoom options to test.

Remember that there are a lot of methods and properties you can work with as well on the `RichTextBox` control itself. If you type the **richTextBox1** and the following period, you will see the total list of properties, methods, and events. You also can use the Object Browser to take a look.

Introducing the Dialog Controls

The standard dialog controls have been around for quite a few versions of Windows. In development environments prior to .NET, you used either Windows API calls or Windows Common ActiveX Controls. Each of these had issues that I won't bother going into, so you will have more time to work with the actual controls. The major controls you will be using, as mentioned in the first sections, are the `OpenFileDialog`, `SaveFileDialog`, `ColorDialog`, and `FontDialog` controls. Each name is pretty self-explanatory as to what they perform.

To use each of these, you can set various properties that are specific to each. The `ShowDialog()` method is used to display each of the controls used in remaining examples. So all you need to do is drag and drop each control onto the form, then set the necessary properties and call the `ShowDialog()` method. Then, depending again on which control you are using, you will utilize the results from the control with the `RichTextBox` control.

To work through the controls, I will take them one at a time as they are placed on the form. I will start off easy with the `ColorDialog` control and then move onto the `FontDialog` control.

Using the ColorDialog Control

You can find the `ColorDialog` control in the Dialogs category of controls in the toolbox. There are not a lot of properties, methods, and events to use on the `ColorDialog` because it is a pretty simple control. As mentioned, the method you will use to display the dialog box will be the `ShowDialog()` method. The dialog box can be seen again in Figure 9-10.

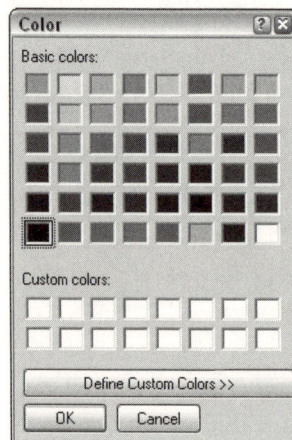

Figure 9-10

Once you have displayed the dialog box, and the user has responded, you set the color of the text selected in the `RichTextBox` control to the color specified. To accomplish these two tasks, you use the following two lines of code:

```
if (colorDialog1.ShowDialog() == DialogResult.OK)
    richTextBox1.SelectionColor = colorDialog1.Color;
```

And that's all there is to it to use it in its simplest form.

Try It Out   **Adding the ColorDialog Control to Your Form**

Using the form you have been working with in this chapter:

1. Drag and drop a `ColorDialog` control from the toolbox into the bottom section of the form editor, beside the `menuStrip1` control. C# Express will organize the control for you. You can see what the designer will look like in Figure 9-11.

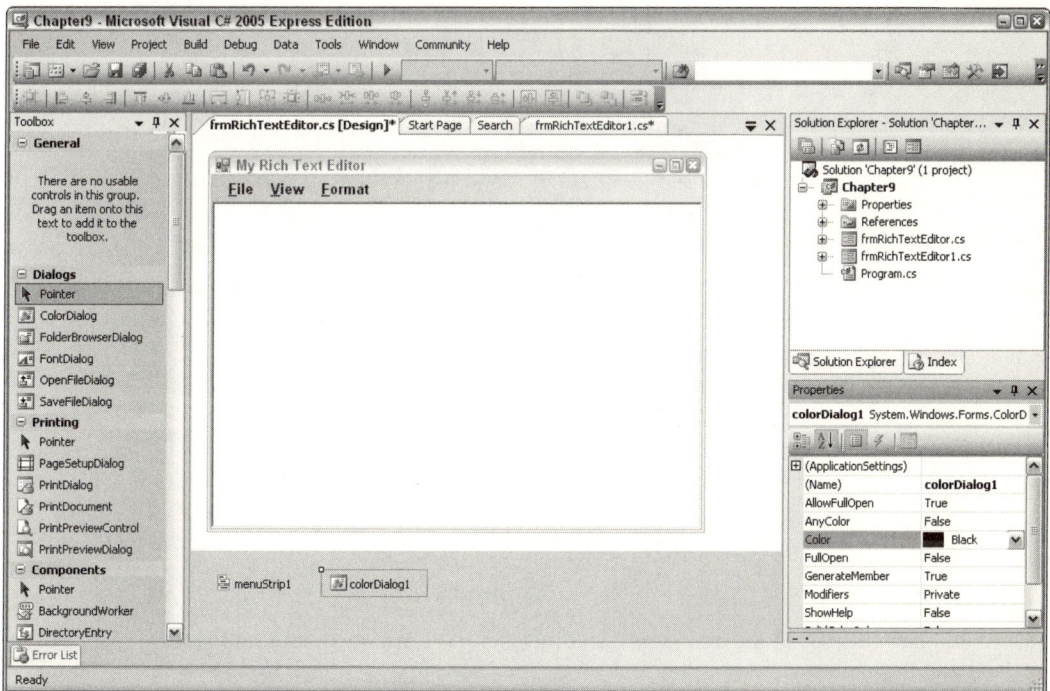

Figure 9-11

2. Double-click the Format ➪ Color choice of the `MenuStrip` control. The code file opens with the `Click` event displayed.

3. Type the following lines of code in the body of the `Click` event routine:

```
if (colorDialog1.ShowDialog() == DialogResult.OK)
    richTextBox1.SelectionColor = colorDialog1.Color;
```

4. Press F5 to test the application.

5. Type text to test; then highlight some of text.

6. Choose Format ➪ Color from the menu on the Rich Text Editor form. The Color dialog box opens.

7. Select a new color, and click OK. The text that was highlighted in the form will be changed to the new color.

Using the FontDialog Control

The `FontDialog` control, just like the dialog box itself, is a little more complicated than the `ColorDialog` control. Because there are more options to the control such as whether or not you want the various buttons, like the Apply button (`ShowApply` property), to be visible. Another worthwhile property is the `ShowEffects` property. This property, set to `True` by default, displays the Strikeout and Underline choices. You can also find the `FontDialog` control in the Dialogs category of controls in the toolbox. You will use the `ShowDialog()` method to display the dialog box. The dialog box is shown again in Figure 9-12.

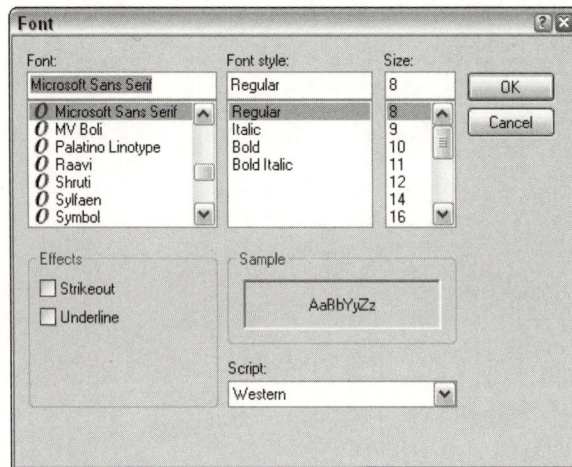

Figure 9-12

Once you have displayed the dialog box, and the user has responded, you set the font settings of the text selected in the `RichTextBox` control to the font specified. To accomplish these two tasks, you use the following two lines of code:

```
if (fontDialog1.ShowDialog()== DialogResult.OK)
     richTextBox1.SelectionFont = fontDialog1.Font;
```

This should look familiar, since it is almost the same as the code used for the `ColorDialog`.

Try It Out   Adding the FontDialog Control to Your Form

Using the form you have been working with in this chapter:

1. Drag and drop a `FontDialog` control from the toolbox into the bottom section of the form editor, beside the `ColorDialog` control.

2. Double-click the Format ⇨ Font choice of the `MenuStrip` control. The code file will open with the `Click` event displayed.

3. Type the following lines of code in the body of the `Click` event routine:

```
if (fontDialog1.ShowDialog()== DialogResult.OK)
        richTextBox1.SelectionFont = fontDialog1.Font;
```

4. Press F5 to test the application.

5. Type in text to test; then highlight some of text.

6. Choose Format ⇨ Font from the menu on the Rich Text Editor form. The Font dialog box opens, as shown in Figure 9-13. (I also used the zoom feature to make the text larger.)

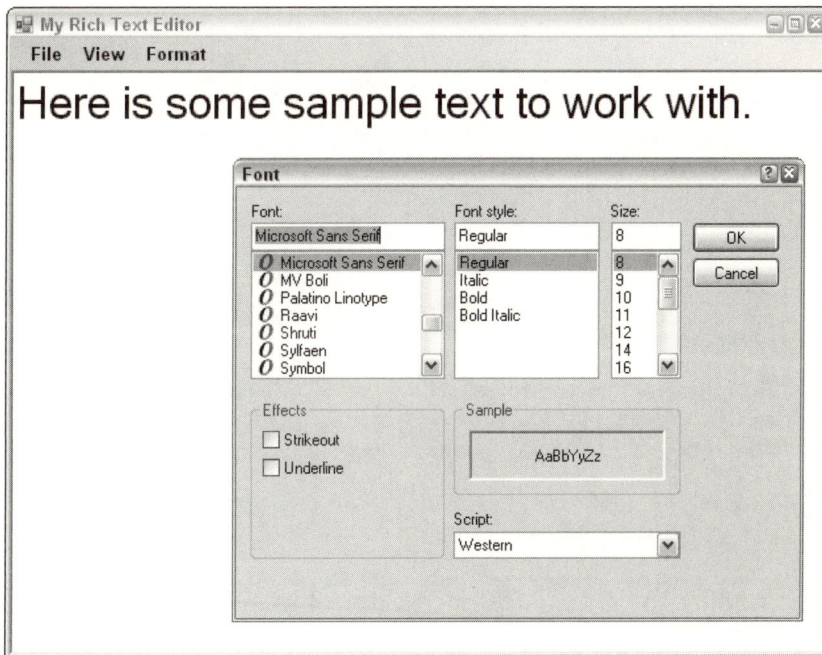

Figure 9-13

7. Select a new font, and click OK. The text that was highlighted in the form is changed to the new font.

There are a number of font options you can specify, including the special effects and sizes. Good stuff.

Using the OpenFileDialog Control

While the controls that have been discussed thus far in the chapter have been great for modifying the different fonts and colors of the text in the `RichTextBox` control, it doesn't do you much good to make all the changes and not be able to save the text to a file. It also is useful to be able to open files as well as save them.

The `OpenFileDialog` has a number of different properties you can set to determine the default settings of the dialog box displayed. Place the control onto the form. You can then highlight the control and see the properties you can work with, as shown in Figure 9-14.

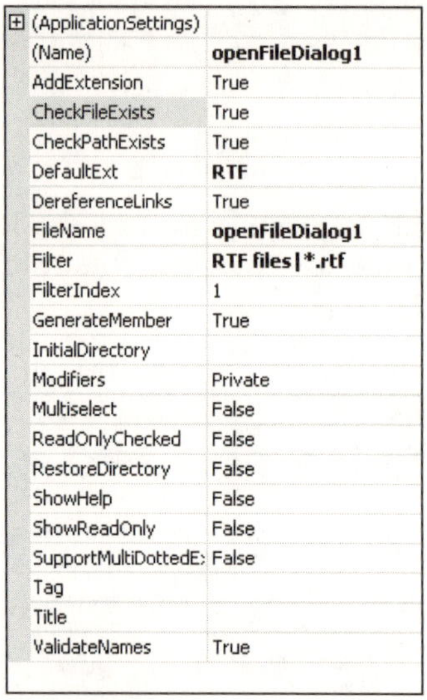

⊞ (ApplicationSettings)	
(Name)	**openFileDialog1**
AddExtension	True
CheckFileExists	True
CheckPathExists	True
DefaultExt	**RTF**
DereferenceLinks	True
FileName	**openFileDialog1**
Filter	**RTF files	*.rtf**
FilterIndex	1
GenerateMember	True
InitialDirectory	
Modifiers	Private
Multiselect	False
ReadOnlyChecked	False
RestoreDirectory	False
ShowHelp	False
ShowReadOnly	False
SupportMultiDottedE:	False
Tag	
Title	
ValidateNames	True

Figure 9-14

For the purposes of this example, you will be setting the `DefaultExt`, `FileName`, and `Filter` to your own specifications. After setting the properties as you want them, you can then call and open the dialog box in code with as little as the following lines of code:

```
if (openFileDialog1.ShowDialog() == DialogResult.OK)
    richTextBox1.LoadFile(openFileDialog1.FileName);
```

Try It Out   **Adding the OpenFileDialog Control to Your Form**

Using the form you have been working with in this chapter:

1. Drag and drop an `OpenFileDialog`, from the Dialogs category in the toolbox.

2. Highlight the `openFileDialog1` control with the Properties window open.

3. Type **RTF** for the `DefaultExt` property. This places "RTF" at the end of your files for the extension by default.

4. Type **RTF Files|*.rtf** in the `Filter` property. This property limits the files displayed in the file dialog boxes to those that meet the criteria — in this case, those with the extension of *.rtf.

5. Double-click the File ⇨ Open menu item in the `menuStrip1` control. The editor opens with the `Click` event displayed.

6. Type the following lines of code in the body of the routine:

```
if (openFileDialog1.ShowDialog() == DialogResult.OK)
    richTextBox1.LoadFile(openFileDialog1.FileName);
```

7. Press F5. The application starts, with the Rich Text Editor you created opened.

8. Choose File ⇨ Open from the form. The Open File dialog box opens, as shown in Figure 9-15.

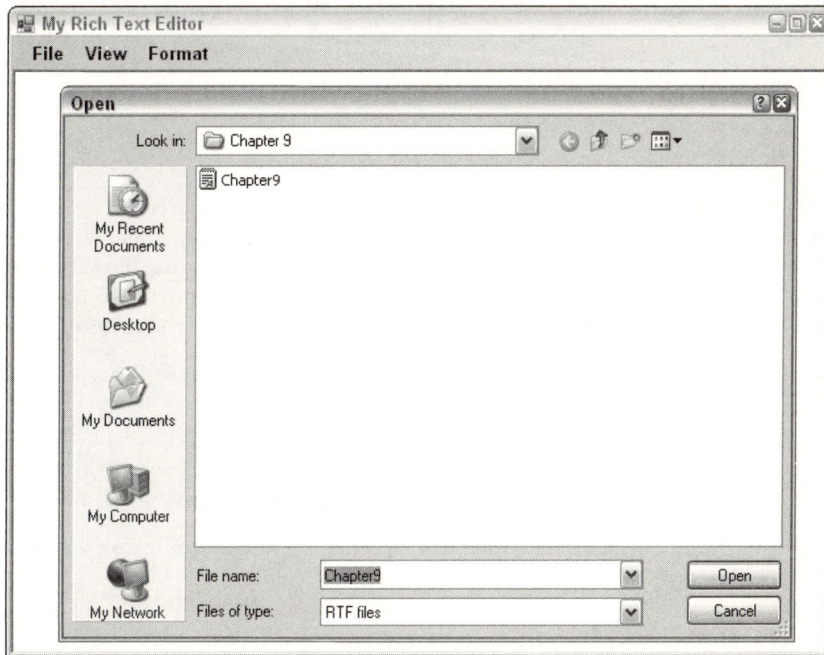

Figure 9-15

9. Click the Open button to open the file.

Note that if you were to click the Cancel button, an exception would occur. You could add code to error-trap whether or not the user has specified a file. But I will leave that to you. Let's move on to saving the file.

Note that the `Chapter9.rtf` *file is a sample file that I have supplied for you. You can find it in the Chapter 9 folder with the other samples for this chapter. If you save this file using the next section, then you will have to download it again if you want to use it as it was originally.*

Using the SaveFileDialog Control

The `SaveFileDialog` control has the same properties as the `OpenFileDialog` does. In fact, to show you how you can utilize both, I have made the code to use the `SaveFileDialog` a little more complicated:

```
string strFileName = openFileDialog1.FileName;

if (strFileName != "")
{
    if (saveFileDialog1.ShowDialog() == DialogResult.OK)
    {
        strFileName = saveFileDialog1.FileName;
        richTextBox1.SaveFile(strFileName);
    }
}
else
{
    richTextBox1.SaveFile(strFileName);
}
```

This code tests to see if the `openFileDialog1` control's `FileName` property has been set, through opening a file. If not and the `FileName` property is equal the name of the dialog box, which is the default, then the `SaveFileDialog` control is displayed, and the user can specify the file to Save As. If a file has been specified in the `OpenFileDialog`, then that name is used. This is how the Save option for a new file generally behaves, by only asking for the filename if it hasn't been saved before.

Try It Out   **Adding the SaveFileDialog Control to Your Form**

Using the form you have been working with in this chapter:

1. Drag and drop a `SaveFileControl` from the Dialogs category in the toolbox.

2. Highlight the `saveFileDialog1` control with the Properties window open.

3. Double-click the File ⇨ Save menu item in the `menuStrip1` control. The editor opens with the `Click` event displayed.

4. Type the following lines of code in the body of the routine:

```
string strFileName = openFileDialog1.FileName;

if (strFileName != "")
{
    if (saveFileDialog1.ShowDialog() == DialogResult.OK)
    {
        strFileName = saveFileDialog1.FileName;
        richTextBox1.SaveFile(strFileName);
    }
}
else
{
    richTextBox1.SaveFile(strFileName);
}
```

5. Press F5. The application starts, with the Rich Text Editor you created opened.

You can now test the application by pressing F5 and opening a file already created, or you can edit text opening a new blank file and then choose File ➪ Save.

Summary

The controls you learned how to use in this chapter can be utilized in just about every application you create using C# Express. The `RichTextBox` control is great when you have an application that you need to edit and work with files other than simple text files. This includes copying information to and from other applications such as Excel or Word documents, with all the formatting intact!

Using the dialog controls, you can do everything from setting fonts to changing text colors. You can open and save files using the `OpenFileDialog` and `SaveFileDialog` controls. With the various properties, you can set the dialog boxes to match the task you are trying to accomplish. You will be using the file dialog boxes throughout the rest of the book, starting in the next chapter.

Exercises

1. What is the name of the enumerator used for setting the `SelectionAlignment` property of the `RichTextBox` control?

2. What is one of the methods you can use in code to display all the dialog boxes displayed in this chapter?

3. Which property on the `RichTextBox` do you use to utilize a font from the `FontDialog`?

4. What happens if you choose File ➪ Open but then click Cancel?

Part III
Using Data in Applications

10

Introducing Database Concepts

There are all sorts of applications you can create to perform various tasks with C# Express. Some of those programs you create are going to need to work with data. Anytime you need to store data or information, you can use a database. A *database* is an electronic method for storing data such as customer information, invoices, mailing lists, and more. While there are methods for storing and working with data on the computer other than databases, it makes the most sense to take advantage of the features a database can give you.

This chapter covers data, primarily that used in databases. While you can use data without managing whole databases, having a good understanding of what databases (or in this case relational databases) are and how to work with them will help you create applications that are more logical, powerful, and easy to work with. In this chapter, I give a quick introduction to databases and discuss the following:

❑   What the parts of a database are and how they compare to real-world databases

❑   Kinds of database systems

❑   Relational databases

Getting Started with Databases

As you work with computers you quickly realize that everything you do on a computer deals with data in one sense or another. Whether you are creating a Word document or crunching numbers with Excel, it is all data. However, not all data belongs in a database, and not all programs are meant to be used as a database, although if you look at some people's documents and worksheets, you may wonder if they are trying to use them as databases. This section explains a few things about databases, as well as shows you how to use real-world databases every day.

If you have been using Microsoft Office products for a while, you have probably had some experience with or at least heard of databases. In fact, even if you haven't used databases on the computer, you have used them in real life.

Looking at Databases in the Real World

In the real world, there are a never-ending number of tasks and subjects that work as an example of databases. Every day from the time you get up until the time you go to bed you are dealing with databases of one kind or another. Here are just a few examples of real-world data:

❑   Mailing lists

❑   School registrations

❑   Checking account information and history

❑   Membership lists

❑   Customer information

And the list goes on and on. While some of these items look like simple topics in themselves, undoubtedly additional data for each topic could be flushed out so that more than one topic, what are called *tables* in database jargon, would be necessary.

The last entry in the list just displayed is a common example of a real-world database, and is worth discussing further. Customer information is stored as business records in manila folders, located in a filing cabinet. In the manila folders customer, information is stored, with either:

❑   One customer's information stored per folder

❑   All customer information sheets in one folder

Both ways can be analogous to an electronic database and have been used for years in the real world.

In accessing the real-world customer database, you:

1.   Open the file cabinet.

2.   Search through the cabinet for the folder you are looking for.

3.   Pull out the folder.

4.   Look through the folder for the information for which you are searching.

5.   Take the piece, or pieces, of paper containing the information.

6.   Read the data on the page.

7.   Modify the data as necessary.

At this point, you also could add new information by filling out a new form or delete information by throwing away information. (Of course, nowadays you would most likely shred the information for security reasons.)

It should be noted that the terms below are generic as far as the various database systems are concerned. These terms are discussed in greater details in the next section.

Tables are used to store data in databases. Fields (columns) are used to store individual pieces of data such as customer name, address, and so on. The information supplied in the fields makes up a record (row) in the table. So in this instance, all customer information, such as name, address, city, state, and so on, together make up a record (row). You will find that these terms are used interchangeably when various database products such as Microsoft Access (fields, records) and Microsoft SQL Server (columns, rows) are discussed.

Database Models

Various models of databases exist, two of which are flat-file and relational databases. The relational model of databases is the most common and is used nowadays for desktop and Web development. However, before going deeper into the relational database model, you should know about the flat-file model, including how they store data and their drawbacks.

Flat-File Model Databases

Flat-file model databases store information in single tables, including repeated data. For example, if a store was selling different kinds of coffee and wanted to track customers, invoices, invoice items, and suppliers, the database would look like Figure 10-1, which is a flat-file type table.

Customer	Invoice Date	Invoice #	Product1	ProductSupplier1	Product1Cost	Product2	ProductSupplier2	Product2Cost
John Smith	9/1/2004	3443	French Roast	Starbucks Coffee	$10.95	House Blend	Starbucks Coffee	$11.95
Sally Jones	9/1/2004	3445	Sumatra	Starbucks Coffee	$11.95	French Roast	Starbucks Coffee	$12.95
Harry James	9/1/2004	3445	Columbia	Seattles Best Coffee	$12.95	Columbia	Seattles Best Coffee	$12.95

Figure 10-1

If you look at this figure closely, you may notice it looks like it was created in Excel, which it was. A lot of new developers and users store data in Excel spreadsheets, thereby creating flat-file tables and databases without realizing it.

There are a number of problems with the flat-file database model. Here are just a few of the issues:

❑ **Redundant data.** Entries often get repeated, taking up more space than necessary. In Figure 10-1, for example, there is no reason to spell out the names of the suppliers each time.

❑ **Error prone.** When data has to be repeated, there is more of a chance to enter erroneous data into the table.

❑ **Limited columns.** Currently, only two products and their information can be entered using the table structure displayed.

❑ **Extra work to update.** With the redundant data issue, if you want to make any updates, you will have to make sure you parse through the other fields and update those values to match.

In addition to the preceding issues, reporting (retrieving) on the data can be problematic as well. Now take a look at what the relational database model looks like.

Relational Database Model

Unlike the flat-file database model, which stores all data, including related data, in a single record and table, the relational database model use tables that are related to one another to store information. For example, instead of having your coffee invoices all stored in a single table called tblInvoices, the information would be stored in related tables, with customer information being stored in one table, invoices information stored in another, product information in yet another, and so on. Figure 10-2 shows an example of how the flat-file table in the previous section could be structured into a relational model.

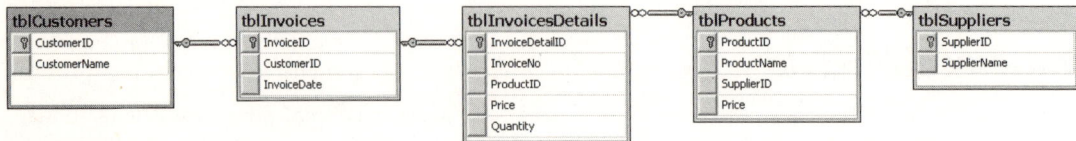

Figure 10-2

This figure was taken from C# Express connected to a SQL Server Express database file called `CoffeeSQL.mdf`, located in the main `Samples` folder. The figure shows the database diagram of the tables the data is now separated out into, as compared to the single table (spreadsheet) in the previous figure.

> *C# Express enables you to connect to both Access databases (*.mdb) and SQL Server database files (*.mdf). SQL Server Express is included with C# Express, so the majority of the data-oriented examples and chapters will be using SQL Server Express database files. These are all located in main `Samples` folder. How to connect to SQL Server Express and Access files is discussed in Chapter 11.*

Take a look at some of the benefits of using relational databases. They are pretty much the opposite of the issues found in flat-file databases:

❑ **Nonredundant data.** Because entries are entered once, and other tables point to the data, there is less redundant data.

❑ **Less error prone.** When data is entered once in lookup tables, data is then picked from lists. This lends greater control and prevents input errors.

❑ **Unlimited data.** Because data is stored in rows (down) versus fields (across), the data is not limited to predefined structures. For example, when you want to add another product to an invoice, you simply add another record to tblInvoiceDetails. In the flat file, you would have had to add a third or fourth product column.

Looking at Figure 10-2, you might think maintaining a relational database involves a lot more work because of the multiple tables, but you very quickly learn to appreciate the benefits of the relational database despite the extra work needed in the beginning.

Next, read about the elements that make up relational databases.

Tables: Where Data Is Stored

As mentioned in a note earlier in the chapter, tables are where your data is stored. Tables have specific elements: fields, primary keys, and indexes.

Columns/Fields

When created, table structures consist of columns (or fields) that represent pieces of data. Columns have properties that give you control over the data that goes into them. Here are a few of those properties common to different database systems such as Access and SQL Server:

❑ **Name.** Column names are what you will refer to when you want to pull information from the column or assign data to the column. You will want to assign your names to make sense. For example, for the tblCustomer table, the two columns displayed in Figure 10-3 are named CustomerID and CustomerName.

❑ **Data types.** Data types tell the database system how to handle the data placed in the column. Which data types there are depends on specific database systems. Microsoft Access calls text data under 255 characters *text datatype*; in SQL Server, it is *nvarchar(255)*.

❑ **Other properties.** There are a number of other properties that help control data going into the columns, and those properties will again depend on which database system you are using. Some properties, such as `Default Value`, are used by most systems, but some, such as the `Caption` property, are used by Access but not SQL Server.

You can see an example of the table structure for tblCustomers listed in Figure 10-3 with the Customer column highlighted. The table structure is displayed in C# Express.

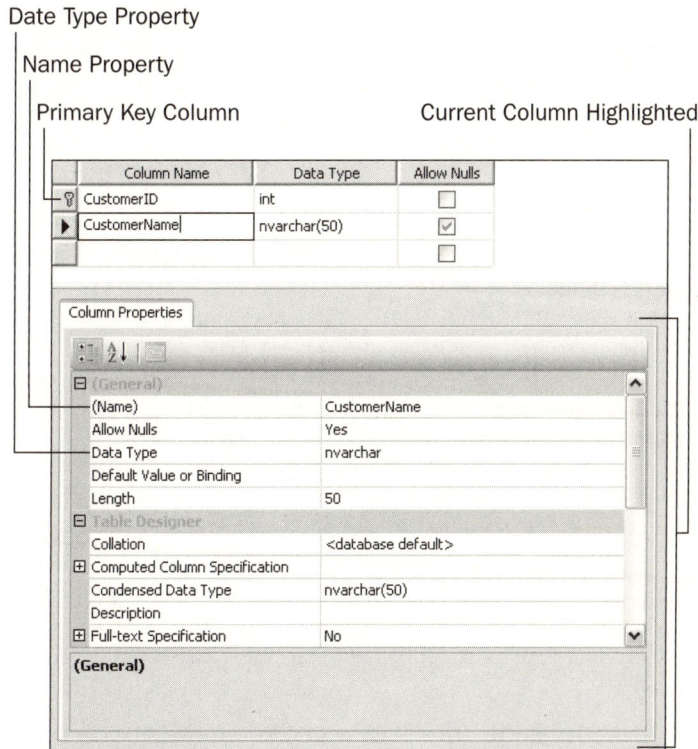

Figure 10-3

Primary and Foreign Key Columns

Notice the callout for the Primary Key column in Figure 10-3. Each table should have a primary key. In the case of tblCustomers the primary key is the column CustomerID. The primary key makes sure that each record in a table is unique, and provides the ability to always find a specific record. How primary keys are specified will again depend on the database system you are using.

Foreign key columns are columns in a table that point to primary key columns in other tables. For example, you will see CustomerID in tblInvoice, which is used to match the primary key column CustomerID, in tblCustomers. Primary and foreign key columns are especially important in the use of relations. When picking a primary key, you must make certain that the data in the field will be unique values in each row of the table. Both Access and SQL Server have a means to auto-generate this field for you. In Access it is called AutoNumber, and in SQL Server it is the Identity column.

It's All about Relationships

Relationships are how you tie (relate) data together using separate tables. In Figure 10-2 you saw a database diagram for `CoffeeSQL.mdf`. In Figure 10-4 you can see the relationships window in Access, displaying the relationships for `Coffee.mdb`, the Access version of the database.

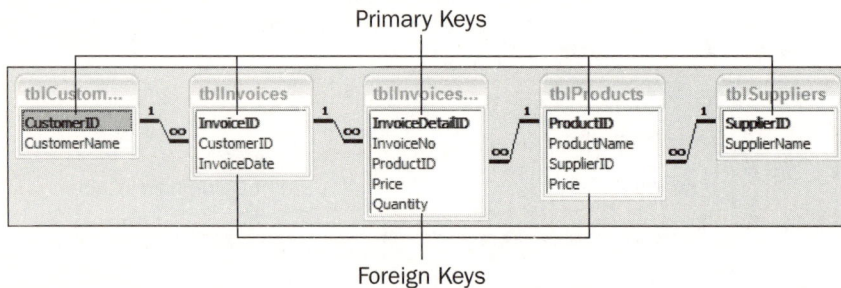

Figure 10-4

Three types of relationships are found in relational databases. Because `Coffee.mdb` mainly uses one type of relationship, other examples are listed outside that database:

❏   **One-to-one relationship.** Used when you want to have records in one table match up with individual records in another table based on the same primary key in each table. An example of this in a banking database is a table that stores private information that would match up directly with a table that stores information that can be viewed by anyone. This is probably the least used type of relationship, because the use of queries (Access) and views (SQL Server) can limit the data you access in tables.

❏   **One-to-many relationship.** This type of relation is used to relate a table such as tblCustomer (a customer) with tblInvoices (the customer's Invoices). The way you look at it is that one customer can have many invoices. Note that the primary key is in tblCustomer, and the foreign key is in tblInvoices.

❏   **Many-to-many relationship.** This is a pair of one-to-many relationships used with three tables. An example of this is an insurance database. Insurance companies can have multiple customers, and customers can have multiple insurance companies.

As far as which type of relationship to use, it will depend on the need. All three can be used in the same database, or just use one type of relationship throughout the database. It really comes down to the data.

Referential Integrity

One of the important aspects of relational databases is maintaining referential integrity of the data. For example, in the coffee database, a record in the tblInvoices table can't be created without a related record in tblCustomers in existence. Another example is that a record in the tblProducts table could not be added with a record already in the tblSuppliers table.

Depending on the database system, you can set referential integrity up to also help maintain data once it is in the database. For example, you can specify that a record can't be deleted in one table, such as tblCustomers, if records exist in tblInvoices that are related to it.

Another use for referential integrity with current data is to have records deleted in related tables, such as tblInvoices, when a record is deleted in the table that contains the primary key, in this case, tblCustomers.

Normalizing Your Data

Normalizing data are the steps taken to take nonnormalized data (flat file) and shape it into what is called normal (relational) form. Here are the steps:

For first normal form (1NF):

❑　Remove duplicate columns from the table.

❑　Create separate tables for each group of related data, identifying each row with a unique column or set of columns. This unique column or set of columns would be the primary key.

In the case of the table displayed in Figure 10-2, the Product1, Product2, and so on, and the product specific information is removed from the main table and broken out into separate rows.

For second normal form (2NF):

❑　Remove subsets of data that apply to multiple rows of a table and place them in separate tables.

❑　Create relationships between these new tables and their predecessors through the use of foreign keys.

In this case, you would remove the customer information and store it in a separate table, then create a relationship between the new customer table and the table containing the invoice information.

For third normal form (3NF):

❑　Remove columns not dependent upon the primary key.

Invoice detail is broken out into separate tables at this point, and each set of data is given its own ID, with a foreign key pointing to the invoice header record.

For fourth normal form (4NF):

❑　Make sure relation has no multivalued dependencies.

Additional forms are possible, depending on how far you want to take the normalization. The majority of databases used are in third or fourth normal form.

Working with Various Databases

You've read about flat-file and relational databases and now know the differences. There is some additional information you need to know about the available relational databases and their platforms. Before getting into the specifics of Microsoft Access and SQL Server specifically, you need to get comfortable with some terminology.

File Server versus Client/Server

File server databases are where the database is stored in a folder on a file server. When you access the database, all the data is brought down over the network and is locally processed. Microsoft Access is a file-server-based database system.

Client/server databases are stored on a server, but when it comes time to process, the processing is performed out on the server, and just the necessary data is brought down over the network. Microsoft SQL Server is a client/server-type product.

> One of the big changes in SQL Server Express 2005 is that the databases files, with the extension of *. mdf, are more mobile than prior versions. So you can have the power of client/server applications but pass around the databases more conveniently.

Although with most development environments how you develop against the two types of database platforms will vary, between C# Express, the data tools included, and .NET, you will develop using the same methods.

Front and Back Ends

When working with database applications, you have front and back ends. The application created to control the input and output of the data is called the *front end*. The database containing the data is the *back end*. The application will contain forms, reports, and other programming elements. When you are connecting to a data source, the data source, such as Microsoft Access or SQL Server databases, are the back end, and the applications you write are the front end.

The next couple of sections describe the two databases for which C# Express includes tools: Microsoft Access and Microsoft SQL Server.

Microsoft Access

Perfect for small- to medium-size solutions when used as a back end, Microsoft Access is a popular database system, with thousands if not millions of installations. Access can also be used as a front end as well, but that is a topic for another book. You can see Access with the `Coffee.mdb` open and tblCustomers displayed in Figure 10-5.

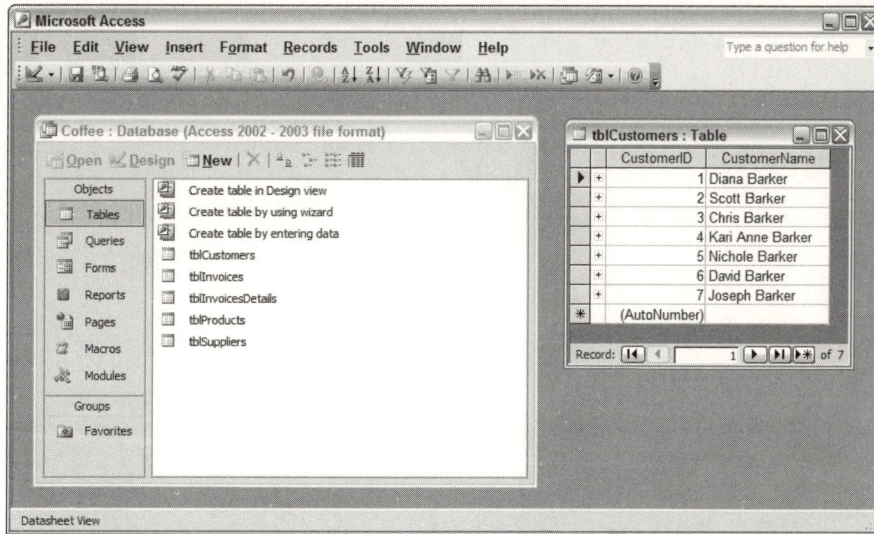

Figure 10-5

Benefits and Issues of Microsoft Access

There are quite a few benefits to use Access over other database products. Some of the positive aspects of Access are as follows:

- ❑ **Established application.** Access has been around for quite a few versions, with Microsoft enhancing the product with each version. The current version is Microsoft Access 2003.

- ❑ **Powerful report writer.** Access is a banded report writer, with bands set up for Report Header/Footers, Group Headers/Footers, Page Header/Footers, and Detail. You can embed reports within reports. The Accesdfs report writer is commonly used by other products to create reports, including Visual Basic and even SQL Server.

- ❑ **Used as front end and/or a back end.** It is almost as common to have Access used as a front end for a SQL Server database as it is to use it strictly with Access. You can link tables in an MDB file or use an Access ADP file, which is a database project specifically set up to be a front end for a SQL Server database.

- ❑ **Macro language for beginners and VBA for developers.** Access provides a powerful forms package with the Visual Basic for Applications (VBA) development language behind it.

- ❑ **Database files easy to transfer.** Just by using Windows' copy and paste functions, you can move/copy Access databases over locally, over a network, or even by storing the database in a compressed folder and e-mailing the folder.

Now that you've seen the benefits of Access, following are some issues that can arise when using Access for your databases:

- ❑ **Large databases bog down.** You can run into problems with large-size databases, if those databases are not carefully created.

❑ **Large number of users bog down.** When creating an application for a large number of users, you need to be very careful about how the application is created. Otherwise, you can get bogged down with the querying and updating of data. This is especially true with large databases, as mentioned in the previous item.

❑ **Forms designer can be confusing to use.** As powerful as they both are, the form and report designers in Access can be confusing to use when moving beyond the basics.

❑ **Not built for use with the Internet.** Because Access is a file server product, and not meant for the truly high volume you get when using database over the Internet, Access is made more for use on a local area network.

Access works very well for C# as a back-end database when you have a limited number of people accessing the data. Access also is a great database to prototype applications in, for later use in another development language such as C#, and to have the data moved to SQL Server. Because you also can utilize the Access database from other products without having to have a version of Access installed, using Access as a back end is even that much more worthwhile.

Microsoft SQL Server

Built for small to enterprisewide databases, SQL Server is built for use with other development products and includes no forms management tools of its own.

In Figure 10-6, you can see the CoffeeSQL database open in C# Express.

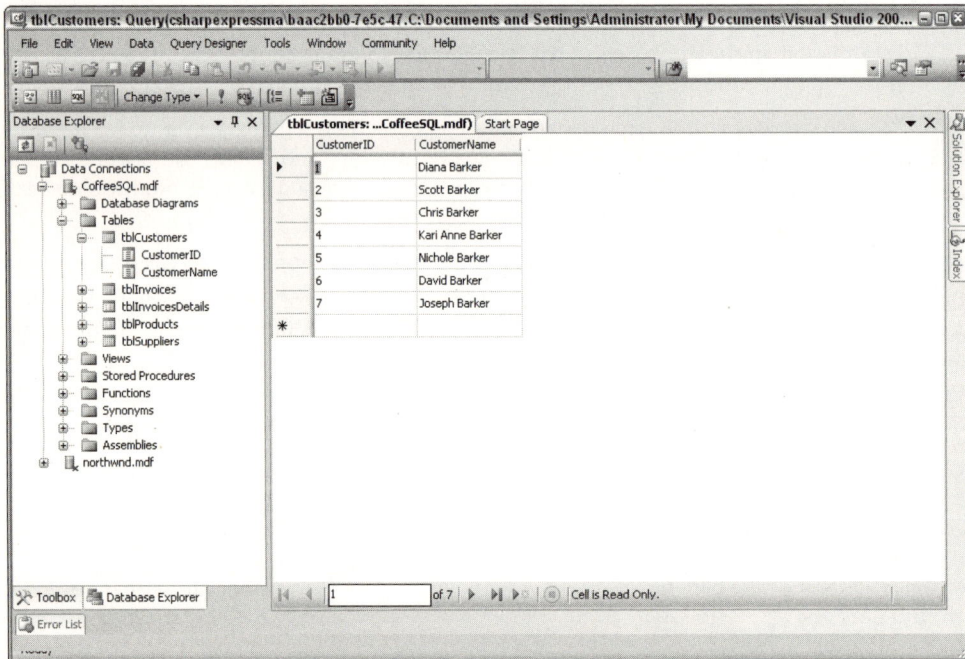

Figure 10-6

Benefits and Issues of Microsoft SQL Server

As with Microsoft Access, there are number of benefits to using Microsoft SQL Server, including the following:

❑ **Established application.** As with Access, SQL Server has been around for quite a few versions. At this writing, SQL Server 2000 is the current version.

❑ **Robust set of client tools for data management.** Spearheaded by Enterprise Manager and Query Analyzer, SQL Server has a number of tools that help you manage data in your databases.

❑ **Extensive SQL language for data manipulation.** Using Transact SQL, you can create stored procedures that can manipulate data in just about any way necessary. Also available is DTS, or Data Transformation Services, which enables you to create packages to schedule tasks for working with the information in your database.

❑ **Can handle large amounts of data.** SQL Server is made for large amounts of data. On a server that has been properly set up, you can store many gigabytes of data. In addition to the proper system, the data needs to be normalized and care must be taken when you are creating views and stored procedures.

❑ **Works well with the Internet.** Because SQL Server works well with large databases, and large number of users, it works well as a database for use with the Internet. Of course, when creating the database, you do need to be conscientious about how much data you are going to be storing and how many people will be utilizing the database at a time.

The majority of the issues with using SQL Server have been related to the lack of tools. C# Express has taken care of those by supplying tools that make it much easier to work with SQL Server databases in the IDE.

Summary

Once you have worked with databases for a while, you will find it a whole new world that can really increase the number of applications and solutions you can create for users. Just about every company has database needs that they are handling through various means such as putting the information in spreadsheets and Word documents. The data stored in these types of applications are generally in the flat-file format. There are a number of benefits to pulling your data into relational databases, and a number of relational database systems are available.

C# Express connects directly to two major databases, Microsoft Access and SQL Server. The same tools are provided for working with either one, as well as classes and controls with C#. The next few chapters go into detail about using SQL Server database with your C# applications.

Exercises

1. What is the process of converting your data from flat-file format to a relational database format called?

2. Name the three types of relationships discussed in the chapter.

3. In Access you have fields and records. What are these elements called in SQL Server?

4. Give a couple of the benefits to using SQL Server databases.

5. Name the extensions of the Access and SQL Server database files.

11

Using SQL Server Express Features within C# Express

In Chapter 10, I discussed various aspects of what databases are and how you can use them within your applications. Microsoft has been working on SQL Server, its premier client/server database, to make it more developer-friendly for tighter use with C# and their other developer languages by providing tools in the development environments. To this end, every version of SQL Server is more scalable, making it easier than ever to pass SQL Server database files. These database files use the `extension.mdf`. SQL Server Express, included with C# Express, is the easiest version yet.

SQL Server Express has a set of tools to help you to manage database files for development and small deployment purposes. In addition to including a copy of SQL Server Express, C# Express includes a set of data tools including the Database Explorer, which provides almost all the functionality needed for maintaining databases from within the C# Express IDE. In Chapter 12, you will see how to use various data controls to manipulate data within your applications. In this chapter, you will:

❑   Be introduced to SQL Server Express and tools included in it.

❑   Learn about the Database Explorer in C# Express.

❑   Work on connecting to an existing database and create new databases within the Database Explorer.

❑   See how to create the various objects in SQL Server databases.

Introducing SQL Server Express

SQL Server has been around for quite a few years and is mainly known as a large client database solution. Unlike Microsoft Access, which has had a full set of user and development tools since version 1.0, SQL Server has generally been considered to be set up and used by big IT departments and larger companies. While it is true that SQL Server can handle very large databases, and servers can be linked together to handle some of the largest, Microsoft has been working for a number of years to deliver a lower-scaled version of SQL Server for single or few users.

The prior version of SQL Server Express was called Microsoft SQL Server Desktop Edition. The latest edition is much more convenient to use, and it can be either downloaded off the Net for installation or included in your own setup.

Access to SQL Server

Microsoft is trying harder than ever to have its SQL Server database files take over where Access database files are now used so heavily. The reason is that after you have created an Access database, you may outgrow it, either by volume of records or number of users, or both. Once this happens, you will need to convert it into a SQL Server database. Converting a database from Access into SQL Server is called *upsizing*. Once you have done this, you need to make a number of changes. If your application, called the *front end*, is set up to utilize Access, then some changes need to be made to applications to then work with the SQL Server database.

Using a database created in SQL Server Express, the database file (*.mdf) can be detached from a SQL Server Express instance. It can then be attached to a full SQL Server instance with very little change or effort. The programming in the application is exactly the same.

SQL Server Configuration Manager

One of the tools included with SQL Server Express is the SQL Server Configuration Manager. Rather than helping you manage databases, this tool helps you manage the system environment on which your databases will be running. When you install SQL Server Express, the parameters are pretty well set up as you need them to be for single system use. The majority of the tasks in the SCM are those that are available with the full-blown version of SQL Server. However, one of the choices, SQL Server, is created for SQL Server Express to create a default instance of SQL Server locally on your computer. The default version is called (SQLEXPRESS) and can be seen in Figure 11-1. You can have more than one instance of SQL Server managed by the SQL Server Configuration Manager. For the purposes of this book, you will just use the default instance.

Some of the services displayed aren't available within the SQL Server Express version. For instance, Report Services are not available. However, you could use SQL Server Configuration Manager to look at an existing full-blown version of SQL Server 2005.

> You should have installed SQL Server Express on your computer when installing C# Express back in Chapter 1. If you have a problem with the following Try It Out, refer back to that chapter and install SQL Server Express with C# Express. You can also download and install SQL Server Express separately.

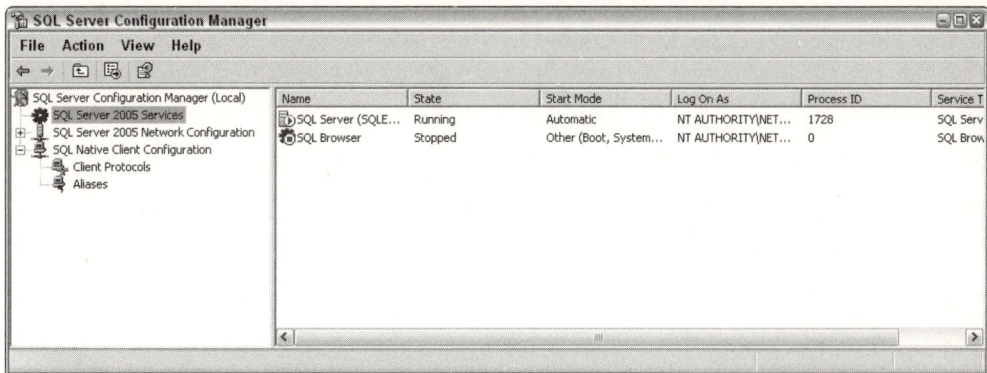

Figure 11-1

Opening and Looking Around the SQL Server Configuration Manager

While at the Windows desktop:

1.   Choose Microsoft SQL Server 2005 ⇨ Configuration Tools ⇨ SQL Configuration Manager from the All Programs menu. The SQL Server Configuration Manager opens.

2.   Click the SQL Server 2005 Services node if it is not already selected. You will then see information displayed in the right pane showing the current status of your local version of SQL Server. This will look as it does in Figure 11-1.

3.   You can click around on the left pane to look at the different services.

I wouldn't really change anything at this point, because it is set up to work as default. As mentioned, for the purpose of this book you really won't have much to do with the SQL Server Configuration Manager.

SQL Server Tools in C# Express

When you are developing a database application, the application can be created using C# or any other development language. If that application works with a database, you are going to need tools for both connecting and using the database within your program, and also possibly create and modify the objects while developing the application.

There is quite a bit you can do with SQL Server from within the C# Express IDE. The purpose of those tools is to make it so that you don't have to switch back and forth between the tools that come with SQL Server to modify the database objects such as tables and views. The following sections list what you can do inside C# Express using the tools provided, and then discuss how you actually use them.

Introducing the Database Explorer

The majority of the work that you need to do as far as working with the structure of a database can be handled using the Database Explorer. You can see the Database Explorer by choosing View ⇨ Database Explorer. You don't even need a project open to work in the Database Explorer within C# Express, once you have the Database Explorer showing in the same area as the toolbox is displayed. One of the first things you will do when using the Database Explorer is either connect to an existing database or create a new database. Once connected to a database, you will have access to the various objects within the database. You can see an example of this in Figure 11-2.

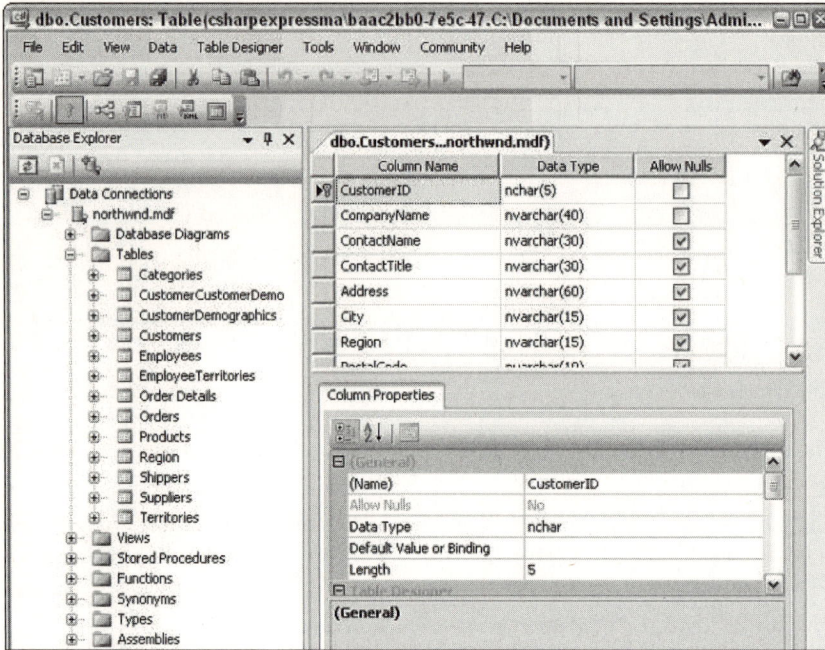

Figure 11-2

Before actually connecting to a database yourself, take a look at some of the features in the Database Explorer.

Database Explorer Features

Within C# Express are a number tasks that can be handled within the Database Explorer. If you need to connect or work with a database when in the editor, you can use the Database Explorer to accomplish most of the tasks.

Task/Object	Description
Connect to Database	Add a database connection to an existing database that resides in a SQL Server instance on your local machine or network.
Create Database	Create a new database and connect to that database; then add objects described below.

Task/Object	Description
Maintain Tables	As described in Chapter 10, tables are where you store the data that is maintained. To store the information, you need to specify the table structure that tells the database what kind of data is to be stored.
Maintain Views	Because data is stored in related tables, you need a way to see and work with the data in a format that represents its original format. For instance, say you want to be able to see the customer name for an invoice, even if only the CustomerID is stored with the invoice. Views let you specify different ways to look at your data.
Maintain Stored Procedures	Procedures written in T-SQL that can be called to modify your data including creating tables; adding, deleting, and updating records; and viewing data.

The majority of the objects mentioned in this table were discussed in Chapter 10. You will be shown how to work with them further in the chapters that follow.

Working with Data Connections

To get started actually using the SQL Server tools within C# Express, you need to connect to a database. This can be a database that exists on your system or one provided with this book. There is a small database called `CoffeeSQL.mdf` that is provided in the `Samples` folder to which you can connect.

When a connection is achieved, you can then perform all the desired actions against the database, either working with database objects or going on to specify ways to use the database with your projects.

After starting C# Express, choose Tools ⇨ Connect To Database. . . . This both opens the Database Explorer and starts the Add Connection dialog box.

In prior versions of SQL Server, databases were required to be already attached to a SQL Server instance. That is no longer the case; you can take a database that someone sends to you and connect to it using the Add Connection wizard. C# Express will create a connection to the database and utilize the SQL Server instance specified, in this case the SQL Express instance specified by default when you installed SQL Server Express.

The first page of the Add Connection dialog box is shown in Figure 11-3.

In the figure, you can see two options for security using the databases in SQL Server. For the purposes of this book, you will be using the default, which is Windows Authentication. You won't have to worry about messing with security that way. When you click the Browse button, you can then locate the database file you want to connect to using a standard File Open dialog box.

Once you have located the database file you want to use, click Open, and the file path and name appears in the Add Connection wizard. Then click OK to open the Database Explorer. Now click the plus sign displayed next to the Data Connections label, and you see the database you choose. If you click the plus sign that appears next to the database, you will see all the object categories in the database, as shown in Figure 11-4.

Figure 11-3

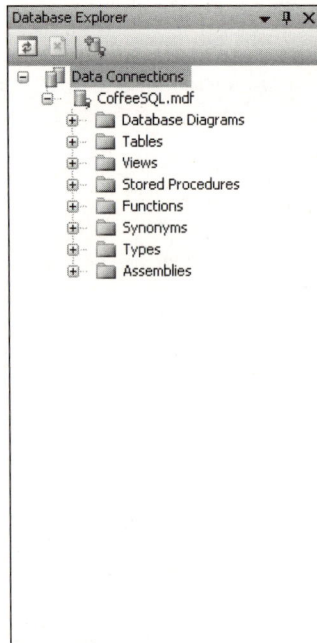

Figure 11-4

Okay, you have seen what it looks like to open a connection. It is time for you get busy and do it yourself.

Try It Open   Add a Database Connection to an Existing Database

If you have your own database you want to connect to, you can use that. Otherwise, as mentioned, you can use a database called `CoffeeSQL.mdf` that is located in the `Samples` folder in your folders for this book.

1. Open C# Express. Don't open a solution at this point.

2. Choose Tools ➪ Connect To Database . . . . The Add Connection dialog box appears, along with the Database Explorer.

3. Click the Browse button. An open file dialog box with the title Select SQL Server Database File appears.

4. Locate the `CoffeeSQL.mdf` or whichever database file you want to connect to. You can see the `CoffeeSQL.mdf` file in Figure 11-5.

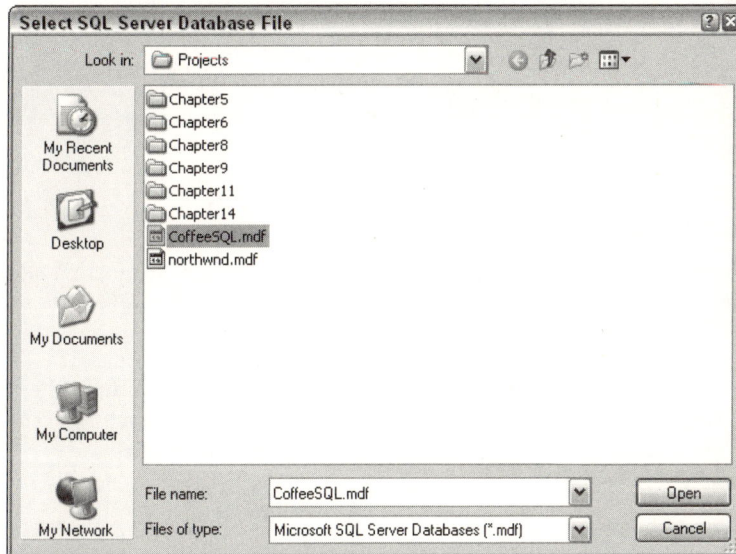

Figure 11-5

5. Click Open. The database file path and filename is now listed in the Database File Name field on the Add Connection dialog box.

6. Click OK. The connection is created, and you can browse to the database in the Database Explorer.

Creating a New Database Using the Add Connection Dialog Box

Creating a new database and a connection to that new database is just about as easy as connecting to an existing database. Of course, you still have the task of creating the objects such as tables that you want to use once the database is created. But the cool thing is you can do all of it from within C# Express.

Instead of specifying an existing database in the open file dialog box, do the following:

1. Give a new name.

2. After giving the new name, click Open. The new name and the path you specified is displayed in the Add Connection dialog box.

3. Now, when you click OK, an additional dialog box opens that you will need to respond to.

The new dialog box displayed informs you that there isn't an existing database file with that name and asks "Would you like to create it?" By responding and clicking Yes, C# Express then creates the database and then the connection to the database. The dialog box is shown in Figure 11-6.

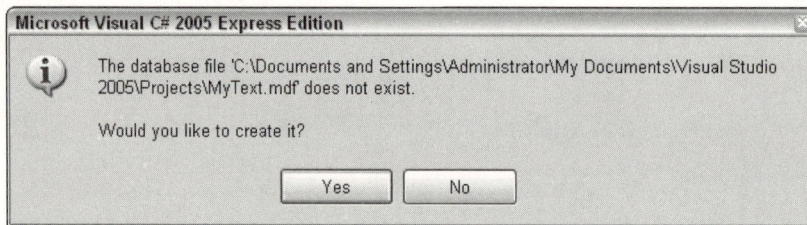

Figure 11-6

Working with SQL Server Objects

Once you have created the data connection by either connecting to a current or a new database, you can then go into the database and start managing objects. The following sections walk through some of the objects you will use most often and how to use them.

Tables are the objects used the most in databases, and because they are actually the objects that hold the data, they are definitely the base place to start our discussion of the various SQL Server objects.

Table Definitions

As discussed in the previous chapter, tables are made up of columns and rows. When you are working in the design view of a table, you will be specifying properties for the various columns, such as last and first name. Depending on what you are trying to accomplish, there are a few ways you can work with tables in the Database Explorer. For example, if you just want to look at what columns are in a table and aren't interested in knowing what the properties are, you can click the desired table, and then the columns will be displayed below the table title, as shown in Figure 11-7.

If you decide you want to see the properties of the columns or even want to edit (modify) a structure of a table, you just need to double-click on the table you are interested in. Once you have double-clicked the table, look at the structure of the table in the middle of the editor where files are normally displayed, with the column in the table listed above. In addition, a property window is displayed showing the properties of the columns. In the main properties window on the right, various properties are displayed for the table itself.

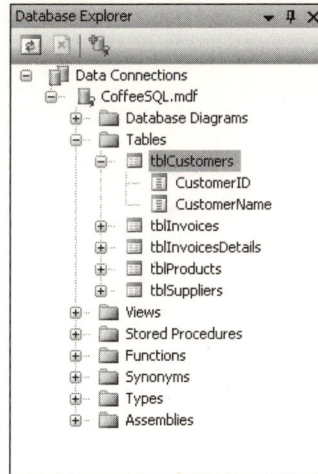

Figure 11-7

Try it Out   Display a Table Structure

In this Try It Out, you display a table's structure and add a column to the table. So, with the CoffeeSQL database displayed in the Database Explorer:

1. Double-click the table called tblCustomers. As described, the table appears in the middle of the IDE, as shown in Figure 11-8.

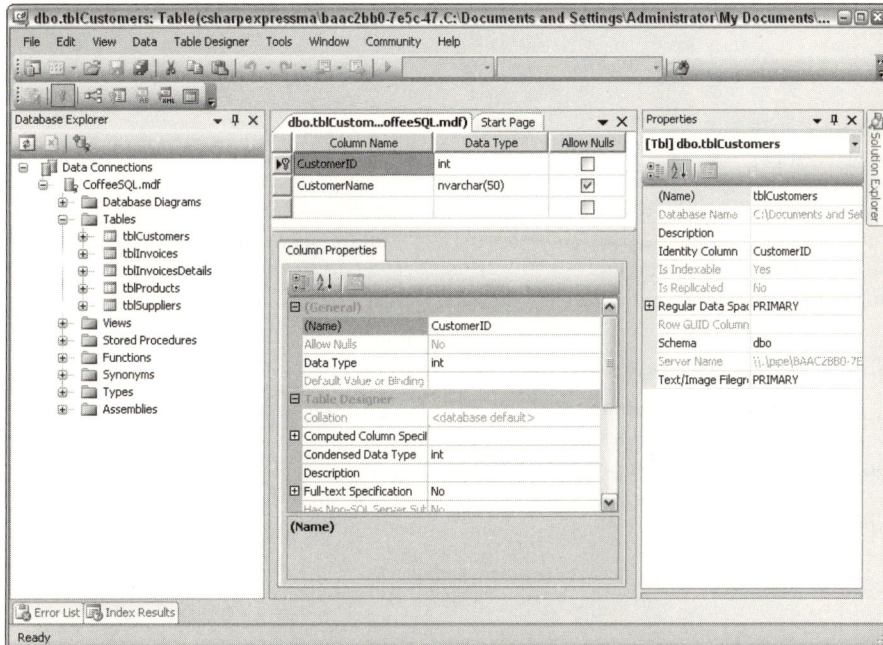

Figure 11-8

2. Place the cursor in the blank field under Customer Name.

3. Type **EmailName** for the Column Name; then press Enter.

4. In the Data Type drop-down list, pick NVarChar(50), as shown in Figure 11-9.

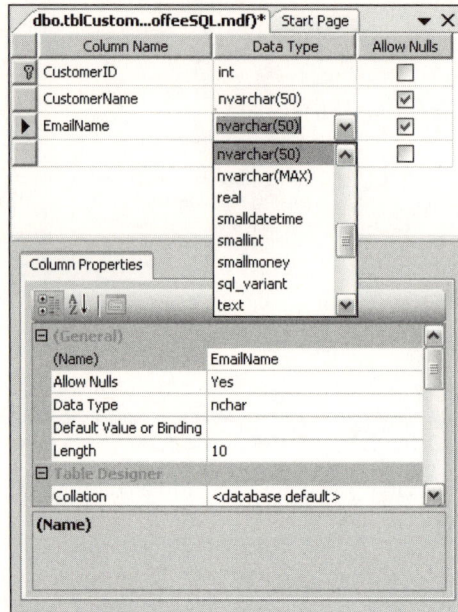

Figure 11-9

5. Save the file by choosing File ⇨ Save All.

Once you have saved the table information, you can now view the data.

> *Note that there are a lot of properties you need to set when are first creating a table, such as indexes and default values. The purpose of this book at this point is to get you started in using C# Express with SQL Server Express. Creating databases and tables from scratch can take entire chapters, so I will let you read up on some of those items on your own and show you how to use some of the tools that you have available.*

Viewing Table Data in C# Express

To view the data in the tblCustomers table, right-click the table and choose Show Table Data. The data is displayed in a data sheet, or grid, format. You can then modify the data as desired. Generally you use this mode to correct or test tables in the database.

One important thing to know at this time is that you can move around the records using controls at the bottom of the screen. You can see this screen in Figure 11-10.

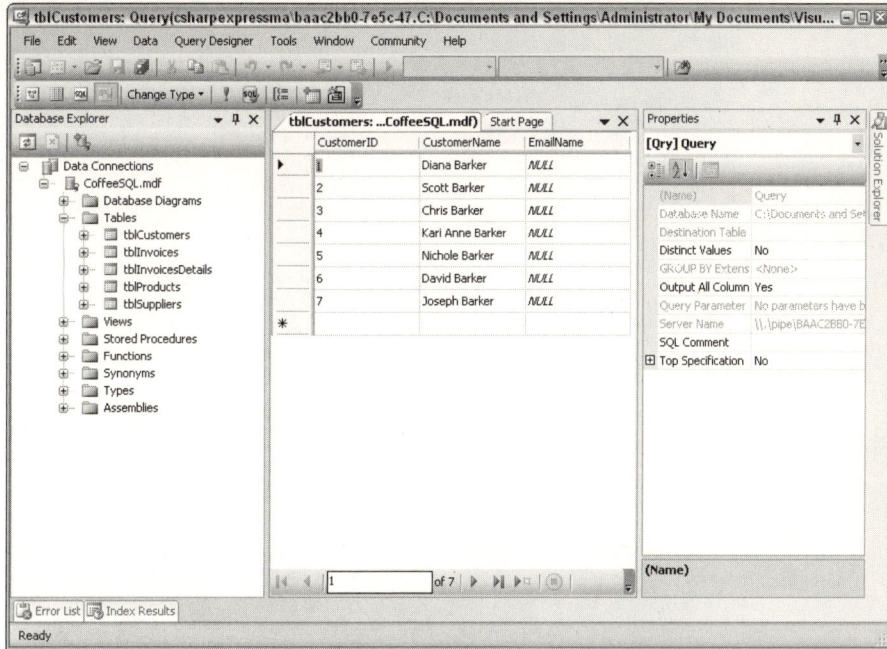

Figure 11-10

Notice that the new column is included and is set to NULL. The NULL value means that a field has not been set and the system does not know what type of value is in there.

There is a powerful toolbar also displayed in Figure 11-11, where one of the choices is Change Type. This toolbar gives you the ability to change the results set you are looking at into a query that is either a type view (selectable data) or a stored procedure (bulk updating), depending on what you want to do with it.

Try It Out   View Table Data

1.   Right-click the tblCustomers table.

2.   Pick Show Table Data from the menu. The table appears in the main pane of the C# Express IDE, as shown in Figure 11-10.

Other SQL Server Objects

There are many other SQL Server objects that you can work with from the Database Solutions, such as views and stored procedures. While more detail is beyond the scope of this text, there are some good books out there that provide more information about creating these objects.

You can also work with views in the IDE, as shown in Figure 11-11. The figure shows a view being created, where you can see the table it's based on as well as the grid of fields to use. Lastly, you can see the result on the bottom of the screen.

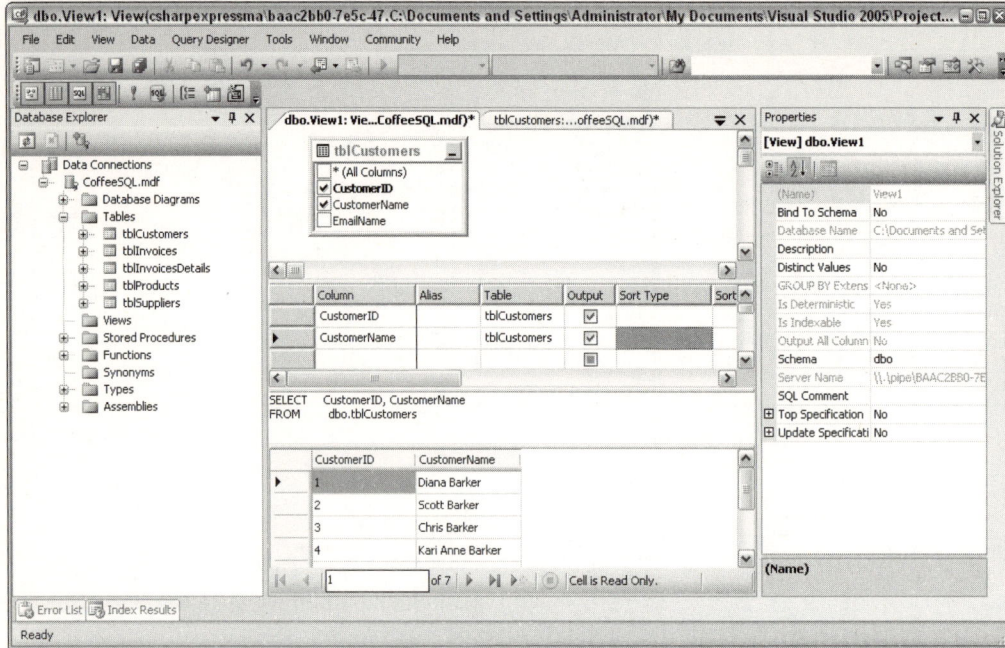

Figure 11-11

You will also learn about some of these features as you continue through the next couple of chapters on learning about data controls and using ADO.NET in your C# applications.

Summary

Microsoft has gone to a great extent to give you the ability to use C# Express to create usable applications without necessarily having to use full-blown versions of Visual Studio 2005 and SQL Server. In fact, to help with this, they have included a scaled-down version of SQL Server with C# Express called SQL Server Express. Formally known as the MSDE, this version provides developer with the ability to use SQL Server on a smaller scale for development purposes or even as single-user solutions. They have even gone as far as to provide the ability to point and connect to a SQL Server database file with the extension of .mdf.

While SQL Server Express has tools to working with SQL Server databases, C# Express also provides a number of tools for allowing you to connect to SQL Server Databases and maintaining them right from within the C# Express IDE using the Database Explorer. With the Database Explorer you can modify the various objects found with databases such as tables, views, and stored procedures.

Exercises

1. What does MSDE stand for?

2. What are the two main tools provided in SQL Server Express?

3. Which tool do you use in C# Express to work with databases in and out of projects?

4. What is the difference between a view and a stored procedure?

12

Utilizing .NET Data Controls

Over the last several chapters, you have been introduced to relational databases and, in particular, to the database tools included in C# Express to use with SQL Server. Besides the tools to work interactively with data, .NET provides classes and, more importantly, data controls to use data in your applications. Typical data applications entail binding different controls to fields in tables of a database, then being able to navigate and work with the data using forms. Editing and updating customer records are a good example of a typical data application.

In using data controls you will have to learn how to use more than one at the time and how to use those data controls with each other. Some of the controls that bind to data include `TextBox`, `ComboBox`, and `ListBox` controls. One of the data controls that you will use on your form is the `DataGridView` control. This powerful control enables you to view your data with practically no programming, just with dragging and dropping it on the form and setting a few properties.

In this chapter, you will read about the `DataGridView` control and other data controls that you now use on your forms. The following topics are discussed:

❑ An overview of the data controls available for use

❑ Using data sources in your application and managing them using the Data Sources panel

❑ Working with the `DataGridView` control

❑ Utilizing `TextBox` controls with the `DataGridView` control to display data

❑ Adding a `BindingNavigator` to manipulate data and save data

Getting Started Using Data in Your Applications

There are a number of ways to utilize data in your applications—some more difficult than others. The techniques and controls discussed in this chapter are some of the easiest ways. There are some people who believe that you should be using code to control everything yourself. This is a great philosophy when you have been building a library of classes to control all the data handling yourself, such as adding, deleting, and modifying records in tables of a SQL Server database. However, when you start out and are just learning, you don't necessary have the luxury to create all your own code.

It is true that a number of code libraries are out there that can take you a long way toward creating the necessary classes. But, again, to use those classes, you really need to understand how to work with data in your applications. In the next chapter, I will go into more details about how to work with ADO.NET, which is used "under the covers" by the data controls discussed in this chapter, to work with data using your code. For this chapter, I will give you a quick overview of the data controls provided by .NET, starting with data sources.

Starting with Data Sources

You may remember the discussion from Chapter 11 on the Database Explorer. Shown in Figure 12-1, the Database Explorer is where you maintain your databases from C# Express.

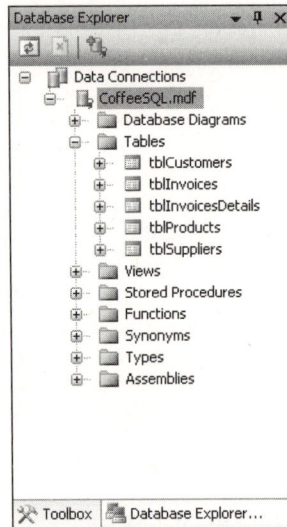

Figure 12-1

If your Database Explorer is not currently displayed, you can do so by choosing View ⇨ Database Explorer. However, while you can manipulate the databases using this tool, it doesn't connect the data to your projects themselves. To do that, you need to use data sources.

Data sources are just what the name implies, the source of data for your projects. When you create a data source, C# Express walks you through the Data Source Configuration Wizard, which first sets up a connection string, usually from databases you have added to the Data Explorer. It then sets up a data set.

Data Sets

A data set is data that you set up to be stored in memory, called *cache*. Data sets are made up of collections of tables and relationships. Although this sounds complicated, C# Express goes to a great deal of trouble to make it so you can use the data controls and not have to deal with specifics of writing each line of code to perform work with the data set. You will just pick the tables you want to include, and C# Express generates the code necessary for you. Once you have created the data source and the data set, then you are able to use them with other controls on the forms by dragging and dropping them onto the forms.

Using the Data Source Configuration Wizard

The simplest way to create a data source is to use the wizard provided. This utility asks you the following questions:

❏ Which type of data do you want to use? The choices are Database, Web Service, and Data Object. For this chapter, you will be using the first option.

❏ Which data connection would you like to use? You will be using the connection string created for the database you specified using the Database Explorer.

❏ Which objects in the database do you want to include? By choosing a SQL Server database, you will have the choices of tables, views, stored procedures, and functions.

Try It Out   **Create a Data Source**

To get going with this chapter's project, create a new Windows application project. Once this project has been created:

1. Select Data ⇨ Add New Data Source . . . . The first page of the Data Source Configuration Wizard appears, as shown in Figure 12-2.

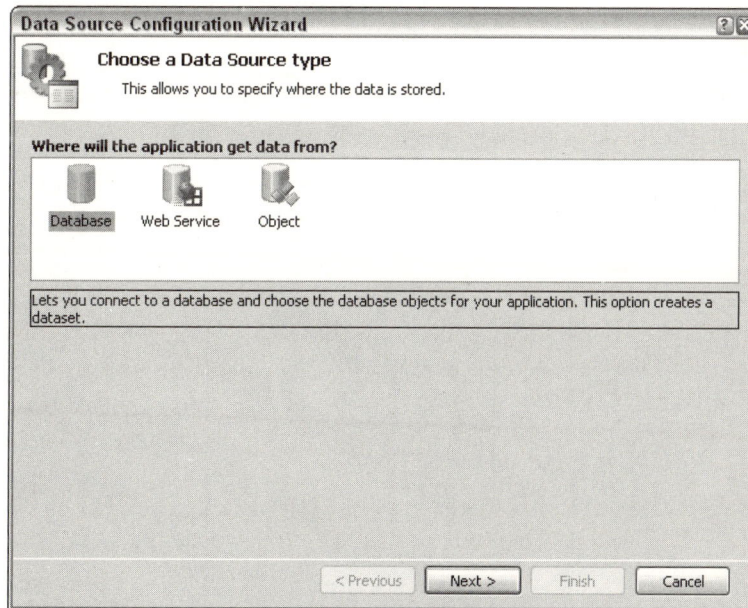

Figure 12-2

2. Click Next, leaving the default value of Database. The next two pages ask which connection string you want to use, which will be the CoffeeSQLConnectionString, created in Chapter 11, and, finally, which objects in the database to include.

3. Select the tables that you want, as shown in Figure 12-3.

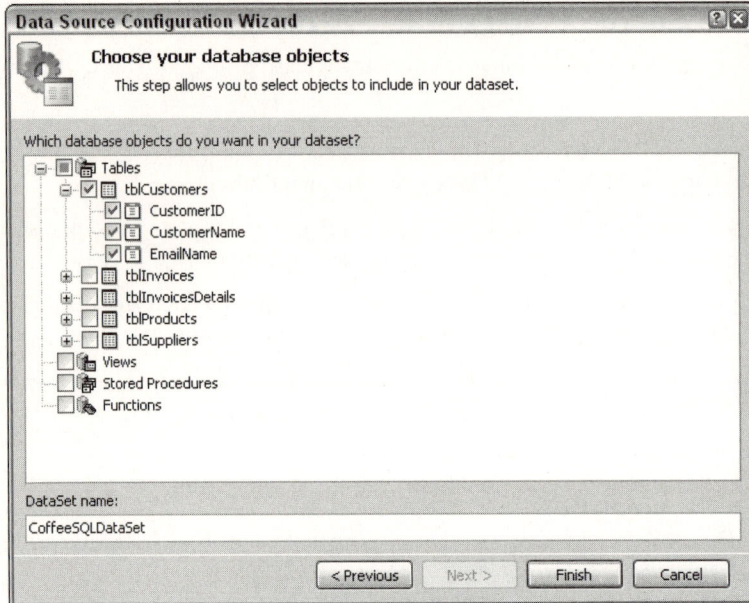

Figure 12-3

4. Click Finish. The data source is created. You will now use that data source for accessing data in your application.

You can keep track of your data sources in your project by choosing Data ➪ Show Data Sources. When you do this, the Data Sources panel appears beside the Data Explorer, as shown in Figure 12-4.

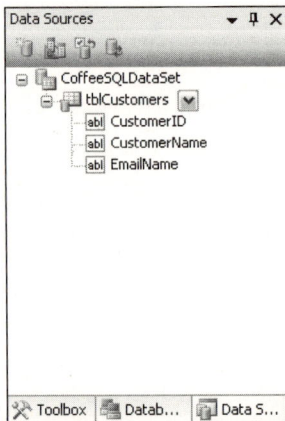

Figure 12-4

Notice that the last portion of the name of the data source created is `DataSet`. `DataSet` happens to be one of the data controls that are included for working with data in .NET.

Data Controls Overview

As mentioned, you will be using the various data controls in one way or another depending on the task you are trying to accomplish. The following table discusses those data controls and their purpose.

Control	Purpose
DataSet	Used to represent data in memory. Multiple tables can be included in a `DataSet` control.
DataGridView	Displays data in a gridlike view, so you can browse through the data.
BindingSource	Binds the `DataSet` control to other controls that can be bound to data, such as `TextBox` and `ComboBox` controls, along with the `DataGridView` control, of course.
BindingNavigator	Provides navigation for forms and data working with the `BindingSource` control.
TableAdapter	Not displayed in the toolbox, this control provides the means to perform updates back to the database. A real workhorse, SQL commands are created and loaded into various properties of this controls for performing various tasks including selecting, deleting, and modifying data.

As with the majority of the controls that you can add to your form from the toolbox, the data controls can also be added just using code. Most of these controls are actually built around ADO.NET classes, which are discussed in the next chapter.

One of the cool things about using these controls is that C# Express will generate most of the code necessary for utilizing them in your applications, which is very helpful, since multiple steps have to occur to set them up. The best way to describe the use of the data controls is to actually add them to the forms yourself. As you walk through the steps, you will also notice that C# Express adds the additional data controls needed to provide the necessary functionality for the control you added.

Using the DataGridView Control

For instance, when you want to use the `DataGridView` control, you just have to drag and drop it onto the form, and the prompt that appears will let you set up most of the necessary properties (see Figure 12-5).

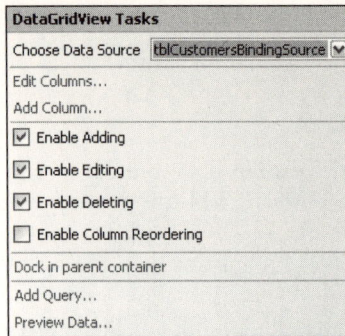

DataGridView Tasks

Choose Data Source [tblCustomersBindingSource ▼]

Edit Columns...

Add Column...

☑ Enable Adding

☑ Enable Editing

☑ Enable Deleting

☐ Enable Column Reordering

Dock in parent container

Add Query...

Preview Data...

Figure 12-5

If all you want to do is display data using the `DataGridView` control, all you have to do is literally drag and drop it onto the form and select some of the items in Figure 12-5. Give it a shot.

Try It Out   Add a DataGridView Control

As has been done in most of chapters before this, you will want to create a main form to use as a switchboard for your sample forms. Once you have done that, you can then create the form that will be used to display a `DataGridView` control.

1. Right-click the project, and select Add New Item from the menu.

2. Select Windows Form for the template to use, and name it as desired. For the purpose of this example, the name frmUseDataGridView was used.

3. Drag and drop a `DataGridView` control onto the form from the Data Controls section of the toolbox. The menu in Figure 12-5 appears, without the Choose Data Source field filled in.

    If you accidentally lost this window by clicking off it, aim for the black and white arrow in the top right of the control. The window will appear again.

4. Click the drop-down menu for the Choose Data Source field. A tree view appears with the top node displaying Other Data Sources.

5. Keep expanding the data sources until you get to tblCustomers, as shown in Figure 12-6.

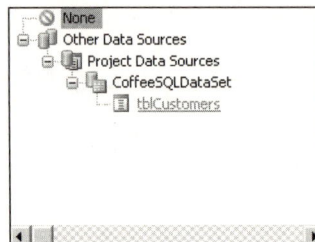

⊘ None
⊟ Other Data Sources
  ⊟ Project Data Sources
    ⊟ CoffeeSQLDataSet
      tblCustomers

Figure 12-6

6. Click on tblCustomers. Back in the `DataGridView` tasks, the Choose Data Source field will then be filled with tblCustomersBindingSource.

7. Click the Dock in Parent Container link. You see the `DataGridView` control fill the form.

8. Click off the task pane onto the form anywhere. The Task pane disappears, and the form is then displayed, with the fields in the tblCustomers table, as well as the new `DataSet`, `DataBinding`, and `TableAdapter` controls shown in Figure 12-7.

9. Click F5 to test the application. Choose the new form to be displayed, and the data is displayed in the `DataGridView` control, shown in Figure 12-8.

If you were to look at the properties of the component used, you would see that they refer to each other. The `BindingSource`'s `DataSource` property is set to the `CoffeeSQLDataSet`, and the `DataMember` property is set to `tblCustomers`. The `DataGridView`'s `DataSource` property is set to the `tblCustomerBindingSource`. So you can see how they are all interjoined by setting properties to each other. Again, it is great that C# Express does all lot of the work for you.

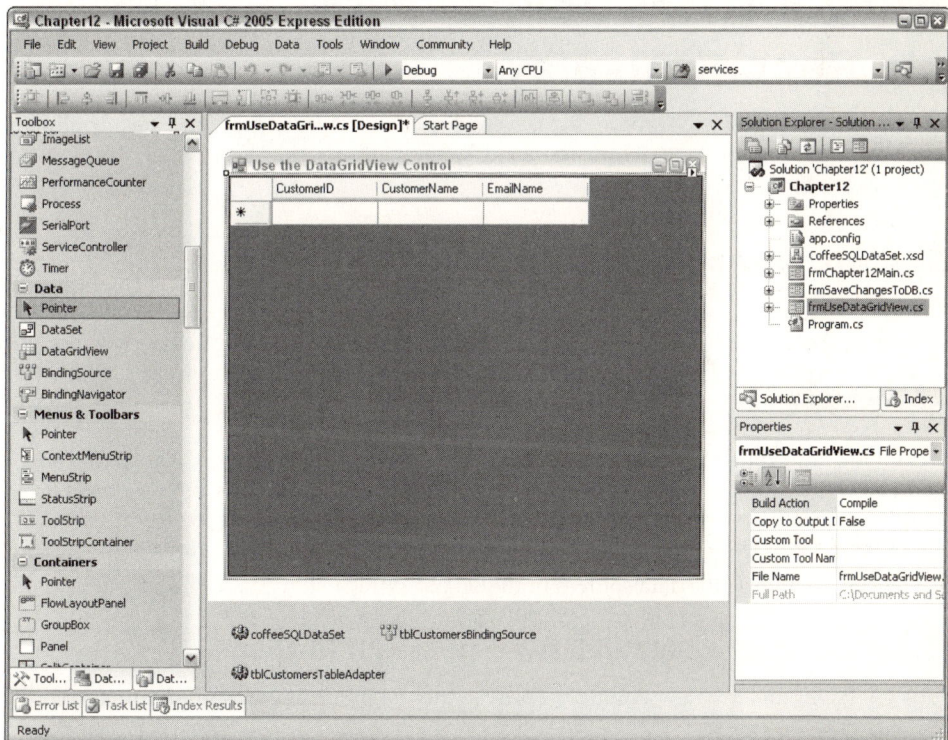

Figure 12-7

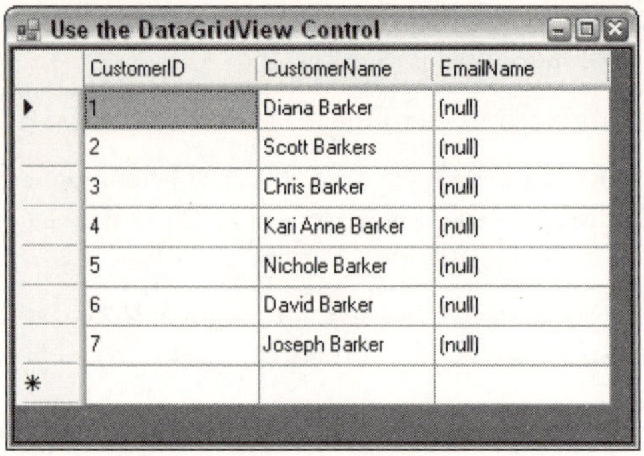

Figure 12-8

Creating a DataGridView with Single Record Display

There will be times when you want to display just a single form view showing one record on the form at a time. Accomplishing this takes a little more work, but it also shows off another one of the data controls, the `BindingNavigator` control.

BindingNavigator Control

The `BindingNavigator` control is an interface to the `BindingSource` control and enables you to display buttons on your forms for adding and deleting records, as well as for moving around the records that you are working with. Once again, it is very straightforward to bind controls to data once you learn the steps to take.

The first thing I do when I am going to create a form using `TextBox` controls that will be bound to data is to add all of the controls on the form first, except the data controls. Then, once the `TextBox` controls and any other that are needed are positioned where you want them on the form, you can start the process of binding them. In fact, you can add a `DataGridView` control onto the form with the text boxes with no programming, just by dragging and dropping and then modifying some properties.

Try It Out   **Display a DataGridView control with TextBoxes**

For this Try It Out, create a new Windows Form, in the example frmDisplayIndividualRecords, and then:

1.   Add three `Label` controls, with three `TextBox` controls, laid out side by side on the form.

2.   Type **Customer ID**, **Customer Name**, and **Email** for the `Label` controls' `Text` property.

3.   Type **txtCustomerID**, **txtCustomerName**, and **txtEmail** for the `Name` property for each `TextBox` control, beside the appropriate label.

4. Position the controls toward the bottom of the form, leaving room at the top for the `DataGridView`.

5. Click the Data Sources pane.

6. Drag and drop the tblCustomers node from the Data Sources pane over onto the top of the form (see Figure 12-9).

That's right. A heck of lot happened right there. Not only did the data source cause the `DataGridView` to be added to the form, but the needed data controls as well, including the `BindingNavigator` control discussed earlier. You can see the buttons that were added because of the control at the top of the form.

7. Click the first `TextBox` control, beside the label Customer ID.

8. Click the + symbol next to the (DataBindings) property category. The category then expands to display (Advanced), Tag, and Text properties.

9. Click the drop-down arrow next to the `Text` property. The same data source dialog box displayed when you were creating the data grid control appears. However, instead of choosing Other Data Sources as you did last time, choose CustomerID from tblCustomersBindingSource, as shown in Figure 12-10.

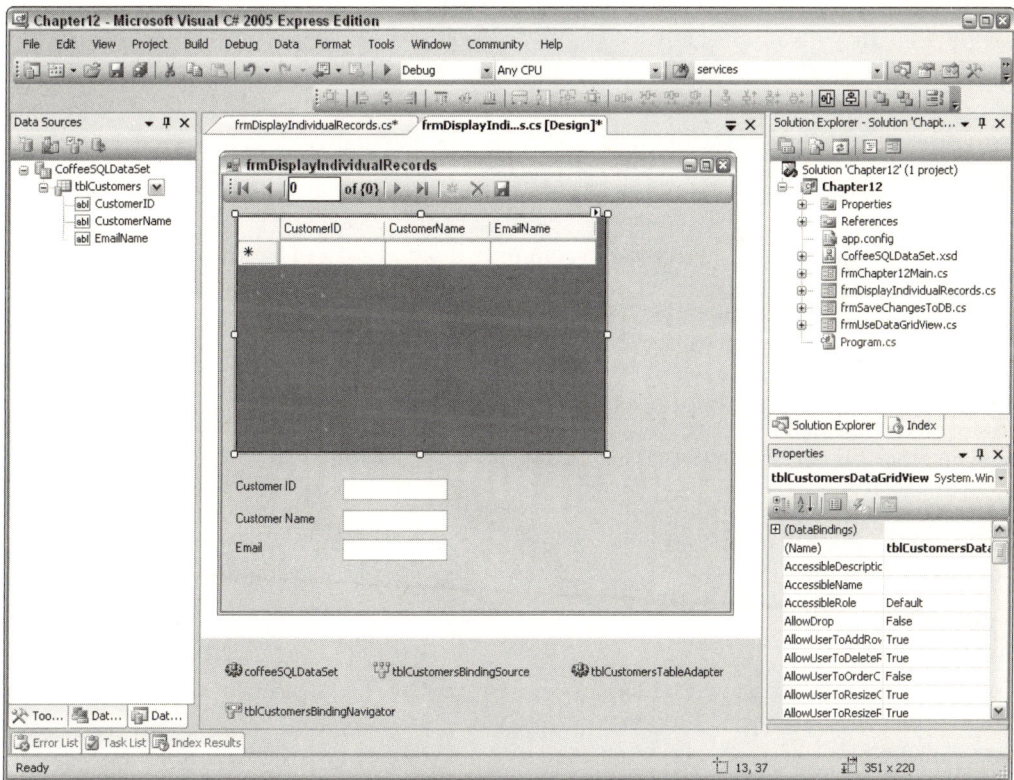

Figure 12-9

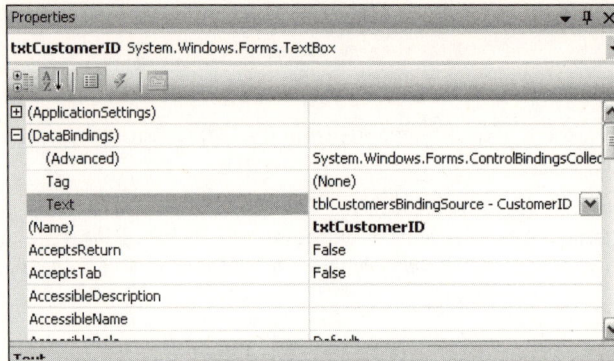

Figure 12-10

When you click CustomerID, the pane closes, and you see the `Text` property filled in as shown in Figure 12-11.

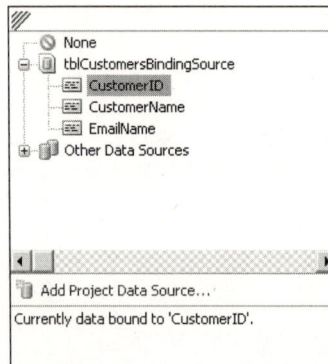

Figure 12-11

10. Repeat Steps 7 through 9 for the `txtCustomerName` and `txtEmail TextBox` controls.

11. Press F11 to build and run the application. Choose the form that you created to display this example.

You can move through the records in the `DataGridView` and see them reflected in the fields below. So you now have your data synchronized among multiple controls. In addition, you also can move around using the buttons provided by the `BindingNavigator` control at the top of the form, displayed in Figure 12-12.

One of the items included in the buttons up on top is the Save button. With this button, you can make your changes and save them back into your database.

There you have it. You have created a form that is bound to data and not only has a browse view but also binds those records to individual fields for data manipulation.

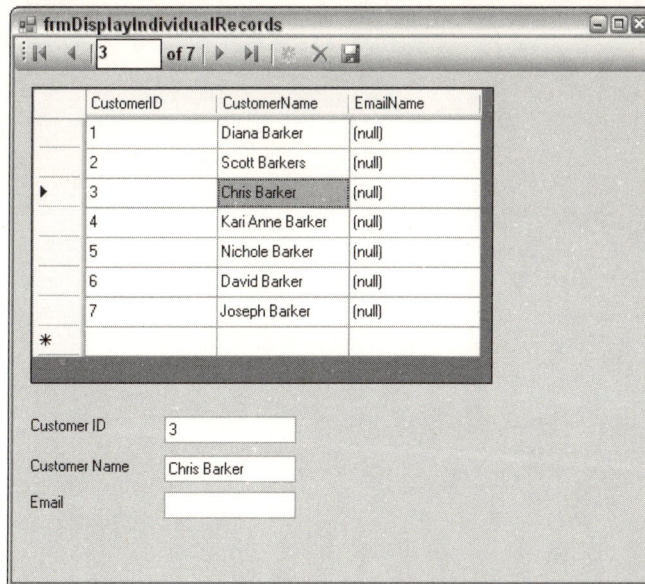

Figure 12-12

Summary

As you are creating applications you will need to work with data from a database. In the past, when using languages such as C#, doing so used to be a lot of work. Now, with C# Express, the necessary controls and code are created for you as you drag and drop the controls onto your form. With these controls you can accomplish just about any task you need, including modifying, adding, and deleting records.

You can add data sources into your project and use them for various forms and controls. These data sources can be viewed using the Data Sources pane. In this chapter you saw how to utilize a DataGridView control on your form, and how to synchronize it with TextBox controls using a BindingNavigator control. When a BindingNavigator control is added to a form, a ToolStrip control is added with buttons for various data actions you need to perform. All of this is performed without one line of code being written by the developer.

Exercises

1. Which objects do you need to add to your project in order to utilize data in your form?

2. Which control (and underlying class) keeps track of data in memory?

3. What control is used to bind data to controls such as the TextBox control and provide navigation?

4. What is the difference between the BindingNavigator and BindingSource controls?

13

Working with ADO.NET

As you drag and drop data controls onto your form, C# Express generates the necessary code to utilize the controls. When you are starting out, this works great for the majority of the tasks you need to accomplish. However, as you become more comfortable with the language and your needs expand, there will come a time when you will want to be able to write your own code to work with data on your own. To accomplish this, you can use ADO.NET. The code created for the data controls when you drop them onto the forms, in fact, uses ADO.NET under the covers to accomplish necessary tasks. ADO.NET (ActiveX Data Objects .NET) are a set of classes provided by .NET for working with data in your applications. The great thing about these classes is that you can use them as you need to or just continue using the data controls. Some of the classes and the object created by them were introduced in the last chapter, including data sets.

In this chapter, you are introduced to some of the classes that make up ADO.NET and how to use them. The following topics are discussed:

- ❑ The history of data access
- ❑ What is ADO.NET?
- ❑ Working with the `DataSet` class
- ❑ Using `SqlConnection` and `SqlCommand` classes
- ❑ Binding ADO.NET objects to Windows controls

Introducing ADO.NET

Over the years there have been a number of ways that Microsoft has been providing tools for developers to access data from their applications. During the last 10 years, there have been quite a few tools provided, such as DAO (Data Access Objects), RDO (Remote Data Objects), and ADO (ActiveX Data Objects). That's right, before ADO.NET there was ADO.

Some Data Access History

DAO was originally created to access the Jet database engine. Jet is the database engine used with Microsoft Access. DAO provided various classes such as the `Recordset` class, which enabled developers to load data into memory from their databases and to work with it as needed. While DAO was great and is still in use today, it was primarily built for use with Jet. When you wanted to use it with other providers such as SQL Server, you had to use another layer of technology called ODBC (Open Database Connectivity) drivers and had additional hoops to jump through to utilize these other databases.

To handle the various databases, Microsoft came out with another data access method called ADO. ADO is a more generic data access method, blending with a layer called OLEDB. OLEDB enables various providers to create their own interface that can then be utilized by the ADO classes. This meant when you created an application using ADO and OLEDB, if you had to switch back ends, provided you wrote your code correctly, all you had to do was change the OLEDB connection. As with DAO, a `Recordset` class was created to help you manage record sets as you loaded them from tables in a database into memory to work with.

At the same time ADO came around, Internet developers wanted to access their data. While ADO worked up to a point, and is used still used quite a bit, developers still needed more functionality in some cases. So RDO (Remote Data Objects) came on the scene, which provided the functionality of accessing remote data.

Welcome ADO.NET

.NET was a huge platform change not only for languages and desktop/Web development but for data access. ADO.NET was introduced to basically combine the best of both ADO and RDO but also to provide a more complete set of classes for working with data. ADO.NET consists of multiple classes providing data controls and data provider classes.

One major change from ADO to ADO.NET is that the main object used for manipulating data is the `DataSet` class, introduced in Chapter 12, rather than the `Recordset`, which merely returns just what the name implies, a single record set. With the `DataSet` you can actually store multiple tables and their relationships in a hierarchical manner. Another big difference is that ADO.NET uses disconnected data. This means that when you are working on the Internet, you can connect to your database and bring data over to work on, disconnecting when you do so. After working with the data, you connect again and update the data. With ADO it all had to be with one opened connection.

When working with ADO.NET, you will use the ADO.NET namespaces provided by the .NET Framework Class Library. Within the ADO.NET namespaces, you will then specify which data provider you need to use. The following section discusses those namespaces.

Some ADO.NET Data Classes and Data Providers

When using ADO.NET classes, the following statement needs to be added to your form when you use the `DataSet` class:

```
using System.Data;
```

For the data provider, it will depend on which one you are using. If you are going to be utilizing data for SQL Server, the using statement will be

```
using System.Data.SqlClient;
```

If you aren't sure which type you are using, or need to use multiple types of data such as from SQL Server and Microsoft Access at same time, you will use:

```
using System.Data.OleDb;
```

The following table outlines some of the classes that are valuable to developers for accessing data.

Control Name	Purpose
DataSet	This control is used in conjunction with the other data controls, storing the results that are returned by commands and the DataAdapter controls. The DataSet control actually brings back a hierarchical view of the data. Using properties and collections in the DataSet object, you can get all the way down to individual tables, rows, and columns.
DataTable	Similar to the Recordset class used in ADO, this control allows you to work with a single record set of data, rather than a whole data set. You can also create DataTable objects from DataSet objects.
DataView	This control lets you create multiple views of the same table. This includes looking at data in various states such as deleted, changed, or sorted.
SqlDataAdapter	This control stores and manages what commands you want to use against a SQL Server database. The commands for selecting, updating, inserting, and deleting records can be used. The connection in which to use the commands against is also tracked.
SqlConnection	Connection information for the SQL Server provider is maintained with this control. Used with the SqlDataAdapter and SqlCommand classes.
SqlCommand	This control enables developers to execute SQL statements or stored procedures to either run bulk operations return data.

The DataSet, DataTable, and DataViews are all available from ADO.NET, whereas the rest of the objects are available via the SqlClient data provider. All of these classes can be used directly in the code of your application.

Using ADO.NET Classes in Your Application

To learn how to use the various objects, you will first add a ListBox control onto a form and then populate the control using ADO.NET classes. The first task will be to create a connection string you can use with the other data provider classes. The string shown in the following code points to the SQL Server Express database first introduced in Chapter 11.

```
string strConn;

strConn = "Data Source=\".\\SQLEXPRESS\";AttachDbFilename=\"C:\\Documents ";
strConn += "and Settings\\Administrator\\My Documents\\Visual Studio ";
strConn += "2005\\Projects\\CoffeeSQL.mdf\";Integrated Security=True;User ";
strConn += "Instance=True";
```

Remember that the extra backslashes cause the characters that follow to be included in the string.

Populating a ListBox Control

Next, after creating two types of the data controls just mentioned, `SqlDataAdapter` and `DataTable`, you will bind them to a list box to display a list of customers.

```
SqlDataAdapter sdaCusts =
        new SqlDataAdapter("Select tblCustomers.CompanyName From tblCustomers",
strConn);

DataTable dtCusts = new DataTable();

sdaCusts.Fill(dtCusts);
```

The first step is to instantiate a `SqlDataAdapter` object, in this case passing the SQL string and the connection string (`strConn`). Next, a `DataTable` object is created. Lastly, the `Fill` method of the `SqlDataAdapter` is used to fill the `DataTable` object with data.

Once this has occurred, the `DataTable` will be used as a `DataSource` for the `ListBox` control. Also, the `DisplayMember` and `ValueMember` are specified.

```
            listBox1.DisplayMember = "CustomerName";
            listBox1.ValueMember = "CustomerID";
            listBox1.DataSource = dtCusts;
```

And that's it code-wise. Now you need to get busy and try this yourself.

Try It Out   Populate a ListBox using ADO.NET

Before performing the steps of creating the form for this Try It Out, you need to create a switchboard to call your forms. After this form is created, you then create another form:

1. Right-click the project and choose Add ⇨ New Item . . ., and name it as desired.
2. Drag and drop a `Label` control onto the form.
3. Type **Customers** for the `Text` property.
4. Drag and drop a `ListBox` control onto the form. The form now looks like Figure 13-1.

Figure 13-1

5. Double-click the main form. This opens the editor with the definition of the `Form_Load` routine created, shown here.

```
private void Form1_Load(object sender, EventArgs e)
{

}
```

6. Under the following line of code:

```
public partial class frmCreatingDataTables : Form
{
```

type the following:

```
private string strConn;
```

7. Under the lines of code that read as follows:

```
private void Form1_Load(object sender, EventArgs e)
{
```

type the following code that was discussed in the section before this Try It Out.

```
strConn = "Data Source=\".\\SQLEXPRESS\";AttachDbFilename=\"C:\\Documents ";
strConn += "and Settings\\Administrator\\My Documents\\Visual Studio ";
strConn += "2005\\Projects\\CoffeeSQL.mdf\";Integrated Security=True;User ";
strConn += "Instance=True";

SqlDataAdapter sdaCusts = new SqlDataAdapter("Select * From tblCustomers",
strConn);
DataTable dtCusts = new DataTable();

sdaCusts.Fill(dtCusts);

listBox1.DisplayMember = "CustomerName";
listBox1.ValueMember = "CustomerID";
listBox1.DataSource = dtCusts;
```

8. Press F5 to build and test the application. Open the desired form. The list box is now displayed with the customers listed, as shown in Figure 13-2.

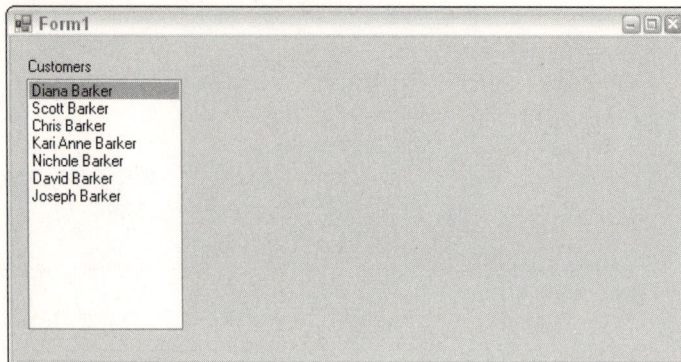

Figure 13-2

The next step is to add a `DataGridView` control to the form and display the data in the `DataGridView` based on the choice made in the `ListBox` control.

Adding a DataGridView Control

Now that you have the customers listed in the `ListView` control, it is time to display the invoices for the selected customer. To do this, you create `SqlConnection` and `SqlCommand` objects to retrieve the data. Using the `SqlCommand` class, the `CommandText` property is set to the SQL string, in this case utilizing the `SelectedValue` of the `ListBox` control. Next, the `Connection` property of the `SqlCommand` object is set to the connection object. Then the connection is opened. You can see the code for all this here:

```
SqlConnection scnn = new SqlConnection(strConn);
SqlCommand scmdInvoice = new SqlCommand();

scmdInvoice.CommandText = "Select * From tblInvoices ";
scmdInvoice.CommandText += " Where CustomerID = " +
                                    listBox1.SelectedValue.ToString();
scmdInvoice.Connection = scnn;
scnn.Open();
```

After these lines of code are executed, the rest is just about the same as the code in the last section, where the `SqlCommand` object is passed to the `SqlDataAdapter` object for the SQL statement. After a new `DataTable` is created, the using the `SqlDataAdapter` `Fill` method, the data is retrieved. Lastly, the `dtInvoices` is set as the `DataSource` of the `DataGridView`.

```
SqlDataAdapter sdaInvoices = new SqlDataAdapter(scmdInvoice);
DataTable dtInvoices = new DataTable();

sdaInvoices.Fill(dtInvoices);

dataGridView1.DataSource = dtInvoices;
```

You can see the result of running the code in Figure 13-3. Now it's time for you to get busy.

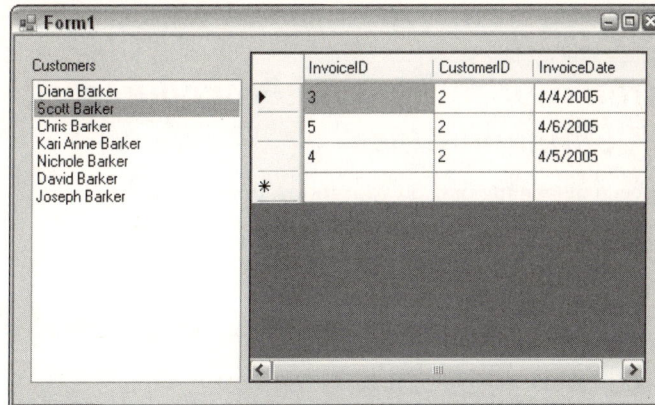

Figure 13-3

Try It Out   Using ADO.NET Classes to Populate a DataGridView Control

Using the form you created in the last Try It Out:

1. Drag and drop a `DataGridView` control onto the form.

2. Click the `DataGridView` control to close the task pane.

3. Double-click the `ListBox` control. This opens the code file for editing and creates a definition for the `ListBox` control's `SelectedIndexChanged`.

```
private void listBox1_SelectedIndexChanged(object sender, EventArgs e)
{

}
```

4. Type the following lines of code between the opening and closing curly brackets:

```
SqlConnection scnn = new SqlConnection(strConn);
SqlCommand scmdInvoice = new SqlCommand();

scmdInvoice.CommandText = "Select * From tblInvoices ";
scmdInvoice.CommandText += " Where CustomerID = " +
                                    listBox1.SelectedValue.ToString();
scmdInvoice.Connection = scnn;
scnn.Open();

SqlDataAdapter sdaInvoices = new SqlDataAdapter(scmdInvoice);
DataTable dtInvoices = new DataTable();

sdaInvoices.Fill(dtInvoices);

dataGridView1.DataSource = dtInvoices;
```

5. Press F5 to build and run the application.

As you select the various names, you will see the orders change.

Executing Parameterized Stored Procedures using the SqlCommand Class

Thus far, you have been displaying data on your forms. But when you need to update data in a table back in the database, you will want to use a stored procedure in a `SqlCommand` object with parameters.

The Stored Procedure

To start, take a look at the stored procedure, found in the `CoffeeSQL.mdf` database:

```
ALTER PROCEDURE dbo.StoredProcedure1
  (@intCustID int,
  @strEmail varchar(50))
AS
  Update tblCustomers Set EmailName = @strEmail from tblCustomers
          Where CustomerID = @intCustID
  RETURN
```

The purpose of this stored procedure is to update a person's e-mail in his or her record. This stored procedure takes the two parameters, `@intCustID` and `@strEmail`, and uses them to specify the `CustomerID` to look for and the new `EmailName` to supply. This stored procedure can be found in the stored procedures of the `CoffeeSQL` database.

The Form

For this form, you use the `ComboBox` control to choose a customer who needs his or her e-mail name updated and then a `TextBox` control. The code for executing the stored procedure will be created for a button on the form. You can see the form in Figure 13-4.

Figure 13-4

The Code

The first code that needs to be written is much the same as was used for loading the `ListBox` control in the last section. The only thing that changes is that instead of using `listBox1` you use `comboBox1`. Even the properties remain the same.

The code for actually executing the stored procedure will be different than what you have seen before. The first code looks familiar in that it instantiates both `SqlConnection` and `SqlCommand` objects.

```
SqlConnection scnn = new SqlConnection(strConn);
SqlCommand scmdUpdate = new SqlCommand();
```

After these lines of code, the `CommandText` property is set to the name of the stored procedure, and the `CommandType` to `CommandType.StoredProcedure`.

```
scmdUpdate.CommandText = "StoredProcedure1";
scmdUpdate.CommandType = CommandType.StoredProcedure;
```

Next, parameters are added to the `SqlCommand` object, one for `@intCustID` and the other for `@strEmail`, using the `AddWithValue` method of the `Parameters` collection. The `Connection` property of the `SqlCommand` object is then set to `scnn`.

```
scmdUpdate.Parameters.AddWithValue("@intCustID",
                                    comboBox1.SelectedValue);
scmdUpdate.Parameters.AddWithValue("@strEmail", txtEmail.Text);
scmdUpdate.Connection = scnn;
```

The `SQLConnection` is then opened. The `ExecuteNonQuery` of the `SqlCommand` object executes the stored procedure. Lastly, the `SqlConnection` object is closed.

```
scnn.Open();
scmdUpdate.ExecuteNonQuery();
scnn.Close();
```

That is all there is to it.

Try It Out   Executing a Stored Procedure with Parameters

Using the project you have been working with throughout the chapter:

1. Add a new Windows form.

2. Add two `Label` controls, a `ComboBox` control, a `Textbox` control, and a `Button` control, as shown in Figure 13-4.

3. Double-click anywhere on the form itself. This creates the Form Load routine definition, as shown here:

```
private void Form1_Load(object sender, EventArgs e)
{

}
```

4. Type the following code between the opening and closing curly brackets:

```
SqlDataAdapter sdaCusts = new
SqlDataAdapter("Select * From tblCustomers", strConn);
DataTable dtCusts = new DataTable();

sdaCusts.Fill(dtCusts);
```

```
comboBox1.DisplayMember = "CustomerName";
comboBox1.ValueMember = "CustomerID";
comboBox1.DataSource = dtCusts;
```

5. Double-click the `Button` control you added. The definition for the `Click` routine is created:

```
private void btnRunCommand_Click(object sender, EventArgs e)
{

}
```

6. Type the following code:

```
SqlConnection scnn = new SqlConnection(strConn);
SqlCommand scmdUpdate = new SqlCommand();

scmdUpdate.CommandText = "StoredProcedure1";
scmdUpdate.CommandType = CommandType.StoredProcedure;

scmdUpdate.Parameters.AddWithValue("@intCustID",
                                    comboBox1.SelectedValue);
scmdUpdate.Parameters.AddWithValue("@strEmail", txtEmail.Text);

scmdUpdate.Connection = scnn;

scnn.Open();
scmdUpdate.ExecuteNonQuery();
scnn.Close();
```

7. Press F5 to build and execute the application.

8. Pick a customer and type an e-mail to update.

9. Click the `Button` control to execute the stored procedure.

Now when you go and look at the data, you will see that the e-mail name is updated for the client you specified, as shown in Figure 13-5.

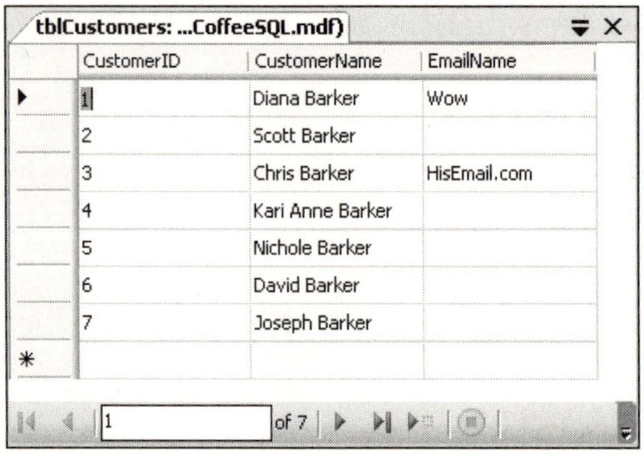

CustomerID	CustomerName	EmailName
1	Diana Barker	Wow
2	Scott Barker	
3	Chris Barker	HisEmail.com
4	Kari Anne Barker	
5	Nichole Barker	
6	David Barker	
7	Joseph Barker	
*		

tblCustomers: ...CoffeeSQL.mdf)

Figure 13-5

You can see this pane in the Database Explorer by right-clicking on the table and choosing Show Table Data.

Summary

C# Express goes to great trouble to create the necessary data controls and to write the code to have your application work with those controls. But there are some cases when you will want to write your code and manage the data yourself. To do so, you need to use ADO.NET and data provider classes. Which object you will use depends on what you are trying to do.

The `DataSet` class with the `SqlDataAdapter` class can be used to retrieve hierarchal data. With command objects you can update data in the database by using parameterized stored procedures. The connection object is used with most of the other classes to create a connection that can be opened and closed as necessary.

Exercises

1. Name the three prior types of access methods provided by Microsoft in the past.

2. In ADO.NET the main object for working with data is the `DataSet`. What was the main object in the prior version?

3. ADO used connected data methodology. What does ADO.NET use?

4. `DataAdapters` are used to load data into `DataTables` and `DataSets`. What are `Command` objects used for?

Part IV
Finishing Touches

14

Getting More Experience with Controls

In a lot of books when you find out about a couple of the more common controls, it is assumed that you will just figure out the rest of the controls by yourself. This is probably very true because you are extremely intelligent. But there are so many very useful controls included in C# Express for use in your C# applications that I wanted to cover as many as possible for you. In Chapter 9, I covered the RichTextBox control and a number of the dialog controls. A total of five controls were covered. This chapter even beats that!

In this chapter there are three tasks that are accomplished: create a file browser using a SplitContainer control, a WebBrowser control, and more. The last two tasks deal with various ways of working with date controls, status bars, and progress bars. This chapter includes about 10 different very useful controls. In it, you will:

❑ Take concepts and command statements you have learned in prior chapters and put them to practical use.

❑ Use a TabControl to include multiple pages (tasks) on one form.

❑ Utilize various controls such as the SplitContainer, ListBox, FolderBrowserDialog, and WebBrowser control to create a file browser utility to display files in a Web browser.

❑ Create a demo to display working graphically with dates using the MonthlyCalendar and DateDrop controls.

❑ Demostrate using ProgressBar controls on a form and in a StatusStrip control at the bottom of a form.

Walking through the Demo Application

As mentioned in the introduction, this chapter is packed with controls—all displayed using a single form. There are three demos, each broken out into its own page using a `Tab` control.

Demo 1: Browsing Web Files

The first page is a utility that enables the user to point to a folder using a `FolderBrowserDialog` control. The folder chosen is then displayed in a `ListBox` control. When the user selects a particular file in the `ListBox` control, that file is displayed using a `WebBrowser` control. An example is shown in Figure 14-1.

Figure 14-1

Another great thing about this demo is that the `ListBox` and `WebBrowser` controls are contained within a `SplitContainer` control. The `SplitContainer` control enables users to control the width of the display of items contained within it—in this case, the list of files and the current file being displayed. There are a number of different types of files you can display using this demo, including text, html, and graphic files, but additional work may be required to display files such as Excel worksheets. File types are determined by current browser plug-ins; images, sounds files, and so on may be accessible via QuickTime, for example.

Demo 2: Choosing and Displaying Dates

The second demo displays a couple of controls that are specifically designed for choosing and displaying dates in your applications. Those controls are the `MonthCalendar` and `DateTimePicker` controls. These controls have been around awhile in the programming world as ActiveX controls before .NET. You can see the demo with a date chosen in the `MonthCalendar` control in Figure 14-2.

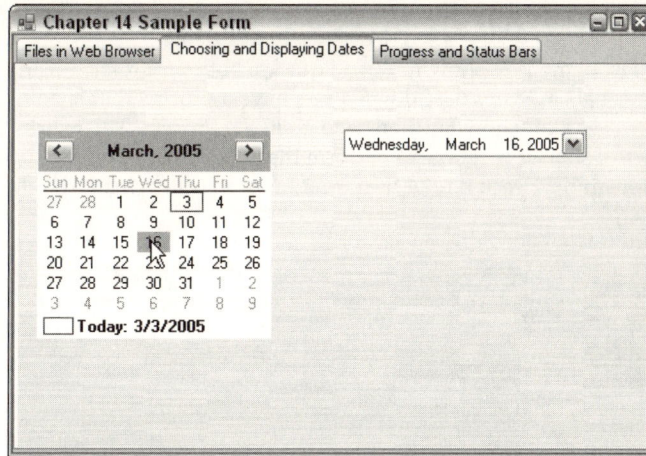

Figure 14-2

The `DateTimePicker` control reflects the date chosen in the `MonthCalendar` control. You also can choose a date in the `DateTimePicker` control, as shown in Figure 14-3.

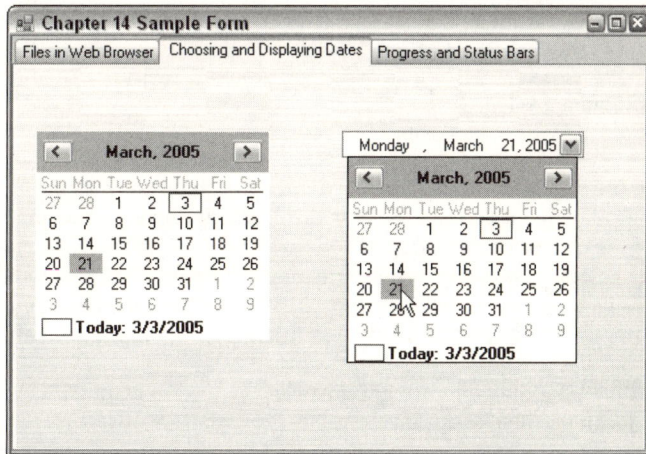

Figure 14-3

When you click a `DateTimePicker` control, another calendar that looks coincidentally like the `MonthCalendar` control drops down. You can pick from the calendar displayed.

There have been times in the real world when I have used both the `MonthCalendar` and `DateTimePicker` controls for different purposes and fields on the same page.

Demo 3: Working with Progress and Status Bars

The purpose of the last demo is to show how you can use both progress bars and status bars in your applications. Progress bars are very useful when you have a process that is going to take a while and you want to let your user know how far there is to go in the process. This works very well when you can calculate the number of steps it will take to perform the action the system is working on. For example, in the case of the demonstration, each day of the current month is iterated through. You can see this in action in Figure 14-4.

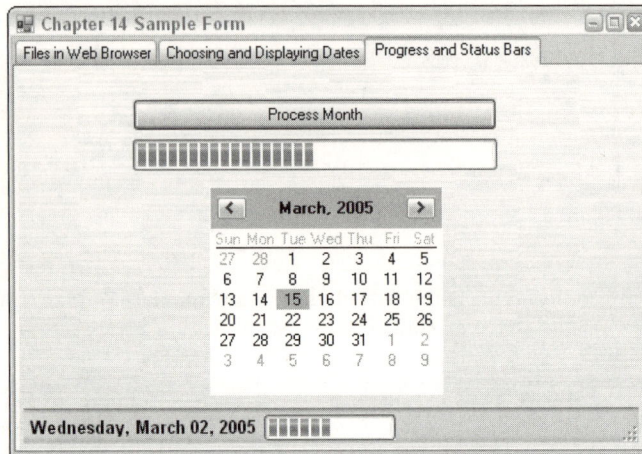

Figure 14-4

In fact, in this demo the MonthCalendar control displays each day as the routine whips though them. A progress bar also is updated in a StatusStrip control, which displays information you want in a status bar at the bottom of the container control specified, in this case a tab page. You also can have it display at the bottom of a form instead if desired. You can display information such as today's date, as seen in Figure 14-4, progress bars, and other information. Creating status bars and what you can display will be discussed further later in this chapter in the section titled "Using ProgressBar and StatusStrip Controls."

It is time to get busy creating the demo. To get started, you need to learn a bit more about the TabStrip control and how you can use it your applications.

Getting Started with the Tab Control

The Tab control is one of those controls that contain other controls. In this case, besides the controls you place on each of the pages of the Tab control, the Tab control is made up of TabPage controls, unlike prior versions of the Tab control such as the ActiveX control called the TabStrip control. This prior version consisted of a strip of tabs, in which you had to change the information displayed yourself by toggling the visibility of boxes and such.

A feature of the Tab control in C# Express is that you can click the tab you want to add controls to and then just place the controls on that tab page. If the Tab control you are adding to a form is going to take up the whole page, then you can set the Dock property to fill the Tab control, and its pages will fill the form. You have seen the way the Tab control looks at runtime in all the figures shown in this chapter thus far.

Try It Out   **Create the Main Form and Add a Tab Control**

In this Try It Out, you see the control in design view as you create the form you will use throughout the rest of the chapter, and place a `Tab` control on it, setting it up for the first demonstration.

1. Open C# Express.

2. Click New Project in the Start Page.

3. Select Windows Application for the template to use, and type in the name of the project you want to call it. For the purpose of this example, it is called `Chapter14`. Pretty original, huh?

4. Rename the main form to what you want it to be. For the purpose of this example it is called `frmChapter14Main.cs`.

5. Resize the main form to be a little larger using the resize handles.

6. Drag and drop a `Tab` control onto the form, clicking where you want the top leftmost corner of the `Tab` control to be.

7. Click where you want to have the bottom right corner of the `Tab` control to be.

    Note that it really doesn't matter where you place the `Tab` control, since you will be setting the `Dock` property of the `Tab` control to be `Fill`, which will cause the control to fill the entire form.

8. Set the `Dock` property of the `Tab` control to `Fill`, as shown in Figure 14-5.

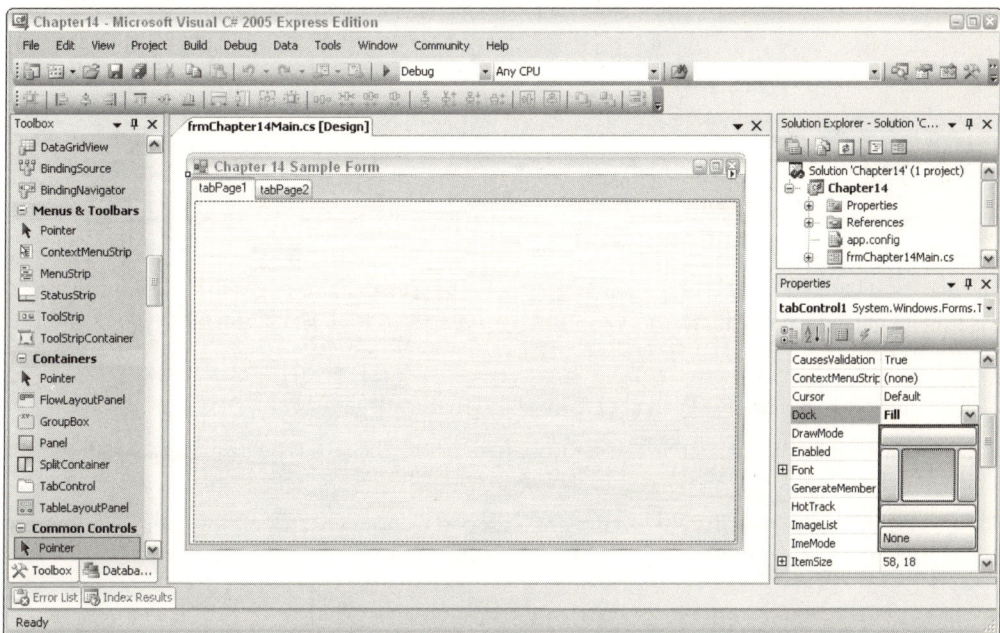

Figure 14-5

If the Properties window doesn't display the `tabControl` as the object to work on, click the blank space beside the tabs on the `Tab` control. This causes the `Tab` control to be selected. To select the individual tab pages, click the tab, then the page of the selected tab. You will work on that next. Remember that the `TabPage` controls are contained within the `Tab` control but have their own properties.

When the `Tab` control is highlighted, you can select various tasks to perform with the `Tab` control such as adding and removing tabs using the right-click menu. Another way to change properties of the `TabPage` controls, contained in the `Tab Pages` collection, is to click the builder button (...) next to the `TabPages` property. When you do this, the Tab Pages Collection Editor is opened, as shown in Figure 14-6, with the second tab page highlighted.

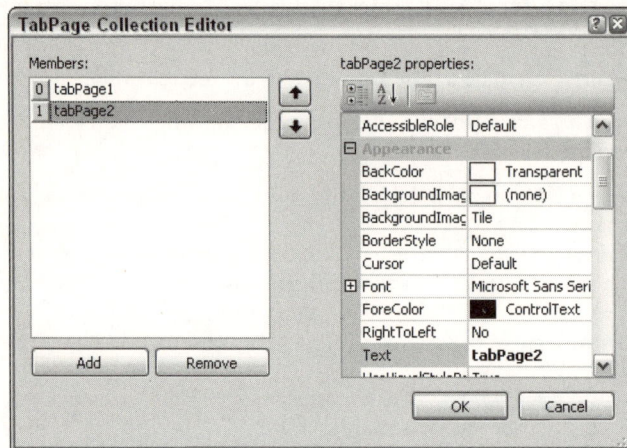

Figure 14-6

Using the arrows beside the list of tab pages, you can rearrange the pages if desired.

Try It Out   **Modify and Add Tab Pages**

For this Try It Out, you will set the `Text` property for the current two pages that exist for the `Tab` control and add a new tab page, setting the `Text` property for that as well. Using the form you created in the last Try It Out:

1. Click the tab with the label (`Text` property) that reads tabPage1.

2. Click the blank area of the `Tab` control down below the tabs. The Properties window reads tabPage1.

3. Type **Files in Web Browser** in the `Text` property, and then click off the property. You now see the text in the tab change as shown in Figure 14-7.

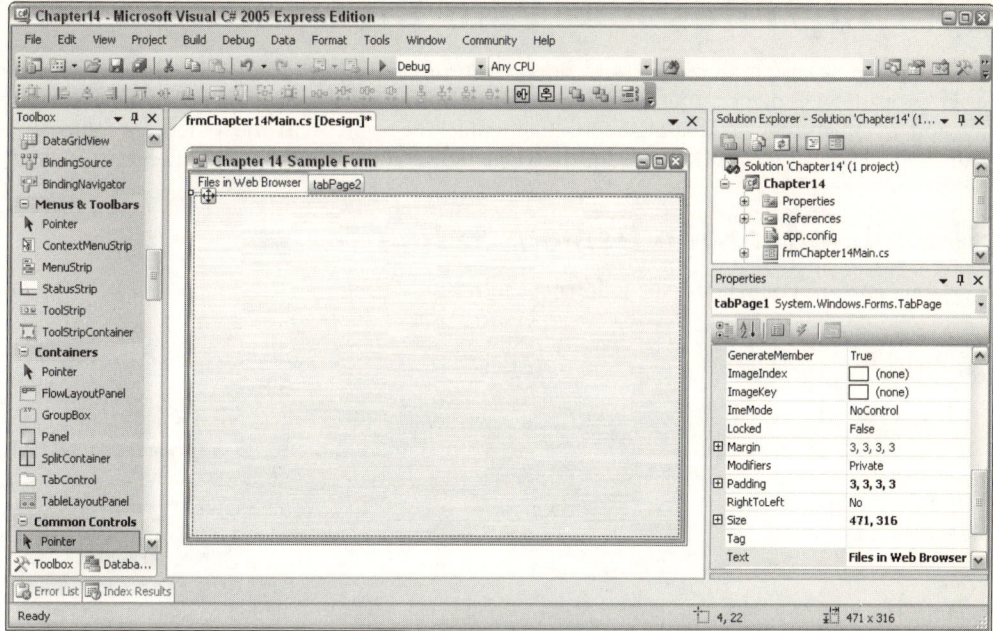

Figure 14-7

Remember that you have just changed the Text *property of the* TabPage *control, not the name itself. Although not used in this chapter, you need to remember this if you are working with the* TabPage *controls using code.*

4. Click the tab labeled tabPage2; then click the page itself below the tab as you did in Step 2.

5. Type **Choosing and Displaying Dates** in the Text property and press Enter. The second tab now displays the text you just typed in.

6. Right-click the Tab control (upper right area next to the tabs).

7. Choose Add Tab from the menu that is displayed. A new tab (tabPage3) is added.

8. Click the blank area in the tab page.

9. Type **Progress and Status Bars** in the Text property of tabPage3.

Now the Tab control is set up to use for the chapter. When you want to add controls to the pages, you will click the tab you are interested in, then drag and drop the controls onto the page. When you run the application, the user can click the tabs and the changing of pages is handled for you.

Now it is time to take a look at the first demonstration, displaying files in a Web browser.

Displaying Files in a Web Browser

While it would be easy to throw the `WebBrowser` control onto a form and hard-code (set using the design properties) to demonstrate showing a file in the `WebBrowser` control, it is not near as interesting, or useful, in my opinion, as creating a form that will let the user specify the folder that contains files, loads them into a list box, and then loads the `WebBrowser` control with the specified file.

Controls Used for the Demonstration

To accomplish this, you will use the following controls:

Control	How Used
Button	Code is written for the `Click` event that calls the `ShowDialog` method of the `FolderBrowserDialog`. The folder returned is then passed to the `GetFiles` method of the `System.UI.Directory` class, which returns the names of files in a string array. The array of filenames is then loaded into the `ListBox` control.
FolderBrowserDialog	The `ShowDialog` method is called to display the Folder Browse dialog box, just the other dialog controls used in the last chapter. After the user chooses a folder, the `SelectFolder` property contains the full path of the folder. Located in the `Dialog` category in the Toolbox.
ListBox	The `AddItem` method is used to load filenames into the `ListBox`. When selected, the current filename is retrieved and used by the `Navigate` method of the `WebBrowser` control.
SplitContainer	Enables the user to have control over the size of both the `ListBox` and `WebBrowser` controls, much like using Frames in a Web site. As with the `Tab` control, this is a container-type control, consisting of multiple panels. It is located in the Container category in the Toolbox.
TextBox	Displays the current folder being loaded into the `ListBox`. Updated in the code behind the `Button` control.
WebBrowser	Using the `Navigate` method displays the file picked from the `ListBox` control in a Web browser on the form. This is located in the Common Controls category in the Toolbox.

While I normally rename each control to be more meaningful depending on the task, for the purposes of this chapter, I am leaving some of the controls with their original name as assigned by C# Express when only one of them is used on the form.

While there is a bit of code used for the controls discussed in the last table, I will walk you through each line so you will understand them as you write them. Also, I have added code to the code sample to discuss the blocks of code. To start with, you need to place the controls on the form.

Try It Out   Adding the Controls for Displaying Files in a Web Browser

To get going, you will want to have the first page of the Tab control display. Once you do:

1. Drag and drop a Button control onto the first page (tabPage1) of the Tab control, naming it **btnSetFolder**.

2. Type **Set Folder** for the Text property of the Button control added in Step 1.

3. Drag and drop a Label control onto the first page of the Tab control, lining it up beside the Button control added in Step 1.

4. Type **Current Folder** for the Text property and **lblCurrentFolder** for the Name property of the Label control added in the last step.

5. Set the AutoSize property of the Label control to False. The reason for this property setting is so that you can resize the label as you want in order to anticipate having text, in this case folder paths, bigger than the text set at design time.

6. Resize the Label control to stretch across the page.

7. Drag and drop a SplitContainer control onto the first page of the Tab control, placing it under the Button control.

8. Set the Anchor property of the SlipContainer to Top, Bottom, Right, Left. This will cause the SlipContainer control to resize itself down the tab page as the form is resized.

9. Resize the SlipContainer using the top middle resize handle so that it starts just below the Button and Label controls, as shown in Figure 14-8.

10. Set the BorderStyle of the SplitContainer to be FixedSingle. This will add more of an emphasis on the two panels when viewing.

11. Drag and drop a Label control into the first panel of the SlipContainer added in Step 8, typing **Files to View** for the Text property.

12. Drag and drop a ListBox control into the first panel, under the Label control added in the last step.

13. Set the Anchor property to Top, Bottom, Left, Right. This will cause the control to grow with the panel it is in.

14. Resize the ListBox control to fill the first panel under the Label control added in Step 10.

15. Drag and drop a WebBrowser control from the Common Control category in the Toolbox in the second panel of the SlipContainer control. Note that the Dock property of the WebBrowser control is automatically set to Fill. This will cause the control to fill the second panel of the SlipContainer.

16. Drag and drop a FolderBrowserDialog control from the Dialogs category of the Toolbox onto the form. As with other dialog controls you won't see anything on the form itself, but a component will be added to the component tray below the form. You can see the final form without code in Figure 14-9.

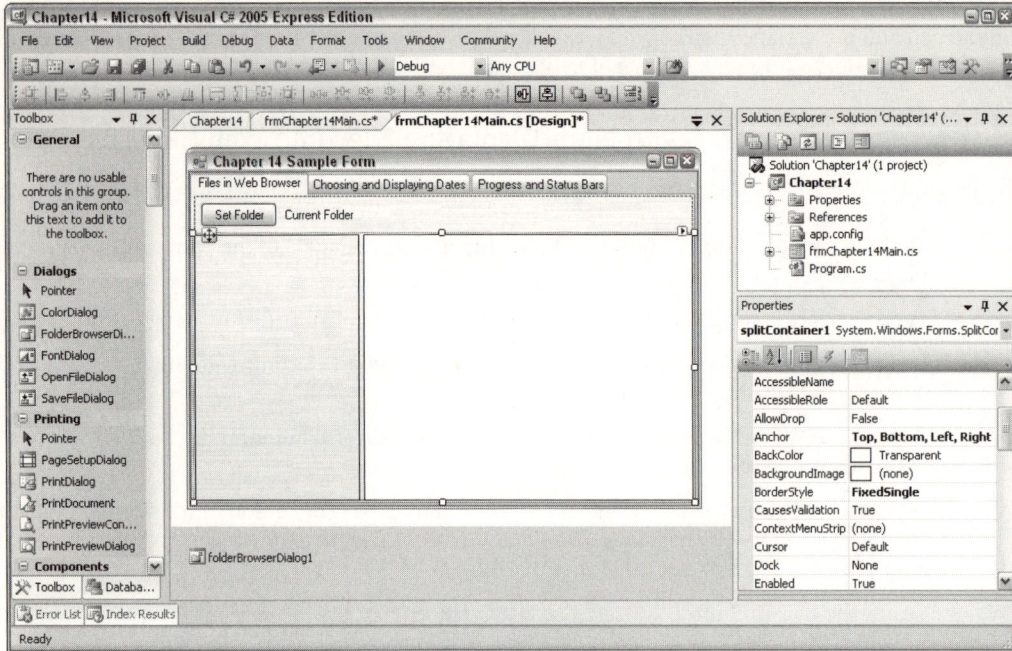

Figure 14-8

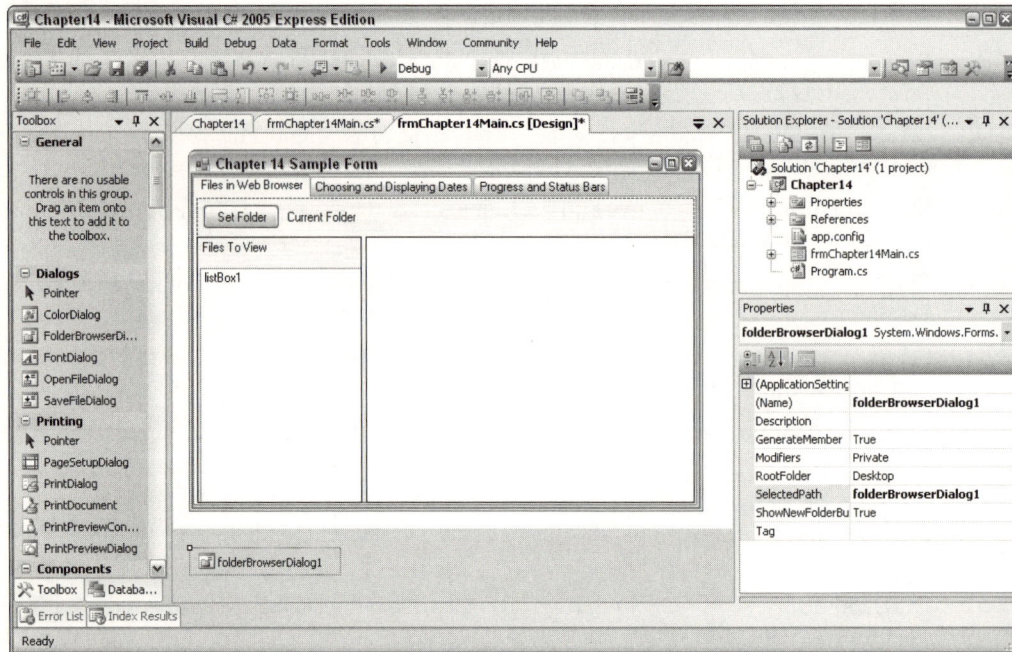

Figure 14-9

Whew, quite a few controls. And this is just for the first demonstration. Now it is time to work on the code for actually using the controls.

Adding the Code for Browsing and Displaying Files

The majority of the commands in this chapter have been discussed at one point or another throughout the book, although there are some new properties and methods of individual controls. I will also review the use of arrays. While I will be discussing the code used for the method a line at a time, I want to go ahead and give you the whole method to look at, which is documented with comments fairly well. Again, don't stress out looking at it, because you will be working on it by sections, or specific tasks, at a time.

```
// Declare the array of strings used for filenames
  string[] aryFileEntries;

  private void btnSetFolder_Click(object sender, EventArgs e)
  {
     // Display the folder browser dialog
     folderBrowserDialog1.ShowDialog();

     // Display the folder selected in the top label
     this.lblCurrentFolder.Text = folderBrowserDialog1.SelectedPath;

     if (this.lblCurrentFolder.Text != "folderBrowserDialog1")
     {
        // Clear the current list of files in the listbox
        // and Web Browser control.
        this.listBox1.Items.Clear();
        this.webBrowser1.Navigate("");

        // Store the filenames into an array
        aryFileEntries =
            System.IO.Directory.GetFiles(folderBrowserDialog1.SelectedPath);


        // Iterate through each of the filenames loaded into the array
        foreach (string fileName in aryFileEntries)
        {
           // strip off the path, and add the filename into the list box
           string strFileNameOnly =
                   fileName.Substring(fileName.LastIndexOf(@"\") + 1);
           this.listBox1.Items.Add(strFileNameOnly);
        }
     }
  }
```

For the steps in Try It Outs of this chapter, I won't be including the comments displayed in the code discussed. Also, remember that the complete code is provided in the sample application for this chapter if you just want to cut and paste it in. Lazy, but it works easier that way and in fact is the way you will learn additional methods and use somebody else's routines.

In the code used with the btnSetFolder Click event, the first step is to display the Folder Browser dialog box and to utilize the folder if one is selected.

Displaying and Utilizing the FolderBrowserDialog Control

To accomplish this, a method and property of the FolderBrowserDialog are used: the ShowDialog method and the SelectedPath property, as follows:

```
// Display the folder browser dialog
folderBrowserDialog1.ShowDialog();

// Display the folder selected in the top label
this.lblCurrentFolder.Text = folderBrowserDialog1.SelectedPath;
```

As explained in the code comments, after displaying the dialog box, the selected path is displayed in the Text property of the lblCurrentFolder label. This shows users which folder they selected. The next step is to look at the Text of lblCurrentFolder and see that it does not equal "folderBrowserDialog1," which is what it will be if the user selected Cancel in the Folder Browser dialog box. This is accomplished with the following lines of code:

```
if (this.lblCurrentFolder.Text != "folderBrowserDialog1")
{
        // Statements in the True block of code.
}
```

Note that instead of using the lblCurrentFolder.Text *value, you could also use the* folderBrowserDialog1.SelectedPath *directly.*

Try It Out   **Add the Code to Use the FolderBrowserDialog**

As the title implies, you will be adding code to use the FolderBrowserDialog, display the selected path, and add a test to make sure a path has been chosen. To get started, open the form that you created on in the prior Try It Outs in the chapter:

1. Double-click the btnSetFolder button. The code file opens, and the btnSetFolder_Click routine is created for you, as shown in the following:

```
private void btnSetFolder_Click(object sender, EventArgs e)
{

}
```

2. Type the following code between the open and close curly brackets of the btnSetFolder_Click routine:

```
folderBrowserDialog1.ShowDialog();

this.lblCurrentFolder.Text = folderBrowserDialog1.SelectedPath;

if (this.lblCurrentFolder.Text != "folderBrowserDialog1")
{

}
```

Notice that the open and close curly brackets were added for the if code block, even though you aren't using it yet. It is a good idea to add these if you know you are going to use a code block even if you test the code in between updating the code.

3. Press F5 to test the application thus far. The application should open with the first page in the Tab control displayed.

4. Click the Set Folder button. The Folder Browser dialog box opens, as shown here in Figure 14-10, where a folder has been chosen.

Figure 14-10

5. Click OK to accept the chosen folder. You now see the path you chose displayed beside the Set Folder button.

6. Close the sample form and return to the C# Express editor.

Clearing the ListBox and WebBrowser Controls

Continuing with the flow of the overall demo code, if the value in the Text property of lblCurrentFolder is a legitimate folder, the next piece of code is executed. The code clears both the Items collection of the ListBox collection, as well as clears the WebBrowser control by passing the Navigate parameter to the empty string (""). You can see the code here:

```
// Clear the current list of files in the listbox
// and Web Browser control.
this.listBox1.Items.Clear();
this.webBrowser1.Navigate("");
```

The purpose of this code is to make the demo usable more than one time when opened. If you didn't include the preceding code, when new items are added, as shown in the next section, they would simply be added onto the current items already in the ListBox. Likewise, if you didn't add the code for navigating to nothing in the last line of code, then the WebBrowser control would reflect the file that was last displayed, regardless of the current list of files.

You will be loading up the `Items` collection of the `ListBox` in the next section, and specifying where to navigate in the Web Control in the section titled "Navigating in the Web Browser Control."

Try It Out   **Clearing the ListBox Items Collection and WebBrowser**

Make sure C# Express is opened in the editor into the `btnSetFolder_Click` routine:

1. Place the cursor in the code block of the `if` statement you added in the last Try It Out as shown here:

```
if (this.lblCurrentFolder.Text != "folderBrowserDialog1")
{

}
```

2. Type the following lines of code:

```
this.listBox1.Items.Clear();
this.webBrowser1.Navigate("");
```

Since this code doesn't really show much until the next section is added, there is no need to run the application again until after the next Try It Out.

Getting the List of Files and Loading the ListBox

The next line of code takes the selected path and passes it to the `GetFiles` method of the `System.IO.Directory` class. The `System.IO.Directory` class provides properties and methods for accessing and working with folders and their content. The `GetFiles` method goes out to the folder passed to it and returns the list of filenames as an array of strings, shown here:

```
// Store the filenames into an array
aryFileEntries = System.IO.Directory.GetFiles(folderBrowserDialog1.SelectedPath);
```

When using this in the real world, you may want to use exception handlers here. For more information on exception handling, reread Chapter 7.

In this case, the array is declared just before the `btnSetFolder_Click` routine at the class level so that the array is available to all the routines in the class. The following line of code is used to declare the array:

```
string[] aryFileEntries;
```

This line of code is place outside of the `Click` event handler, just above in the sample code. By specifying `string[]`, you are telling C# that the variable named is going to be an array of strings. This means that there will be more than one entry in the variable. You can get to the entries using an index starting at 0. So if the list of filenames was `FileA`, `FileB`, and `FileC`, the array will look like this:

```
aryFileEntries[0] = "FileA"
```

```
aryFileEntries[1] = "FileB"
```

```
aryFileEntries[2] = "FileC"
```

You can load items into an array individually. However, there are some methods and statements that enable you to load the elements into the array, and others that iterate through the array to access all the elements. The code in this demonstration has examples of both. For instance, as mentioned, the `GetFiles` method loads the list of filenames into the `aryFileEntries` array for you by passing it as the return value.

Once the filenames have been loaded into the array, you can then go through the array and load them into the `ListBox` control using the `foreach` statement to iterate through the array. The lines of code to iterate through the array looks like the following:

```
// Iterate through each of the filenames loaded into the array
foreach (string fileName in aryFileEntries)
{
  // Statements performed for each array element that is loaded into fileName.
}
```

with the statements performed in the block of code discussed in a moment. This `foreach` statement iterates through the array called `aryFileEntries`, and creates a variable used within the code block called `fileName`. This variable is only seen within the code block, and as with variables stored in the `for` statements, can be declared for each iteration in the loop. `For` statements were first discussed in Chapter 7.

The last thing to discuss before actually walking you through the Try It Out is how to take the filenames and load them into the `ListBox` control. Before loading the name into the `ListBox` `Items` collection, you need to strip the path of the filename off of it. To accomplish this, you will two methods of the string type `Substring` and `LastIndexOf`, both of which were discussed in Chapter 5.

```
// strip off the path, and add the filename into the list box
string strFileNameOnly = fileName.Substring(fileName.LastIndexOf(@"\") + 1);
```

The previous line of code creates a new variable and takes the filename of the path and filename by locating the position of the last "\" character in the current array element that was stored in the `fileName` variable. Remember that by not supplying the length of the substring to return, which is the second parameter, the `Substring` method returns the rest of the string beginning at the starting location, in this case provided by the `LastIndexOf` method.

The @ is necessary when you want to use the literal "\" value. Otherwise, the "\" is considered to be the newline character.

Finally, you will use the `Add` method of the `ListBox` `Items` collection to add the current filename, now stored in `strFileNameOnly`.

```
this.listBox1.Items.Add(strFileNameOnly);
```

Remember that the last couple of lines of code are located inside the code block for the `foreach` statement. Once each of the elements has been added, the `ListBox` control will then show the filenames.

Try It Out   Load the ListBox Control

Now is your chance to add the code specified here and load the `ListBox` control for yourself. Open the form that you created on in the prior Try It Outs in the chapter:

1. Placing the cursor above the line of code that reads

```
private void btnSetFolder_Click(object sender, EventArgs e)
```

type the following line of code to declare the array:

```
string[] aryFileEntries;
```

2. Place the cursor in the `if` statement after the lines of code that read:

```
if (this.lblCurrentFolder.Text != "folderBrowserDialog1")
{
    this.listBox1.Items.Clear();
        this.webBrowser1.Navigate("");
```

Then press Enter. This creates a blank line.

3. Type the following lines of code:

```
aryFileEntries =
    System.IO.Directory.GetFiles(folderBrowserDialog1.SelectedPath);

foreach (string fileName in aryFileEntries)
{
    string strFileNameOnly =
            fileName.Substring(fileName.LastIndexOf(@"\") + 1);
    this.listBox1.Items.Add(strFileNameOnly);
}
```

The final lines of code should look like this:

```
// Declare the array of strings used for filenames
string[] aryFileEntries;

private void btnSetFolder_Click(object sender, EventArgs e)
{
    // Display the folder browser dialog
    folderBrowserDialog1.ShowDialog();

    // Display the folder selected in the top label
    this.lblCurrentFolder.Text = folderBrowserDialog1.SelectedPath;

    if (this.lblCurrentFolder.Text != "folderBrowserDialog1")
    {
        // Clear the current list of files in the listbox
        // and Web Browser control.
        this.listBox1.Items.Clear();
        this.webBrowser1.Navigate("");

        // Store the filenames into an array
```

```
       aryFileEntries =
           System.IO.Directory.GetFiles(folderBrowserDialog1.SelectedPath);


       // Iterate through each of the filenames loaded into the array
       foreach (string fileName in aryFileEntries)
       {
          // strip off the path, and add the filename into the list box
          string strFileNameOnly =
                  fileName.Substring(fileName.LastIndexOf(@"\") + 1);
          this.listBox1.Items.Add(strFileNameOnly);
       }
    }
}
```

Comments have been added to this display so that you can add them yourself at this point if you want.

4. Press F5 to run the application.

5. Click the Set Folder button to choose a folder. The Folder Browser dialog box opens.

6. Pick a folder and click OK. The list of files in the folder is displayed in the `ListBox` control as shown in Figure 14-11.

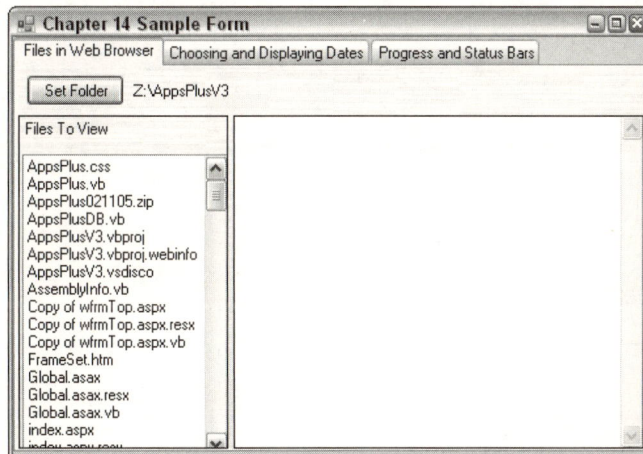

Figure 14-11

The speed in which the files are displayed in the `ListBox` will depend on the number of files in the folder you are pointing to.

Okay, down the home stretch for this demo. The last thing to discuss is displaying a file in the Web browser.

Navigating in the Web Browser Control

Actually navigating in the WebBrowser control is as simple as calling a single method called Navigate, which, as discussed earlier in the chapter in the section called "Clearing the ListBox and WebBrowser Controls," was executed with the empty string ("") to clear the browser. In the case of using it for displaying a file, you will pass the literal "file://" with the full path of the file.

To retrieve the full path of the file you want to display, you take SelectIndex property of the ListBox control and use it as an index for aryFileEntries. You can see how this portion of the command would look here:

```
aryFileEntries[listBox1.SelectedIndex]
```

Taking the literal discussed in the first paragraph ("file://") and adding that to the command just displayed, you will pass the two to the Navigate method as such:

```
this.webBrowser1.Navigate("file://" + aryFileEntries[listBox1.SelectedIndex]);
```

This line of code will be executed using the SelectedIndexChange event of the ListBox. So the complete routine, with comments, will look something like the following:

```
private void listBox1_SelectedIndexChanged(object sender, EventArgs e)
{
    // Use the WebBrowser control to displayed the selected file
    this.webBrowser1.Navigate("file://" +
                    aryFileEntries[listBox1.SelectedIndex]);
}
```

Try It Out   Add the Code to Display the File in the WebBrowser Control

Using the form you created for this chapter:

1. Double-click the ListBox control. This causes C# Express to open the code file for the form and create the header for the SelectedIndexChanged routine:

```
private void listBox1_SelectedIndexChanged(object sender, EventArgs e)
{
}
```

2. Type the following line of code in between the curly brackets:

```
this.webBrowser1.Navigate("file://" +
                aryFileEntries[listBox1.SelectedIndex]);
```

3. Press F5 to run the application.

4. Click the Set Folder button to choose a folder. The Folder Browser dialog box opens.

5. Pick a folder and click OK. The list of files in the folder is displayed in the ListBox control.

6. Click one of the files in the `ListBox` control. The file should then be displayed in the browser if it is of the right type as mentioned in the section titled "Demo 1: Browsing Web Files," found in the beginning of the chapter. Figure 14-12 shows what the form will look like after picking a file.

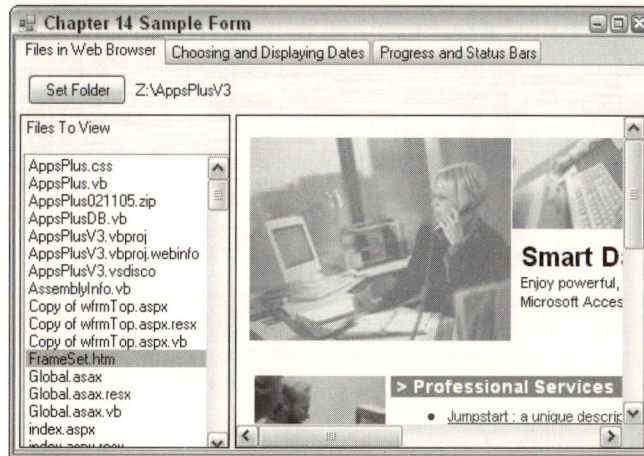

Figure 14-12

There you have it, a very useful utility with not much code written. There are definitely ways to improve upon this design. One way would be to record the index in `aryFileEntries` in the list items. That way you'd be able to sort files in different ways without relying on list item indices to locate the full path to the files. I will leave this to you to work on, before moving on to the next section.

Working with Date Controls

The second tab on the chapter form, Choosing and Displaying Dates, is a lot easier to create than the first tab's topic. Although in my opinion, even though using date controls is much simpler to understand and implement, I honestly think you will use them more often than displaying files in a Web browser in your form.

A lot of your applications will utilize dates, such as order dates for invoices or schedule dates for employee schedules. While you can input a date into a `TextBox` control and control how it is inputted, it is much more professional to give the user a graphic representation for the date. You can see an example of the controls in Figure 14-13.

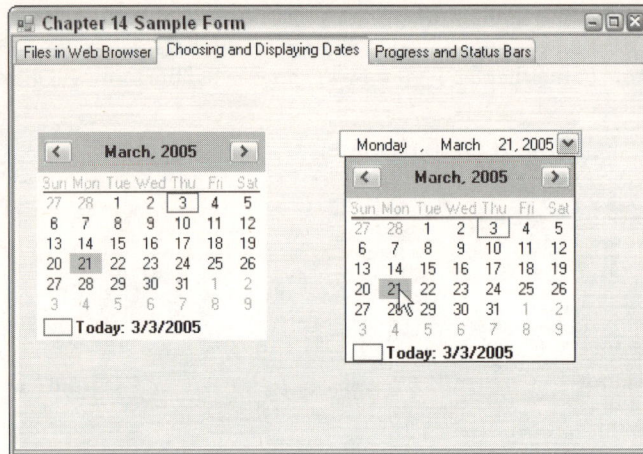

Figure 14-13

Before adding the two controls used for this demonstration, the MonthCalendar and DateTimePicker controls, yourself, I want to discuss a little further how you can use each of them.

Looking at the MonthCalendar Control

With the MonthCalendar control, displayed on the left in Figure 14-13, users can click a date and change the current date selected. You can move back and forth using arrows at the top of the control to change the month. The control displayed in Figure 14-13 has been placed on the form using the default properties. Using the properties provided you can set everything from the title color to whether or not to display today's date.

The main property you will be using in the code is the SelectionStart property. Instead of just providing a single date that you can pick from the calendar, the MonthCalendar control provides the ability to select a range of dates. The other property you would use for that would be the SelectionEnd property. This is useful if you want to use the calendar for specifying To/From dates on a report. However, for this example, you will be using only the SelectionStart property. You also will set the MaxSelectionCount property to 1, because this example is only interested in one day. You can see some the properties mentioned here and more of the possible properties to use in Figure 14-14.

As with other controls, the MonthCalendar control has a number of methods (which you won't be using) and events to use at your disposal. In this example, you will be using the DatePicked event to execute a line of code that updates the value in the DateTimePicker control.

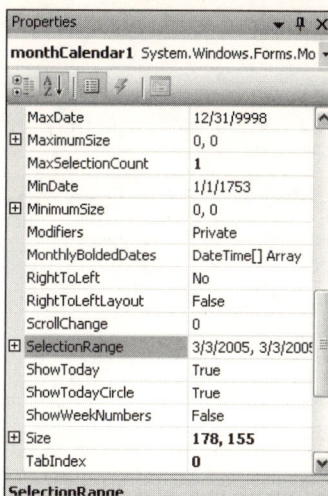

Figure 14-14

Looking at the DateTimePicker Control

The `DateTimePicker` control enables the user to enter or choose dates a few different ways depending on how properties are set:

❑ **Text box.** Using this method of input, users enter the date they are interested in as they would in a `TextBox` control. The data is then evaluated to make sure it matches the correct format.

❑ **Drop-down calendar.** When the drop-down arrow is clicked, a `MonthCalendar` control is displayed and the user can pick from the displayed dates on the calendar.

❑ **Date up/down.** Similar to the numeric up/down control, up and down arrows are displayed in place of the drop-down arrow. Users can then click up and down to move through dates.

Entering as a text box is included in both of the two other choices. To get the up and down arrows, you set a property called `ShowUpDown`. The two arrows then replace the single drop-down arrow. The drop-down calendar choice is the default use of the `DateTimePicker` control and the one used for this example.

The default event that used for executing code for the `DateTimePicker` control is the `ValueChanged` event. To get or set the `DateTimePicker` date in code, you use the `Value` property.

It's time to get going creating this example.

Try It Out   Create the Date Controls Example

Since there are only two lines of functional code, you will have to write to create this example, you will add both controls and the code used to update each based on the other's value all at once in this Try It Out. So with the form used for this chapter, in the design view:

1. Click the tab in the `TabControl` that has the text: Choosing and Displaying Dates.

Chapter 14

2. Drag and drop a `MonthCalendar` control onto the form from the Common Controls category in the Toolbox.

3. Set the `MaxSelectionCount` of the `MonthCalendar` control you added to 1, using the properties window. You can see the control added and the `MaxSelection` property in Figure 14-15.

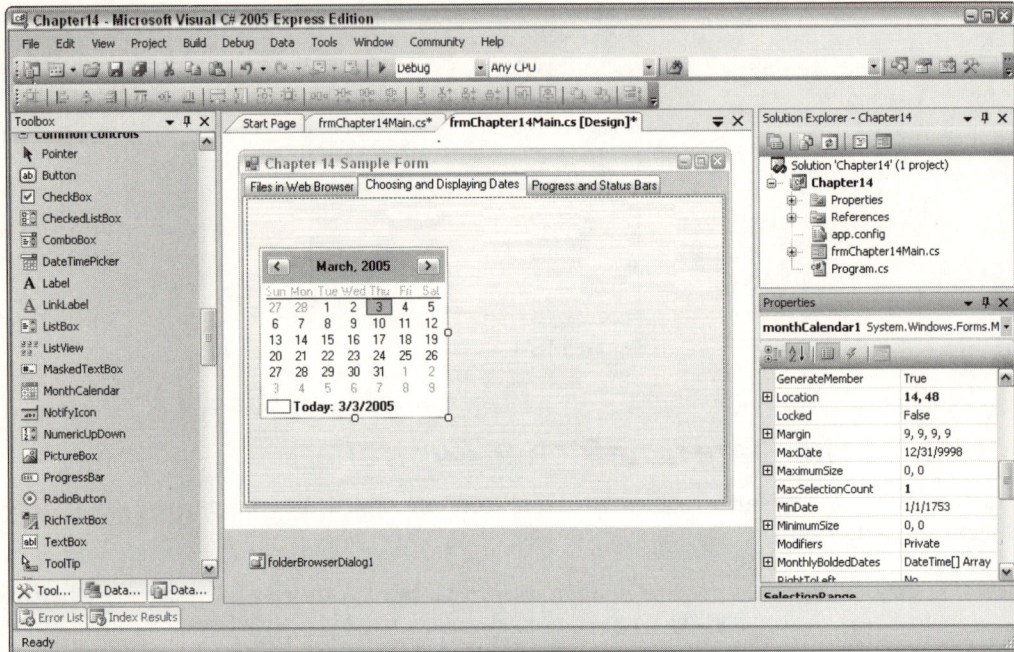

Figure 14-15

4. Drag and drop a `DateTimePicker` control from the Common Controls category in the Toolbox, dropping it beside the `MonthCalendar` control you added.

5. Double-click the `MonthCalendar` control you added in Step 2. The code for the routine of the `DateChanged` is displayed as follows:

```
private void monthCalendar1_DateChanged(object sender, DateRangeEventArgs e)
{

}
```

The cursor is placed in the blank line.

6. Type the following code:

```
// Set the DateTimePicker value to the month calendar date.
this.dateTimePicker1.Value = this.monthCalendar1.SelectionStart;
```

This now causes the `DateTimePicker` control `Value` property to be updated when a new date is chosen in the `MonthCalendar` control. The next steps will show how to add code to accomplish the opposite, having the `SelectionStart` control updated when the `DateTimePicker` value is updated.

7. Switch back to the form design file of the example form.

8. Double-click the `DateTimePicker` control to create the code for the `ValueChanged` event, as shown:

```
private void dateTimePicker1_ValueChanged(object sender, EventArgs e)
{

}
```

9. Type the following code in the blank line provided:

```
// Set the first date of the month calendar control
this.monthCalendar1.SelectionStart = dateTimePicker1.Value;
```

10. Press F5 to build and execute the application.

11. Click the Choosing and Displaying Dates tab.

12. Play with the two date controls and see the response to the other by choosing a date from the `MonthCalendar` control and then from the `DateTimePicker` control.

This fairly straightforward demonstration has showed you how you can not only display dates in different types of date controls but also change them and have them affect other controls. In the next and final demonstration, you will be using a `MonthCalendar` control to set the max values on a couple of different `ProgressBar` controls.

Using ProgressBar and StatusStrip Controls

`ProgressBar` and `StatusStrip` are useful controls that don't always get covered in books. Because these controls are so easy to use, authors think you can just figure them out yourself. While this may be true, unless you have someone show you their differences, you may not see that they are both useful.

Before I go into more detail on each of these controls, take a look at the demonstration created for the purpose of introducing the `ProgressBar` and `StatusStrip` controls.

Describing the Progress and Status Bars Demo

To show you how you can use both of these controls, a demo has been created that places a `MonthCalendar` control on a form with `ProgressBar` and `StatusStrip` controls. In the `StatusStrip` control are two other controls: `StatusLabel` control, which displays today's date, and another `ProgressBar` control. These are discussed in the section titled "Using the StatusStrip Controls," later in the chapter. The last control on the form is a `Button` control that executes the code to iterate and update the progress bar.

The purpose of the `MonthCalendar` control is to provide the maximum values for the progress bars. For example, if you are in February and you click the `Button` control, the progress bars' `Maximum` will be set to the number of days in February, 28 (unless it is a leap year, of course), and a `for` loop is executed for the `Maximum` value of the first `ProgressBar` control.

For fun, the days in the MonthCalendar control are updated as the days are incremented. Lastly, a message box is displayed saying that the process is complete, and then the progress bars values are set to 0 and the MonthCalendar control's SelectedStart property is set to 1. You can see an example of the demonstration after completing the loop, where it displays the message box shown in Figure 14-16.

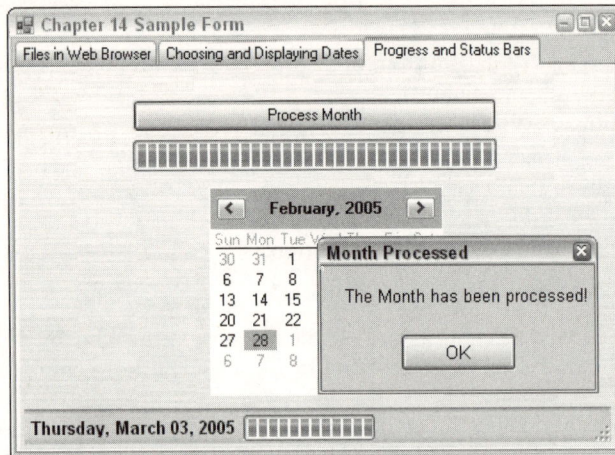

Figure 14-16

To get started on building the demo itself, I want to discuss using ProgressBar controls.

Working with ProgressBar Controls

As mentioned, using a ProgressBar control is pretty easy, taking primarily three basic steps:

1. Drag and drop it on the form.

2. Set the Maximum property for the ProgressBar control, either in the design view in the properties window or using code.

3. Inside the iterative process (loop) that you are executing, increment the Value property of the ProgressBar control you are using.

That's it. You can modify the ProgressBar control's properties if you want to use different features such as changing the Style property of the ProgressBar. The choices are Blocks (default), Continuous, and Marquee. For the purpose of this example, the default style was used.

As with the first demonstration with the File Browser utility, I will break this demonstration up into a few Try It Outs to make it easier to follow. To start with, you will be adding the Button and MonthCalendar controls onto the form along with the first ProgressBar control. The next Try It Out and section goes through the code you will use for using the progress bar. Finally, the last Try It Out has you add the StatusStrip control and the controls included on it, as well as discuss the code used for setting the controls values at runtime.

Try It Out   **Add the Controls for Using the First Progress Bar**

Use the form created for the demonstrations in this chapter, in the design view of the form itself. For positioning of the controls you can use Figure 14-16 as an example:

1. Click the Progress and Status Bars tab.

2. Drag and drop a `Button` control from the Common Controls category in the Toolbox, sizing it to your desired width and height.

3. Set the `Name` property to `btnProcessMonth` and the `Text` property to **Process Month**.

4. Drag and drop a `ProgressBar` control onto the form from the Common Controls category in the Toolbox, again sizing it as desired.

5. Drag and drop a `MonthCalendar` control onto the form, again from the Common Controls category in the Toolbox.

6. Set the `MaxSelectionCount` of the `MonthCalendar` control you added to 1, using the properties window.

Okay, before adding the controls for the status bar, I want to have you add the code that sets up and iterates through the days of the current month.

Adding the Code to Setup and Update the ProgressBar Control

The first thing you need to do is set the `ProgressBar` up to reflect the current month. To accomplish this, you will create a routine called `UpdateCal2Day` that will take the day passed, which is of the `int` type, and assign that value to the `Value` property of the progress bar. Here is what that line of code will look like:

```
this.progressBar1.Value = intDay;
```

The complete code for using the main progress bar and `MonthCalendar` controls is as follows:

```
private void UpdateCal2Day(int intDay)
{
    // Update the two progress bars with the current value (day)
    this.progressBar1.Value = intDay;

    // If the current day is 0 (reset) set the calendar control to day 1,
    // otherwise set it to the day specified.
    if (intDay == 0)
    {
        this.monthCalendar2.SelectionStart =
            new System.DateTime(monthCalendar2.SelectionStart.Year,
                        monthCalendar2.SelectionStart.Month, 1);
    }
    else
```

```
        {
            this.monthCalendar2.SelectionStart =

            new System.DateTime(monthCalendar2.SelectionStart.Year,
                        monthCalendar2.SelectionStart.Month, intDay);
        }

    }
```

After assigning the passed day into the `Value` property of the `ProgressBar` control, the code sets the `Calendar` control on this page to the current day of the month based on the value passed into the routine. You will see that an `if` statement is used to check to see if the `intDay` is 0, reset the `ProgressBar`, and cause code to be run that sets the date to the first day of the month. This is accomplished with the following line of code:

```
        this.monthCalendar2.SelectionStart =
            new System.DateTime(monthCalendar2.SelectionStart.Year,
                        monthCalendar2.SelectionStart.Month, 1);
```

Notice that the `Year` and `Month` properties of the `SelectionStart` property is combined with the 1 constant and is converted into a `DateTime` type using the `System.DateTime` class. If `intDay` wasn't 0, the same basic line of code is used, with `intDay` taking the place of 1.

```
        this.monthCalendar2.SelectionStart =
            new System.DateTime(monthCalendar2.SelectionStart.Year,
                        monthCalendar2.SelectionStart.Month, intDay);
```

Now this routine is first called when the form is loaded so that the `MonthCalendar` control is set to the first day of the month. You can see how the routine is called from the `Load` routine of the form.

```
    private void frmChapter14Main_Load(object sender, EventArgs e)
    {
        // Initialize the progress bar set of controls
        // for the second calendar.
        UpdateCal2Day(0);
    }
```

Before getting into actually creating the code that processes all the month's days, I want you to go ahead and add the code for the routine that updates the progress bar and calendar. When the form is opened and the tab page clicked, you will see the box shown in Figure 14-17.

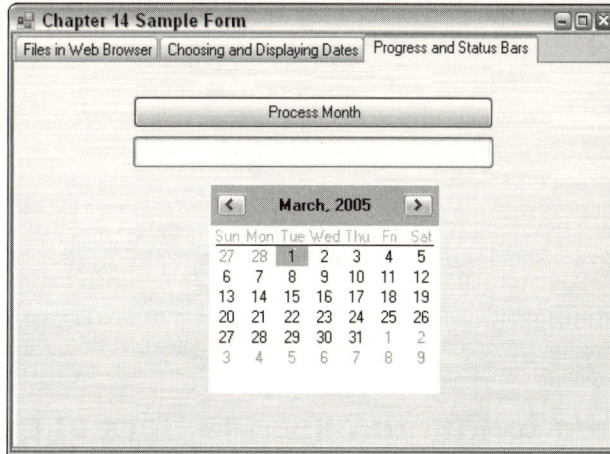

Figure 14-17

Try It Out Add the Code to Set Up Controls

Using the form you created for this chapter:

1. Double-click the title bar of the form. This creates a Load routine for the form as shown here:

```
private void frmChapter14Main_Load(object sender, EventArgs e)
{

}
```

2. Type the following line of code in the blank line:

```
UpdateCal2Day(0);
```

If you were to try and build the application at this point, you would get an error, so don't.

3. Position the cursor just after the closing curly bracket, and press Enter to add a blank line.

4. Type the following code provided here without comments:

```
private void UpdateCal2Day(int intDay)
{
    this.progressBar1.Value = intDay;

    if (intDay == 0)
    {
        this.monthCalendar2.SelectionStart =
          new System.DateTime(monthCalendar2.SelectionStart.Year,
                              monthCalendar2.SelectionStart.Month, 1);
    }
    else
```

```
        {
            this.monthCalendar2.SelectionStart =
               new System.DateTime(monthCalendar2.SelectionStart.Year,
                            monthCalendar2.SelectionStart.Month, intDay);
        }


    }
```

5. Press F5 to test the application. When you click the Progress and Status Bars tab, the calendar appears with the first day of the month highlighted.

You have created code to update the progress bar and calendar based on the value passed to it. Now it is time to add code to the button on the form that runs though the days of the current month chosen.

Adding the Code to Run through the Days of the Month Chosen

Before you actually run through the days of the current month used in the calendar, the `Maximum` property of the `ProgressBar` control needs to be set. To accomplish this, the following line of code is used:

```
    this.progressBar1.Maximum =
            System.DateTime.DaysInMonth(monthCalendar2.SelectionStart.Year,
            monthCalendar2.SelectionStart.Month);
```

This code uses the `System.DateTime` class again by calling the `DaysInMonth` method, which takes the year and month passed to it and returns the days in the month.

Remember that the `System.DateTime` class has a number of different methods and properties that deal with date and time information. It is worth your time to experiment with this class and look it up in the Object Browser.

After establishing the maximum value for the `ProgressBar` control, the code increment the values in the progress bar, causing the progress bar to fill up with blocks. To accomplish this, a `for` loop is used, with 1 as the minimum value and the `Maximum` property of the `ProgressBar` control as the maximum value of the loop. You can see the complete loop here, with the necessary code specified inside:

```
        //  Iterate through each tick in the progress bar,
        //  Which was set based on the # of days in the current month.
        for (int i = 1; i <= this.progressBar1.Maximum; i++)
        {
            // Update the calendar control date to display the current date.
            UpdateCal2Day(i);

            // The following for loop is to slow down the progress bar.
            for (int j = 1; j <= 5000000; j++) ;
        }
```

In addition to calling the `UpdateCal2Day` routine, you will see an additional loop specified. Note that this loop is used to slow down the filling of the progress bar for demonstration purposes. You won't need this when you use it for a real-life situation.

The last thing this routine needs to do is let the user know when the task has been completed, in this case when the days have been looped through.

```
MessageBox.Show("The Month has been processed!", "Month Processed");
// Reset the values.
UpdateCal2Day(0);
```

Try It Out   Add Code to Process Each of the Days

Making sure that the form you created in this chapter is opened in design view with the third tab page displayed:

1. Double-click the `Button` control called `btnProcessMonth`. The code file for the form opens, with the `Click` routine done for `btnProcessMonth`.

```
private void btnProcessMonth_Click(object sender, EventArgs e)
{

}
```

2. Type the following code:

```
this.progressBar1.Maximum =
        DateTime.DaysInMonth(monthCalendar2.SelectionStart.Year,
        monthCalendar2.SelectionStart.Month);

for (int i = 1; i <= this.progressBar1.Maximum; i++)
{
    UpdateCal2Day(i);
    for (int j = 1; j <= 5000000; j++) ;
}

MessageBox.Show("The Month has been processed!", "Month Processed");
UpdateCal2Day(0);
```

3. Press F5 to test the application.

4. Click the Progress and Status Bar tab.

5. Click the Process Month button. You now see the progress bar fill up and the days whip through in the calendar. After completing, the message box appears.

6. Click OK. The progress bar is cleared and the date is positioned on the first day of the month.

Now that you have gotten the progress bar working on the form, it is time to look into using the `StatusStrip` control.

Using the StatusStrip Control

While progress bars are primarily used for displaying the progress of a specific task, such as performing end-of-month processing, status bars are displayed on a form or at the bottom of an application to display the overall information about the current status of the application you are in. You have seen progress bars when you download a file from the Internet or copied a file on your local system. For an example, look at the status bar located at the bottom of the C# Express editor when in a code file, shown in Figure 14-18.

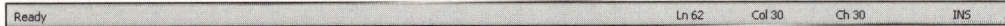

| Ready | | Ln 62 | Col 30 | Ch 30 | INS |

Figure 14-18

This status bar displays actions that are occurring, such as building the application. In C# Express, you will use the `StatusStrip` control to display a status bar.

`StatusStrip` controls are made up of panels. When you add a `StatusStrip` control, a drop-down is displayed that lets you choose from four different types of controls you can display: `StatusLabel`, `ProgressBar`, `DropDownButton`, and `SplitButton`. For the purpose of this example, you will be using the first two types of controls. The actual types are `ToolStripStatusLabel` and `ToolStripProgressBar`.

Once you have specified the controls to use on the `StatusStrip` control, you can utilize them at run-time as you would any other control. For example, now that you have a label on the status bar, you can update it when the form loads to display today's date just as you would a regular label:

```
this.toolStripStatusLabel1.Text = DateTime.Today.ToLongDateString();
```

The same goes for the progress bar used in the `StatusStrip` control. The following lines of code, used in two different routines, set the `Maxium` and `Value` properties of the `ToolStripProgressBar` control:

```
this.toolStripProgressBar1.Maximum = this.progressBar1.Maximum;

this.toolStripProgressBar1.Value = intDay;
```

You will be guided as to where the lines of code will go.

Try It Out   **Add the StatusStrip Control and Code**

Using the same tab you used in the last Try It Out:

1. Drag and drop a `StatusStrip` control on to the form from the Menus & Toolbars category in the Toolbox.

2. A status bar appear across the bottom of the form with a drop-down arrow is displayed.

3. Click the drop down arrow and select `StatusLabel` from the list. The label appears in the first spot in the status bar, and the drop-down arrow appears to the right.

4. Click the drop-down arrow; the screen should appear as it does in Figure 14-19.

5. Click the `ProgressBar` item in the list. The progress bar appears in the status bar. At this point if you test the application, you would just see the current text in the status bar label displayed in the status bar. You need to now add the code. The three lines of code shown in the section are all you need.

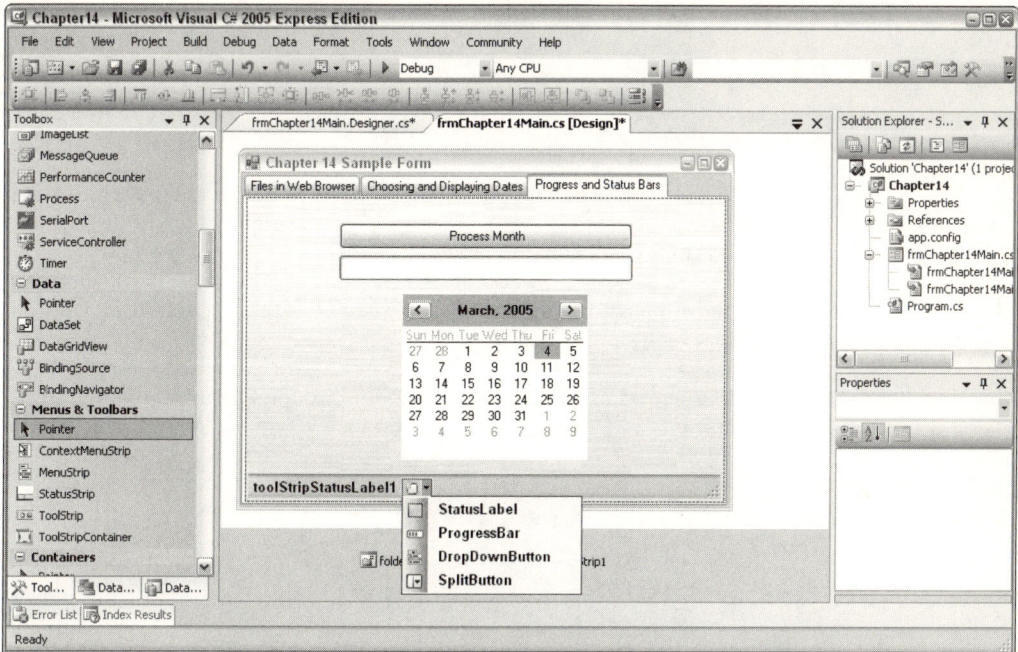

Figure 14-19

6. Double-click the top of the form to open the code with the `Load` routine opened. You can see the current code here:

```
private void frmChapter14Main_Load(object sender, EventArgs e)
{
    // Initialize the second set of controls for the second calendar.
    UpdateCal2Day(0);
}
```

7. Place the cursor after the opening curly bracket and press Enter to add new line.

8. Type in the following lines of code in the new blank line:

```
// Display the current date in the label ini the status bar.
this.toolStripStatusLabel1.Text = DateTime.Today.ToLongDateString();
```

9. Switch back to the form, and double-click the `btnProcessMonth` button. The form opens with the current code displayed. Here are the first few lines of code from that routine:

```
private void btnProcessMonth_Click(object sender, EventArgs e)
{
    this.progressBar1.Maximum =
        DateTime.DaysInMonth(monthCalendar2.SelectionStart.Year,
        monthCalendar2.SelectionStart.Month);
```

10. Type the following code in the line after the last line of code just displayed:

```
this.toolStripProgressBar1.Maximum = this.progressBar1.Maximum;
```

11. Now locate the `UpdateCal2Day` routine, which starts off with the following code:

```
private void UpdateCal2Day(int intDay)
{
    // Update the two progress bars with the current value (day)
    this.progressBar1.Value = intDay;
```

12. Add the following line of code to update the `Value` property of the progress bar in the status bar.

```
this.toolStripProgressBar1.Value = intDay;
```

13. Press F5 to execute the application.

14. Click the third tab. Today's date appears in the status bar.

15. Click the Process Month button. The routine should run through the process, updating both progress bars on the screen as shown in Figure 14-20.

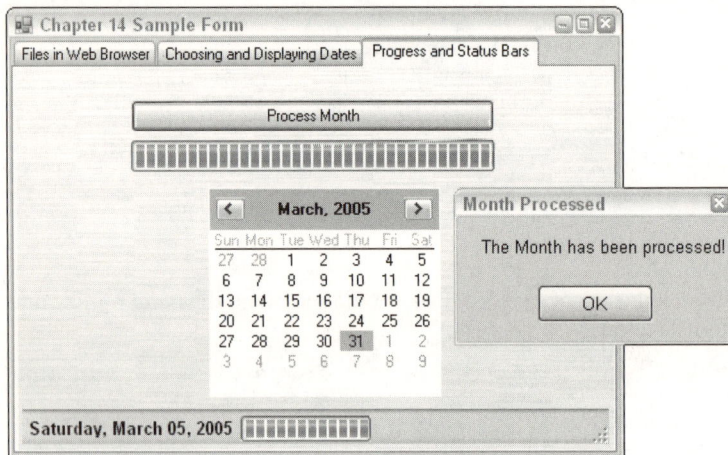

Figure 14-20

And there you go. You now have progress bars and status bars working on your form.

Summary

There are so many excellent controls that come with C# Express for your use, whether you are trying to browse folders, load the files in the folder into a list box, or even click one of the files and have it display in a `WebBrowser` control. It is all very doable, as you can see in this chapter. Once you have become accustomed to adding controls, modifying them to meet your needs more concisely is a lot easier.

An example of how you could combine the examples give here is to display a progress bar when you are loading the files into the Items collection of the list box. That way, the form wouldn't just sit there when you had to load folders with a higher number of files. As you create your forms, you can use one of the many controls you have access to, and then using the object browser, study the various methods, properties, and events available. So it's time to get to work!

Exercises

1. What are the two properties for setting the range on a `MonthCalendar` control?

2. What is the control for displaying two different objects in it and letting them be resized separately?

3. Name the four types of controls that can be used in the `StatusStrip` control.

4. Which method on the `System.DateTime` class returns the number of days in a month, and what are the parameters it requires?

15

Using Web Services from Your C# Application

Over the years, one of the big dilemmas facing software developers and big corporations is how to make data available to those who are both on the inside and outside without giving up security and make it efficient. When information was supposed to be shared, you had to create tapes and disks, mail them, and then import the data. Another issue for software developers is giving their users powerful features without having to spend hundreds of hours trying to give the users want they want. Web Services, also called XML Web Services, gives developers these abilities and much more.

Besides, exposing data developers can also provide and perform actions at a distance by creating a Web service that people from other locations can take advantage of. An example is a Web service hooked up to a Web cam at the Seattle Mariners baseball stadium (called Safeco Field) that allows me to watch the ballgame from my computer in my office.

One of the really great features of Web Services is that you can create them with .NET and C# if you have the full version of Visual Studio .NET.

Web services provide solutions to tasks either that don't make sense for you to create or even maintain the code for, or for which you would have to have access to outside data available from another company or facility. A couple of examples of utilizing Web services are getting stock quotes from a stock service or weather information for anywhere in the world. These examples are used in this chapter to discuss what Web services are and how you can utilize them in your applications.

In discussing the topics just mentioned in this chapter:

- ❑ Gives an overview of Web services and how you can use them in C# Express.

- ❑ Discusses what Web services are available and how to locate them.

- ❑ Shows how to create references in your application to desired Web services.

- ❑ Shows how to use Web services in your own applications, with examples of adding stock quotes and weather information Web services.

Overview of Web Services

Sometimes when I discuss implementing Web services in applications my students get a quick look of panic on their faces. This shouldn't be the case, because Web services are actually no more difficult to use than any of the other .NET classes located in the Framework. The only difference is you need to locate the service and set a reference to it in the applications (more on that in a minute). Right now take a look at one of the examples discussed in the introduction.

Looking Further at a Web Service Example

Before getting into how Web services work, I want to show you one of the examples discussed in the introduction of the chapter. With literally typing only five lines of code, I was able to type in a stock symbol, such as MSFT, and retrieve the screen shown in Figure 15-1 from a stock quote Web service.

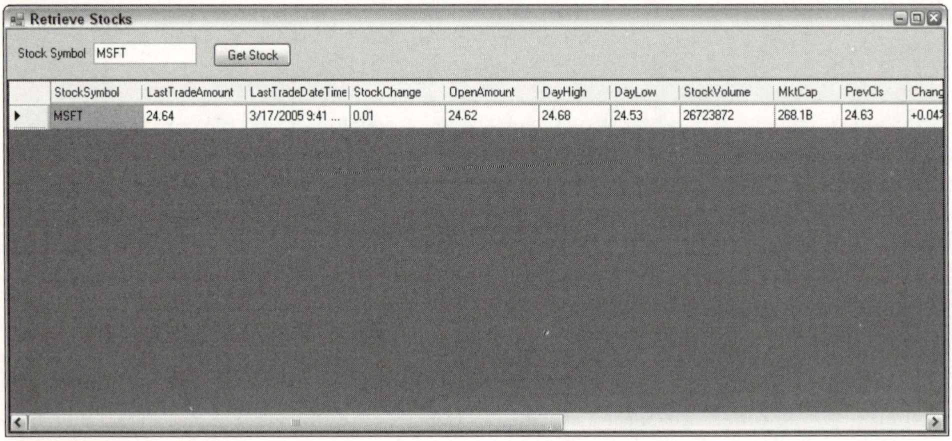

Figure 15-1

It took me all of 15 minutes to locate a Web service to perform this task and create the form to call the service and display the information. I then said to myself, "Well this is cool, but what if I want to get more than one quote at a time?" With this in mind I typed **MSFT, FOX** and then clicked the Get Stock button. Wouldn't you know I got the screen shown in Figure 15-2 without any additional programming?

Now, while not all Web services are as easy to use, I have found most of them not too hard to figure out. You will be creating this form and seeing how to access the Web service later in this chapter. For now, you need to create the starting project.

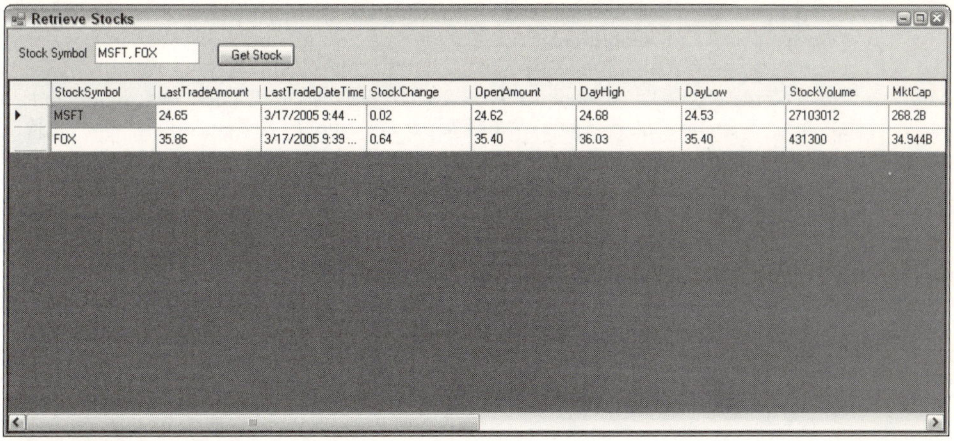

Figure 15-2

Try It Out   Create the Project and Main Form for the Chapter

By now this is pretty old hat. For this chapter, once again you will create a project that has a main form with buttons to open the various forms used for the examples in the chapter.

1. Open up C# Express and while in the Start Page, choose New Project.

2. Choose Windows Application for the template to use, and name the project as desired. For this chapter the project is called Chapter 15.

3. Click OK to create the project and the default form.

4. Using the skills you have learned throughout the book, add two buttons that will be used to call the two sample forms used for this chapter.

You are now ready to read further about how to use Web services. To get started, I will talk further about how Web services are used and what they are.

What Are Web Services?

Even with Windows XP and later operating systems, Web services are utilized without you even knowing about it. Features such as Windows Update and other Internet services use Web services. A lot of companies also now use Web services to expose their databases to outside developers when necessary. For instance, when a financial services company needs to allow certain information be accessible by their clients, they will create a Web service, with security in place that provides the information needed.

When using a Web service, the application on the local machine, also called the *consumer*, under the covers is using Internet protocols such as HTTP and SOAP (Simple Object Access Protocol) to communicate with the Web service located on a Web server. This communication will transpire either locally, on an intranet, or on the Internet. When the Web service is communicating back to the consumer, HTTP and SOAP are also used. The information itself is passed back and forth as XML.

Before you panic thinking you have to learn all of these technologies, one thing you should know is the majority of the work for all the communications between your computer and the Web services is handled by .NET when you use C#. All you will have to do is set a reference to the Web service you are using. You can then make use of .NET types defined in the Web service via their WSDL description, or by a shared class library reference The first part of this chapter is mainly to give you an idea of what Web services are all about and what happens under the covers.

One of the great things about using Web services is that as long as the consumer can create and consume messages defined for the Web service, it doesn't matter what the consumer is written in or even what platform the Web service is run on. The term used for this is "loosely coupled" or, in other words, nonproprietary. Figure 15-3 displays this concept.

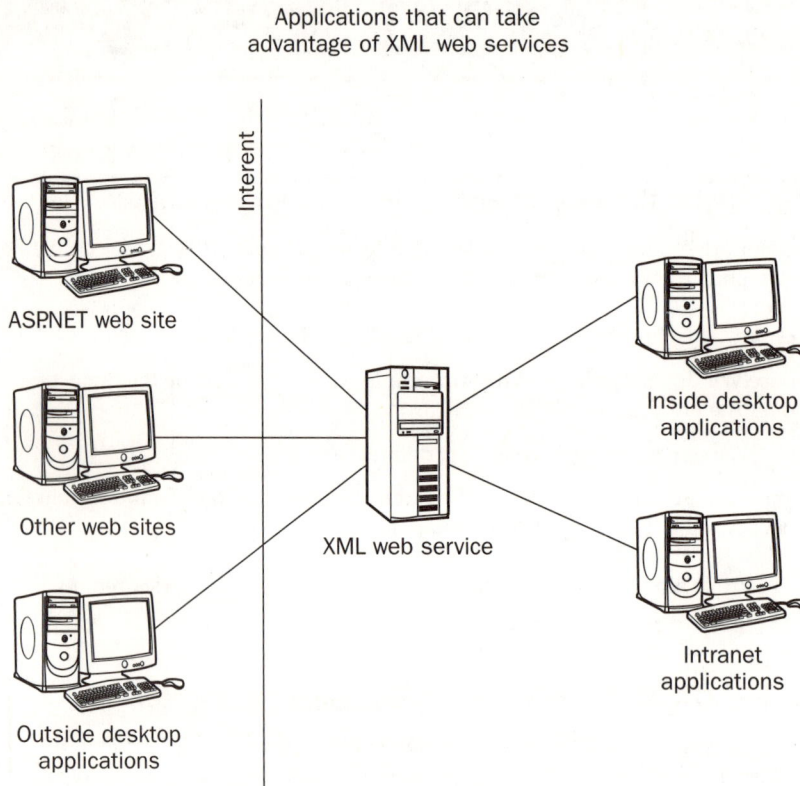

Figure 15-3

Notice that no specific languages or platforms are named in this graphic, except to point out ASP.NET, of course. The Web service can be created using ASP.NET or any other language that works with SOAP.

You can create a Web service using ASP.NET with C#. However, since C# Express doesn't include ASP.NET, you can only be a consumer and use Web services, not create them yourself in C# Express.

Web Services Infrastructure

The infrastructure of Web services includes four main areas:

- ❑ **XML Web Services Directories.** Central location to locate XML Web services created by outside organizations. The UDDI (Universal Description, Discovery, and Integration) registry is an example of one of these directories. Your Web service client may not even need to use these if you know the address of the Web service you are accessing.

- ❑ **XML Web Service Discovery.** Discovering documents that describe a particular XML Web service using the WSDL (Web Services Description Language). The DISCO specification defines an algorithm for locating service descriptions. Again, if you know the location of the service description, you can avoid this process.

- ❑ **XML Web Service Description.** Defines what types of methods the XML Web service uses. Tells clients how to interact with an XML Web service so they know how to use it.

- ❑ **XML Web Service Wire Formats.** To be able communicate with all platforms and languages, XML Web services use open wire formats. These are protocols understandable by any system capable of supporting the most common Web standards. SOAP is the main protocol used.

You can see each of these parts of the infrastructure in Figure 15-4.

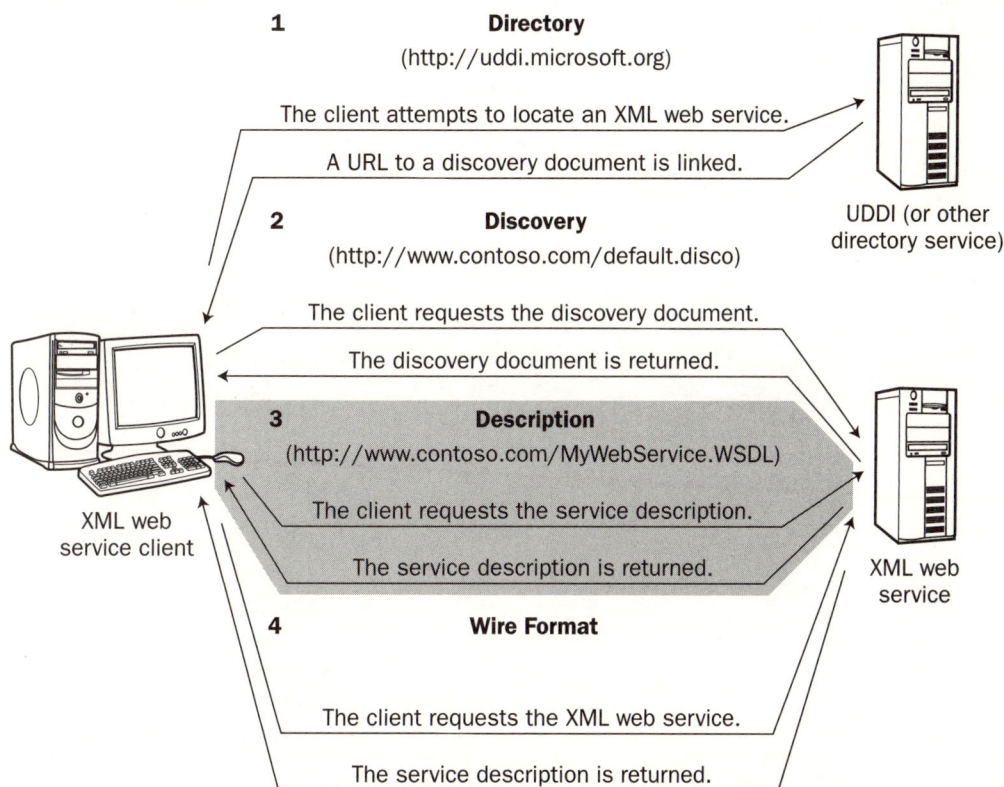

1 Directory
(http://uddi.microsoft.org)

The client attempts to locate an XML web service.

A URL to a discovery document is linked.

UDDI (or other directory service)

2 Discovery
(http://www.contoso.com/default.disco)

The client requests the discovery document.

The discovery document is returned.

3 Description
(http://www.contoso.com/MyWebService.WSDL)

The client requests the service description.

The service description is returned.

XML web service client

XML web service

4 Wire Format

The client requests the XML web service.

The service description is returned.

Figure 15-4

Again, Microsoft has gone to great pains to make sure that you don't have to go through all these steps yourself. These steps are performed when you create Web references in your applications.

Locating and Referencing Web Services

There are actually several ways to locate available Web services: being notified, utilizing the UDDI inside C# Express, and searching on the Web.

Locating Web Services through Notification

This way most often happens if you are using Web services through an intranet in a corporation and the IT department has created a Web service to expose a database used by the company. Also, some financial services companies come up with Web services and notify their clients when they have a Web service available. Since there are a number of ways to consume Web services besides programming code, some companies have gone to Web services to let their people, usually developers, access their databases.

Using C# Express to Locate and Create a Web Reference

When first starting out with Web services, you may find it easier to locate and create a reference to a Web service using the dialog boxes in C# Express. The reason is that it will walk you through the steps to searching for and creating a reference to the Web service. After you create your application, before you can use a Web service to create a reference, actually a Web reference, to the Web service. There are a couple of ways to accomplish this: by choosing Project ⇨ Add Web Reference . . . or by right-clicking while on the Project or Reference node in the Solution Explorer, and then choosing Add Web Reference . . . .

Once you have done either of these methods, the Add Web Reference dialog box appears, as shown in Figure 15-5.

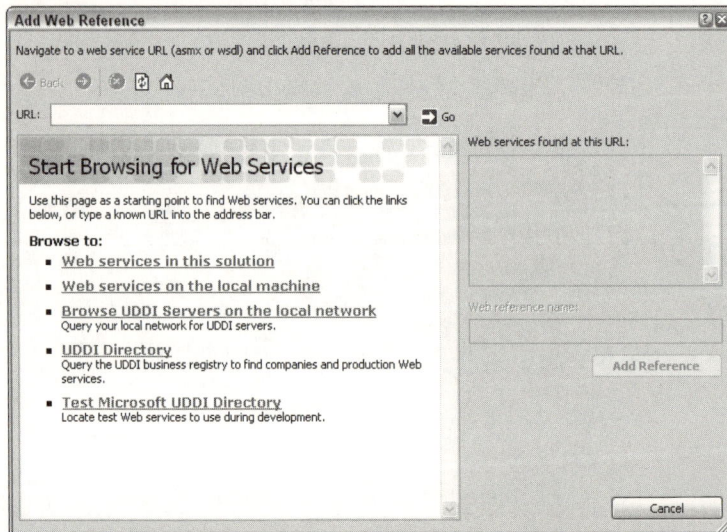

Figure 15-5

Figure 15-5 shows the five links to locate Web services. The first two choices would be used if you were testing out your own Web service, and the third would be if someone at your company had a Web service they created, or you were again utilizing one of your own that you are hosting on a server located on your local network. The last choice, Test Microsoft UDDI Directory, lets you test Web services that are off-site.

The choice of UDDI Directory will be the one you want to use to locate a useful Web service that is actually in production.

> Be aware that unless you know the company putting out the Web services, if you are using the Web service, it may not be available for future use if the company decides not to have it there any longer. The Web services provided in this chapter have been available for a couple of years or are part of a group large enough that they should be available for you. However, just be on notice when you use Web services in your own applications.
>
> I am not recommending one Web service provider over another, and no inference as to the credibility of the Web services or their providers one way or another is implied.

Once you have clicked the UDDI Directory, you are brought to the first page of the directory, shown in Figure 15-6.

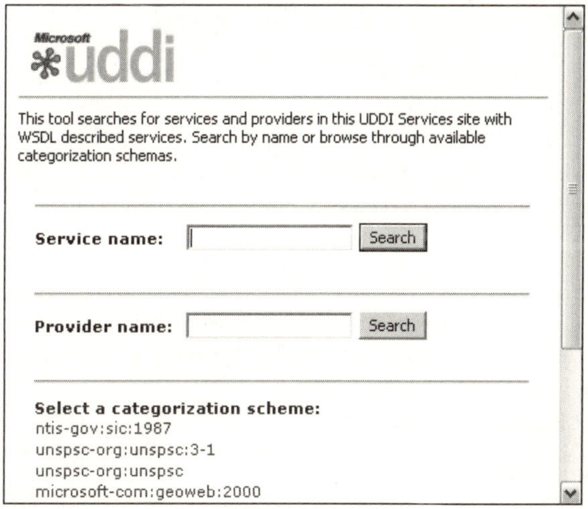

Figure 15-6

At this point, if you know the name of the Web service you want or provider to find, you can fill it in or click the following links. When you scroll down a bit, you will see the choice "VS Web Service Search Categorization." This option then presents some categories for you to choose from. One category is Financial. If you were looking for a Web service that returns stock quotes, this is where you would expect to find one.

At this point the UDDI takes you to possible subcategory screens, and then displays a list of different possible Web services that handle financial tasks. In the case of what you will be using for the next Try It Out, CDYNE Corporation has a Delayed Stock Quote Web service that works nicely. You can see the information for the Web service in Figure 15-7.

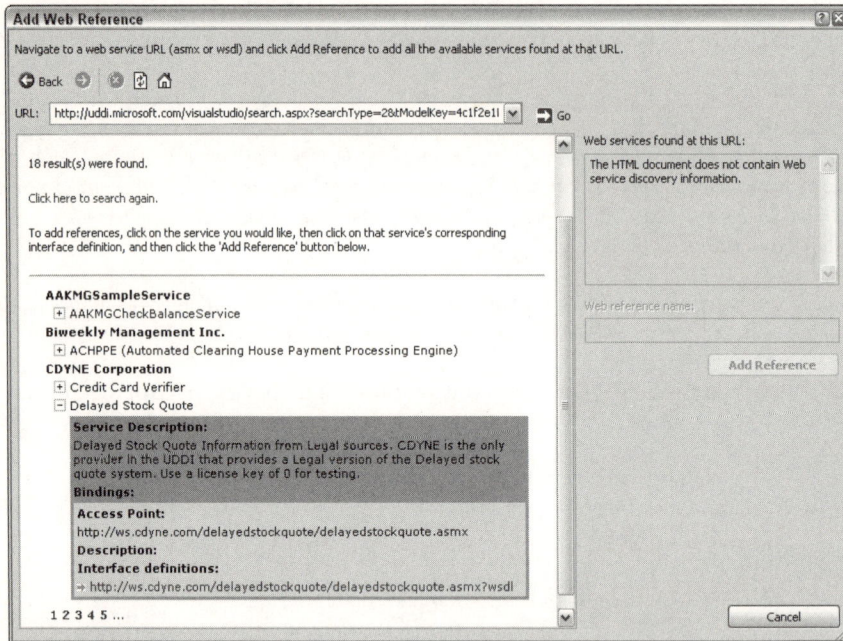

Figure 15-7

After you click the link displayed in Interface Definitions, the Web service details are displayed, and you can then decide to click Add Reference. The Web reference is then created in your project, and you can use the classes, properties, and methods provided by the Web service. In fact, you can even access them using the object browser, as shown in Figure 15-8.

Now that you have seen how to do it, it is time for you to go ahead and add your own Web reference to a Web service. You will utilize the Web service provided by CYNE Corporation.

Try It Out   Create the Web Reference Using C# Express

Using the project you created for the chapter, follow the steps presented here to create a Web reference to the Delayed Stock Quote Web service.

1. Select Project ⇨ Add Reference . . . .
2. Click the UDDI Directory link under the Start Browsing for Web Services label.
3. Scroll down in the UDDI directory page, and click VS Web Service Search Categorization.
4. In the categories displayed, click Financial.

5. Click Search on the next page displayed, since there are no subcategories. The initial choices are displayed, in which CYNE Corporation is included, with the Delayed Stock Quote listed below, as shown in Figure 15-9.

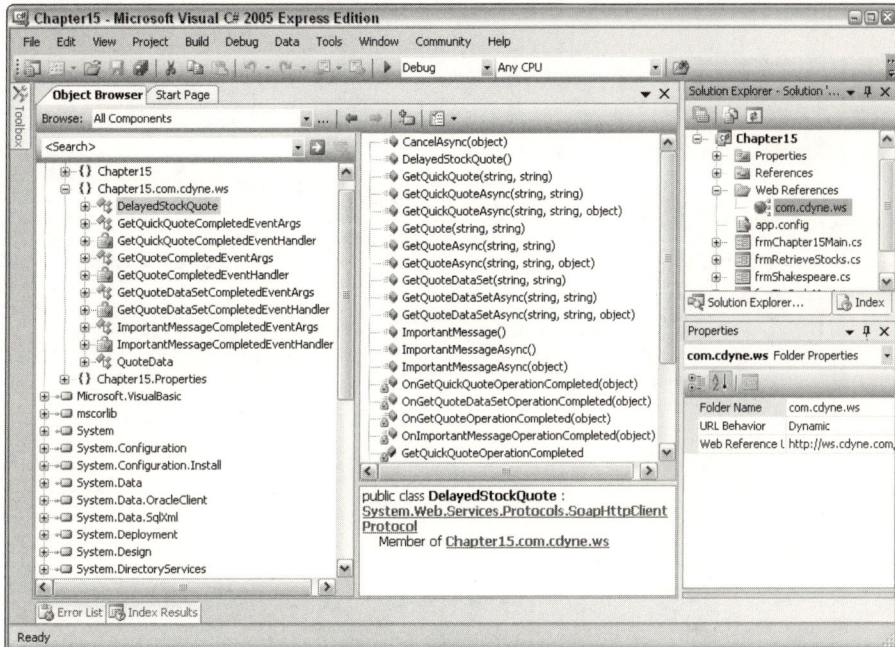

Figure 15-8

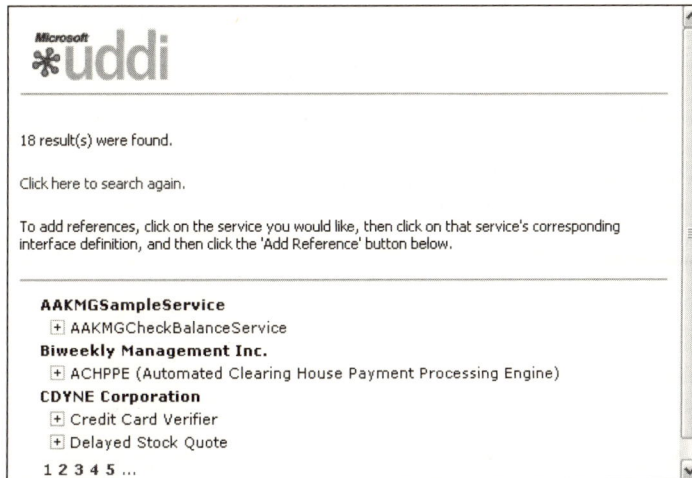

Figure 15-9

6. Click the plus sign next to the Delayed Stock Quote, and scroll down in the browser. You now see the full description of the Web service, as shown in Figure 15-7.

7. Click the http:// address displayed as the Interface Definition. You now see the definition displayed, and the Add Reference button is enabled. The definition for the Web service is shown in Figure 15-10.

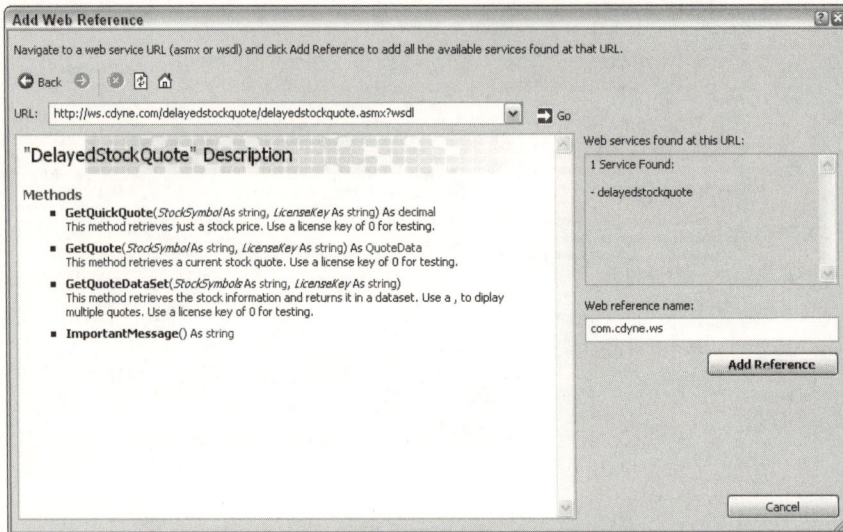

Figure 15-10

It is not a bad idea to copy and paste the information displayed here into a text file, or better yet, press Ctrl + Print Screen and save it to a file. While you can look in the object browser to get this information, it is nice to have it displayed in this format. Otherwise, you will have to go to the provider's Web site to locate this information, and a lot of times they won't have it documented as well.

8. Click Add Reference. The Web reference is now created in your project.

Because the UDDI is so dynamic, here is the actual URL for the Web service as well: http://ws.cdyne.com/delayedstockquote/delayedstockquote.asmx.

At this point, you won't be actually using the Web service that you have created a reference to. You will use it shortly, but before that, I want to show you how to locate and use a reference that you get from searching the Internet directly. I will come back to this Web service to show you how to use it in your code.

Searching for Web Services on the Web

This task and the task covered in the next section use nearly the same method, except here you use a search engine such as Google to locate a particular type of Web service. For example, if I want to locate a weather Web service that could give me the weather for particular locations, I would go to Google and search for "weather Web service". When I do, I see the results shown in Figure 15-11.

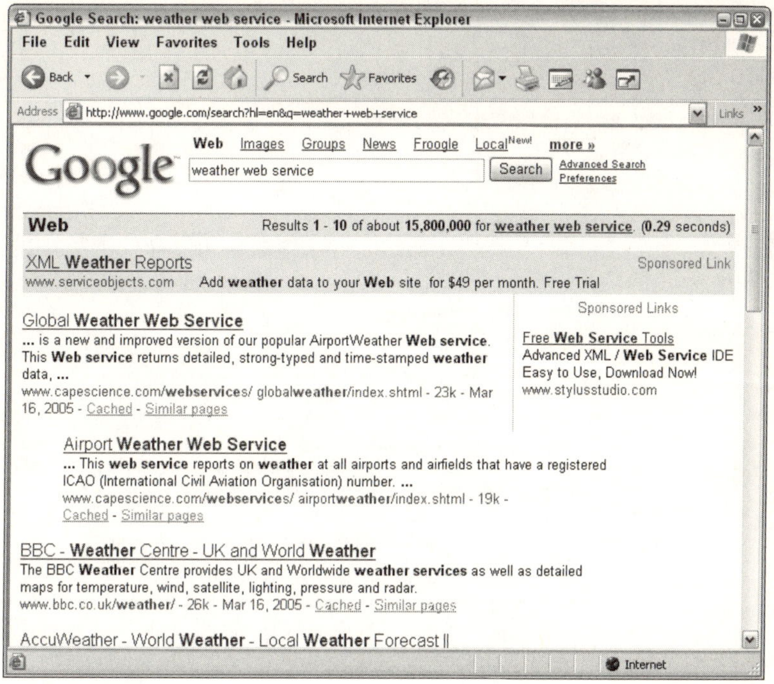

Figure 15-11

As you can see from 15-11, I immediately found a Web service that is what I am looking for. In fact, this service is used in an example that you perform later in this chapter, so you will see how to include a Web service that isn't found using C# Express directly. When clicking the link for GlobalWeather Web Service, the Web services page is displayed with a link to the Web service itself. Further information about the service is given, as shown in Figure 15-12.

> *The data for this Web service is supplied by NOAA, which is pretty amazing if you think about the fact that you are actually using data provided by the National Oceanic and Atmospheric Administration with less then an hour between updates.*

Scrolling down the page, you can see the exact details on how to use this Web service in an application. You can see the methods and properties that are exposed for the Web service, as well as details on the link you need to create a Web reference, in Figure 15-13.

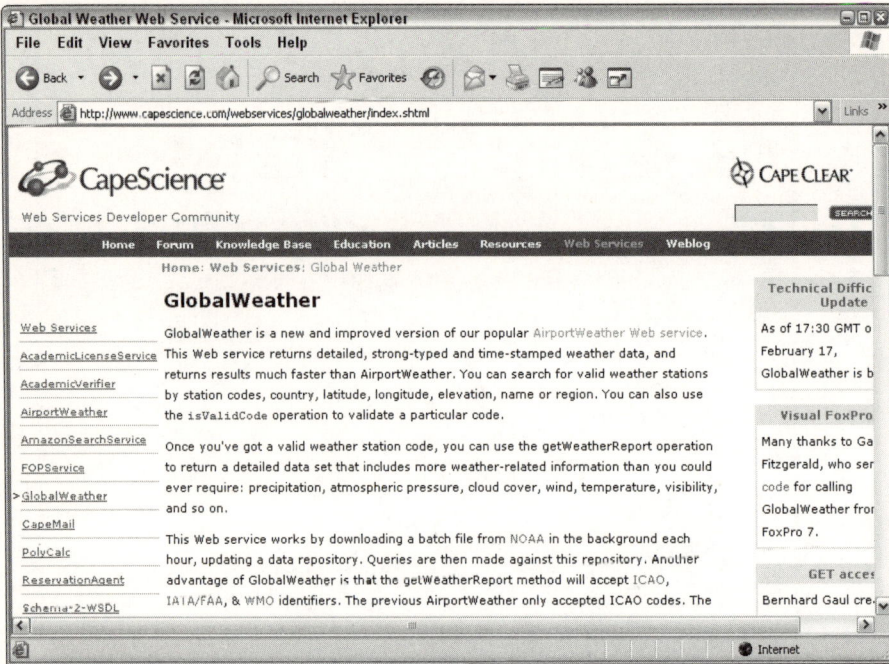

Figure 15-12

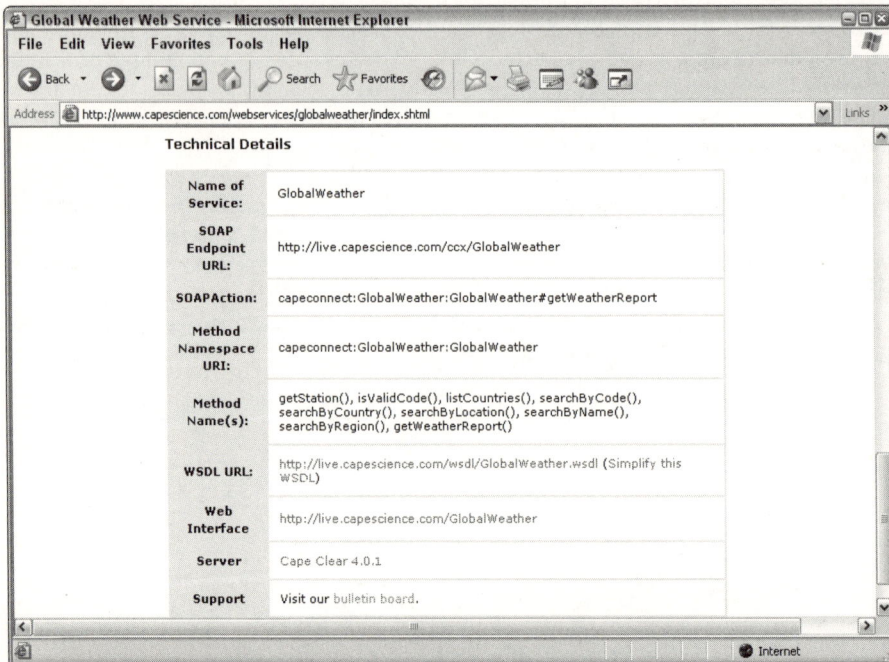

Figure 15-13

When on the page displayed in Figure 15-13, you can see the WSDL URL listed. At this point you can highlight the string, up to where it says (Simplify this WSDL). Then copy and paste it into the address in the Add Web Reference dialog box discussed in the previous section. Once you do that and press Enter, the Web server details appear, as shown in Figure 15-14.

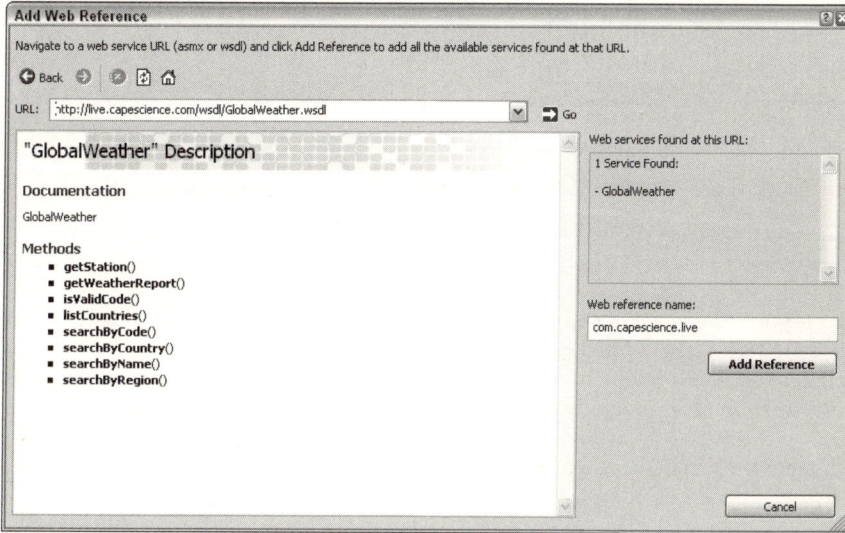

Figure 15-14

This saves you from all the steps taken in the previous section to locate the WSDL URL that was eventually provided by the UDDI directory.

Notice that the description for this Web service isn't as detailed as the one displayed for the Delayed Stock Quote Web service in Figure 15-10. Also, not all Web services are as easy to find or as nicely supported as the ones described in this book. Also, all Web services are subject to change at the whim of the developers who create them.

Try It Out   Add a Web Reference Searching the Web

Now it is your chance to create a Web reference to the GlobalWeather web service. For this Try It Out you use your Web browser along with the project that you have been using in this chapter.

1.   Open your browser.

2.   Type **www.google.com** in the address bar.

3.   Type **Weather Web Service** in the Search field.

4.   Click the Google Search button. The list of search results appears.

5.   Click the first choice in the list, GlobalWeather Web Service. You are taken to the Web site for the Web service.

6. Scroll down the Web page until you now see the definition for the Web service as was displayed in Figure 15-13.

7. Highlight the WSDL URL.

8. Choose Edit ➪ Copy.

9. Switch back to the C# Express project you created for this chapter.

10. Choose Project ➪ Add Web Reference . . . .

11. Place the cursor in the URL field, and click Edit ➪ Paste. The WSDL URL is copied into the URL field of the Add Web Reference dialog box.

12. Click Go. The Global Web Service definition is displayed in the browse window.

13. Click Add Reference. The Web reference is created in the project, and you are ready to go with two Web services in your project.

There you go; you have now created Web references using two different methods. The method you use to locate the Web service will depend on whether you can find the Web service faster using one way than the other. The way just shown it is my preferred method, since you can specify what you are looking for a little bit more precisely than the first method you used in C# Express.

One last thing to keep in mind when comparing Web services is to make sure they have the various methods that you need to accomplish the job.

Now that you have the Web references in your project, it is time to do something with them. To make it as straightforward as possible, start off by creating the form and utilizing the DelayedStockQuote Web service, for which you set the Web reference earlier in this chapter. The form used to display the information from the Web service is shown in Figure 15-15.

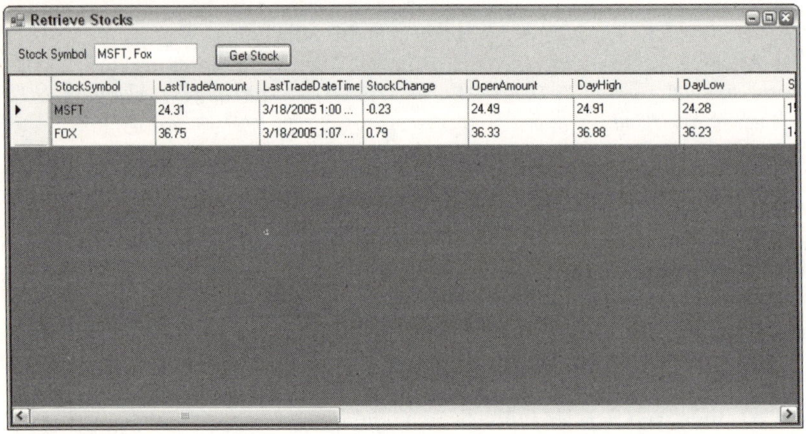

Figure 15-15

Using the Web Service in Your Code

The really cool thing about using Web services in your applications is that they don't take much more to use than any of the other classes in .NET, and a lot less than many. Of course, how much work it takes to utilize them will depend on what features are included. The more features a Web service has, then possibly the more effort it will take to use them—although this is not necessarily true. Many services, such as the GlobalWeather Web service, have an extensive object model, but also provide some methods and properties that can be used in a fairly straightforward manner.

Coding for the DelayedStockQuote Web Service

To get going, you will learn how to integrate the DelayedStockQuote in your application. When working with a Web service, you need to learn what classes and their methods and properties are available for use. One of the ways to do this is to examine the Web service classes in the Object Browser. If you were to do so with `DelayedStockQuote`, you would see that it is in fact only one of the classes that is used. The other useful thing to note is that the method you will want to use is called `GetQuoteDataSet`. This method takes a stock symbol as a parameter, and a license. Since you are only going to be testing the Web service, you will pass "0" as the license key. By double-clicking the new Web reference in the Solution Explorer, you can see that the Web service references have defined a namespace with types for you to use in your program.

> *While not all Web services do so, many let you test their services out for a trial period.*

Knowing what you now know about the Web service, you can declare the necessary objects and get to work. Now it is just a matter of using the same syntax you have been using throughout the book:

```
com.cdyne.ws.DelayedStockQuote wsStock = new com.cdyne.ws.DelayedStockQuote();
```

Once this occurs you, get full IntelliSense on the properties and methods, as you can see in Figure 15-16.

You should be very familiar with the code displayed. I tend to use the full path of the Web services I use so I can remember them as I work with them. The line of code declares the variable `wsStock` as a `DelayedStockQuote` object. Next, you assign a `DataSet` object that is returned from the `GetQuoteDataSet` method:

```
DataSet dsStocks = wsStock.GetQuoteDataSet(this.txtStockSymbol.Text, "0");
```

`DataSet`s were first introduced in Chapter 12. The last thing to do is to assign the `dsStocks DataSet` to the `DataGridView` control on the form. The `DataGridView` was also discussed in Chapter 12.

```
this.dataGridView1.DataSource = dsStocks.Tables[0];
```

Some code can be added for exception handling and such.

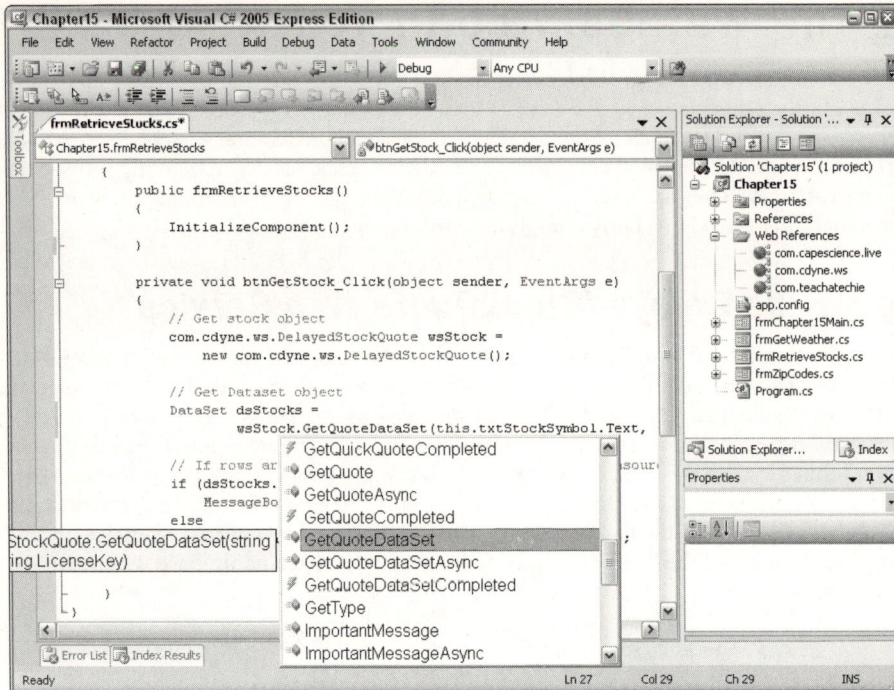

Figure 15-16

Try It Out   **Create a Form for Using a DelayStockQuote Web Service**

By now, creating this form, and even the code introduced in this section, should be pretty old hat. As you keep using these examples and others, you will start to find it is just a matter of learning how to use the new classes that have been created. Using the project you created in this chapter:

1.   Select Project ⇨ Add Windows Form . . ., and name it as desired. For the purpose of this example, I named it `frmGetQuotes.cs`.

2.   Add a `Label` (`Text` property set to "Stock Symbol"), `TextBox` (`Name` property set to `txtStockSymbol`), and `Button` (`Name` property set to `btnGetStock`) control as displayed in Figure 15-17.

3.   Drag and drop a `DataGridView` control from the Toolbox onto the form, positioning as shown in Figure 15-16. Leave the name of the `DataGridView` of the control as it was, and just make a note of it.

4.   Set the `Anchor` property to be Top, Bottom, Left, and Right.

5.   Double-click the `btnGetStock` button. The code file is displayed with the `Click` routine created as shown here:

```
private void btnGetStock_Click(object sender, EventArgs e)
 {

 }
```

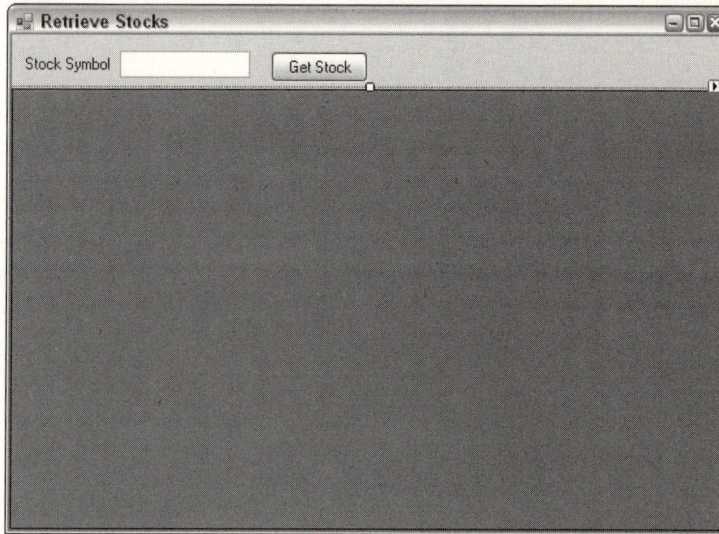

Figure 15-17

6. Type the following lines of code inside the opening and closing curly brackets:

```
com.cdyne.ws.DelayedStockQuote wsStock =
                new com.cdyne.ws.DelayedStockQuote();

DataSet dsStocks =
        wsStock.GetQuoteDataSet(this.txtStockSymbol.Text, "0");

this.dataGridView1.DataSource = dsStocks.Tables[0];
```

The complete code now looks as follows:

```
private void btnGetStock_Click(object sender, EventArgs e)
 {
    com.cdyne.ws.DelayedStockQuote wsStock =
                    new com.cdyne.ws.DelayedStockQuote();

    DataSet dsStocks =
            wsStock.GetQuoteDataSet(this.txtStockSymbol.Text, "0");

    this.dataGridView1.DataSource = dsStocks.Tables[0];
 }
```

7. Add a button to the main form created for the chapter. Add the following line of code, changing the name of the form called to what you named it:

```
        private void btnCheckStocks_Click(object sender, EventArgs e)
        {
            frmGetQuotes frmCurr = new frmGetQuotes();
            frmCurr.Show();
        }
```

8. Press F5 to build and run the application.

By typing in a stock symbols such as MSFT and FOX, you can test the Web service. Another good extension of this would be to access a Web service to populate a drop-down with the stocks available. When you want to bring back information on more than one stock, separate the symbols in the text box with a comma.

I have noticed that with most Web services the first time you call them in an application, the performance is somewhat slower than I liked. However, when you call them a consecutive time in the same instance of the application, the performance is much improved. This will, of course, depend on the Web services themselves.

Coding for the GlobalWeather Web Service

While the coding for the example using this Web service is a little more extensive, it is because more information will be displayed. Even then, it is actually pretty straightforward to display quite a bit of information. In this example, with an airport code supplied, not only will you display the current temperature but also the current station information for sky coverage, visibility, and wind. You can see the form in action in Figure 15-18.

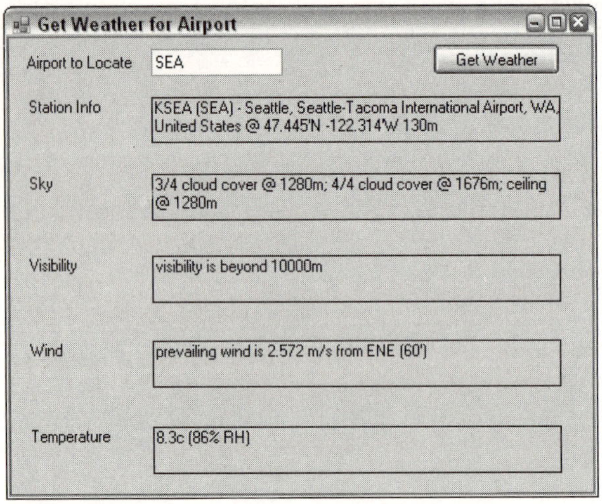

Figure 15-18

The example in Figure 15-18, which you will create, shows not even the tip of iceberg of the information available in this Web service, but maybe a seagull sitting on the tip of the iceberg. Each piece of weather information displayed in Figure 15-18 is made up of smaller properties strung together for convenience.

Each of the lines displayed happened to reflect a class of the WeatherReport class, which you can see in the Object Browser, shown in Figure 15-19.

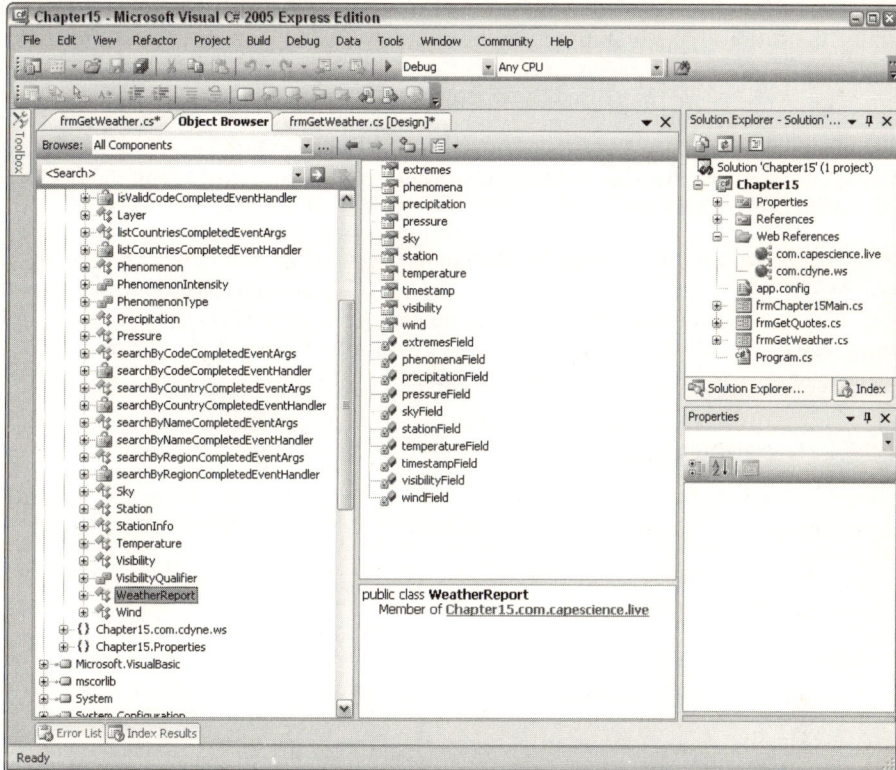

Figure 15-19

You can see the information used in the example, and more. For this Web service, there are several steps you need to take when utilizing the classes within the service. The first object you need to create is a GlobalWeather object, as shown with the following code:

```
com.capescience.live.GlobalWeather wsWeather =
                new com.capescience.live.GlobalWeather();
```

Once you have instantiated this object, you then have a number of methods you can execute to retrieve information various ways. For the purpose of this example, you will use the getWeatherReport method to retrieve the properties of the WeatherReport object. The instantiation of the WeatherReport object and calling of the getWeatherReport method can be seen here:

```
com.capescience.live.WeatherReport wsReport =
            wsWeather.getWeatherReport(this.txtAirportToLocate.Text);
```

Once you have the `WeatherReport`, as referenced by `wsReport`, you can then access the various classes representing the various types of information:

```
lblStation.Text = wsReport.station.@string;
lblSky.Text = wsReport.sky.@string;
lblVisibility.Text = wsReport.visibility.@string;
lblWind.Text = wsReport.wind.@string;
lblTemperature.Text = wsReport.temperature.@string;
```

Interestingly, to get the complete string of information, you will use the `string` property of the particular class you are retrieving. However, since the word *string* is a key word in C#, you will have to tell C# to use the literal value of "string" instead of the keyword meaning, in this case the property, not the keyword. To specify this, you use the @ symbol, as you do when you want to use the "\" as a backslash instead of as a control character, such as in \n the newline command.

Try It Out   Creating the Form and Code for the GlobalWeather Web Service

Continuing to work with the form created in the chapter, you will add the form and code necessary to call the methods in the GlobalWeather Web service:

1. Select Project ➪ Add Windows Form . . . , and name it as desired. For the purpose of this example, I named it `frmGetWeather.cs`.

2. Add a `Label` (`Text` property set to "Airport to Locate"), `TextBox` (`Name` property set to `txtAirportToLocate`), and `Button` (`Name` property set to `btnGetWeather`) control as shown in Figure 15-20.

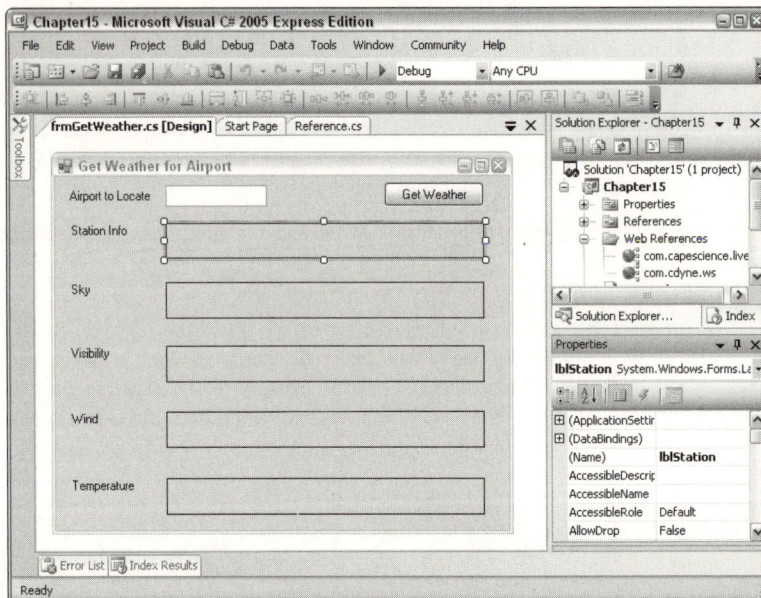

Figure 15-20

274

3. For each of the five pieces of information, also displayed in Figure 15-20, add labels down the left side of the form, which the `Text` properties set to "Station Info," "Sky," "Visibility," "Wind," and "Temperature."

4. On the right side of the form you will add five additional `Label` controls, corresponding to the label added in Step 3, with the `Name` property: `lblStation`, `lblSky`, `lblVisibility`, `lblWind`, and `lblTemperature`.

5. Set the `AutoSize` property on each of the `Label` controls added in Step 4 to False. This will allow you to adjust the height and width of the controls.

6. Double-click `btnGetWeather`. The code file for the form opens, and the new routine is created for the `Click` event of `btnGetWeather`, as shown here:

```
private void btnGetWeather_Click(object sender, EventArgs e)
{

}
```

7. Type the following code inside the code block for `btnGetWeather_Click` routine.

```
com.capescience.live.GlobalWeather wsWeather =
               new com.capescience.live.GlobalWeather();

com.capescience.live.WeatherReport wsReport =
           wsWeather.getWeatherReport(this.txtAirportToLocate.Text);

lblStation.Text = wsReport.station.@string;
lblSky.Text = wsReport.sky.@string;
lblVisibility.Text = wsReport.visibility.@string;
lblWind.Text = wsReport.wind.@string;
lblTemperature.Text = wsReport.temperature.@string;
```

The final routine looks as follows:

```
private void btnGetWeather_Click(object sender, EventArgs e)
{
    com.capescience.live.GlobalWeather wsWeather =
                   new com.capescience.live.GlobalWeather();

    com.capescience.live.WeatherReport wsReport =
               wsWeather.getWeatherReport(this.txtAirportToLocate.Text);

    lblStation.Text = wsReport.station.@string;
    lblSky.Text = wsReport.sky.@string;
    lblVisibility.Text = wsReport.visibility.@string;
    lblWind.Text = wsReport.wind.@string;
    lblTemperature.Text = wsReport.temperature.@string;
}
```

8. Press F5 to build and execute the application. The form opens waiting for you to enter an airport code for which to retrieve weather information.

9. Type an airport code such as SEA or LAX.

10. Click the `btnGetWeather` button. The information is displayed.

For a list of other airport codes, you can go back to the GlobalWeather Web service Web page, shown in Figure 15-13.

Note that if you were using this for a real application, you really ought to check for a null return value, which you get for a nonexistent airport code. Without checking, you get a null-reference exception.

Summary

The limitations on how data is transmitted and received in a convenient yet secured manner has been an issue since information started being traded among companies and locations. The latest method, Web Services, provides both convenience and security for developers in a way like never before.

When companies provide Web services, developers can use various languages for the consumption of the Web service, provided the language supports it. In C# Express and the other Visual Studio products, adding Web services to your applications is as simple as adding a Web reference, declaring objects using the classes provided by the Web service, and utilizing the properties and methods of those types provided by the Web service.

This chapter showed you how to locate Web services both on the Web and using C# Express. It then went on to discuss how to create Web references and use them inside your applications, giving examples of retrieving stock quotes and weather information.

Exercises

1. What does UDDI stand for?
2. What are the four sections of Web services infrastructure?
3. Name two of the ways to locate Web services that you can use in your applications.
4. What utility enables you to discover the various classes, methods, and properties once a Web reference has been established for a Web service?

16

Publishing Your Application and Next Steps

No book on development is complete nowadays without discussing how to publish your applications, also called *deployment*. When you publish or deploy your application, you are making it available for other people's use. In the past it was a big deal to create and maintain the files to distribute applications. I remember in the early Microsoft Access days when I distributed an application, it took 10 floppy disks to hold all the parts of the program.

What you want to do with your final application will determine how you want to publish it.

This chapter wraps up everything I have been talking about with regard to C# Express and what you can do with it. In this chapter, you will:

- ❏ Find out how to deploy your application.

- ❏ Look at some of the next steps you want to take, such as developing C# Web applications.

- ❏ Read about some of the specific features of Visual Web Developer Express.

- ❏ Take a look at some third-party tools.

Publishing Your C# Express Applications?

Unfortunately, no deployment tools are included in the Express products. With the full versions of Visual Studio products project setup templates are included to help your deploy (distribute) your applications. If you want to give your application to someone to use, then you will need to give them all the files in the Bin\Release folder (or Bin\Debug) located under your project folder.

The person using your application will then need to have the .NET Framework 2.0 installed on their machine. Generally, the idea behind using the Express products is to get you going in development and then have you move on if you are going to be distributing the applications you create.

Where to Go from Here?

You have learned so much in this book. I have tried to put you on the path to really enjoying what you are doing with C# Express and to understand the power you have available. These next sections take a look at what are the next steps to working with C# besides just getting as much experience as possible with the product.

Developing for the Web: Visual Web Developer 2005 Express Edition

As mentioned, not only can C# be used in Windows forms as has been shown throughout the book but also for Web development. Along with the other .NET products, Microsoft has created a Web development environment called ASP.NET. There are a couple of ways to get into ASP.NET:

❑ Upgrade to the full version of Visual Studio .NET and use ASP.NET, discussed in the section entitled "Moving Up to Visual Studio .NET," found later in this chapter.

❑ Download Visual Web Developer 2005 Express Edition. Like C# Express, this product has been created to introduce students, hobbyists, and other new developers to the world of programming, in this case programming on the Internet.

Of the two alternatives, the later is the cheapest way to get going in ASP.NET. Built on ASP 2.0, Visual Web Developer 2005 Express Edition (VWD) gives developers tools they need to build Web applications. Much like C# Express, the Web Developer 2003 Express includes the following:

❑ **Visual designers.** Let you drag and drop controls onto Web forms, just as you would Windows forms.

❑ **Code editor.** Makes writing HTML quicker and more conveniently than ever and includes that great product with the silly name of IntelliSense. HTML tags, including methods and properties, are listed as you write your code.

❑ **Microsoft SQL Server 2005 Express.** Integrated using the Database Explorer, similar if not the same data controls are included so that you can drag and drop them onto your Web forms with little or no coding.

❑ **Starter kits.** These are included to help you get going, including the Personal Web Starter Kit.

When using the full version of ASP.NET, you can create your own XML Web Services, as discussed in Chapter 15.

In addition to the similarities with C# Express, VWD includes the capability of installing a personal Web server not requiring IIS.

One way to get started using VWD is to buy *Wrox's ASP.NET 2.0 Visual Web Developer 2005 Express Edition Starter Kit*. Another is to download a copy as shown in the next Try It Out.

| Try It Out | **Downloading and Installing Visual Web Developer 2005 Express Edition** |

Using your favorite browser:

1. Type **http://lab.msdn.microsoft.com/express/vwd/default.aspx**. You are taken to the home page for VWD, as shown in Figure 16-1.

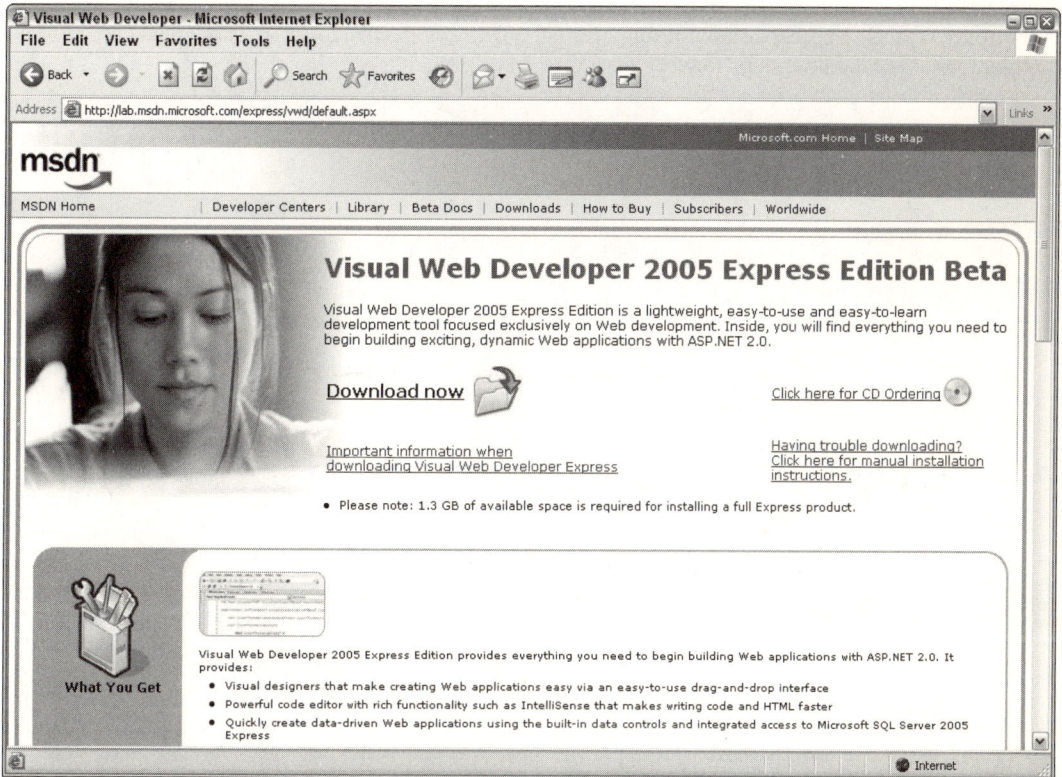

Figure 16-1

2. Click Download now.

3. After filling out the survey, click Download. The standard Run, Save Internet dialog box appears.

4. Click Run. The Setup program starts, as shown in Figure 16-2.

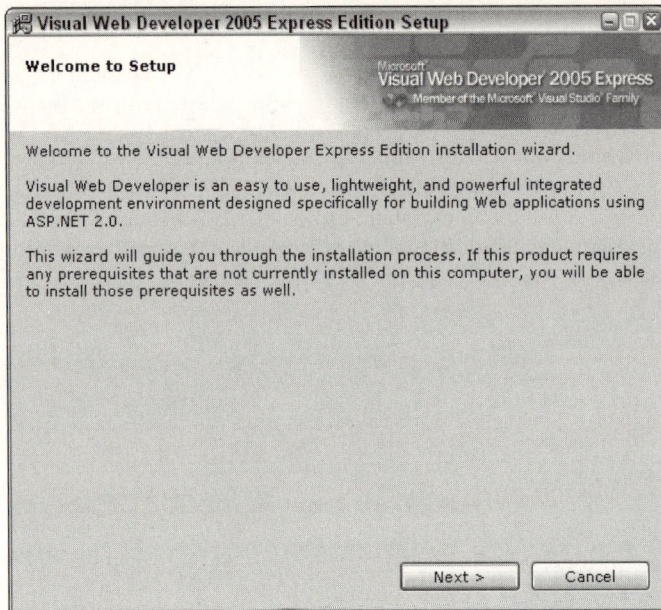

Figure 16-2

5. Click Next. The next page on the setup form asks which destination folder you want to install VWD into, as shown in Figure 16-3.

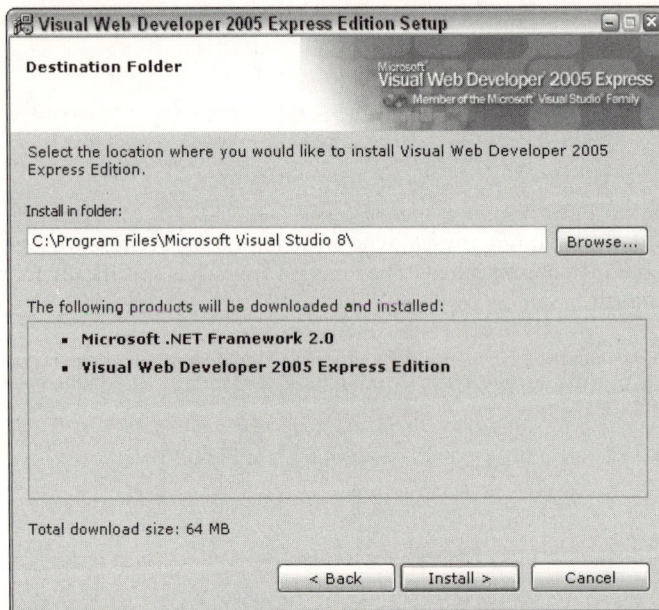

Figure 16-3

6. Click Install. The setup program downloads and installs VWD.

Moving Up to Visual Studio .NET

The other possibility is to move up to the big time and make an investment in Visual Studio .NET 2005. Everything you learned in this book about C# and the tools for development apply to the full-blown version. You will find the IDE almost exactly the same but with additional tools.

With Visual Studio .NET you can use ASP.NET 2.0 to create Web sites as well as Web services. You can take your applications and use them in Visual Studio .NET 2005. You will also notice quite a few more templates, allowing you to create additional types of applications such as Windows service applications and installation packages.

Using Third Party Tools and Other Sources of Information

A number of third-party tools and libraries are available for your use. Here are just a few of the companies that sell tools, and the uses you can put them to:

❑   **FMS Inc. — Total .NET Developer Suite.** These tools provide various services for everything from analyzing your .NET applications to making best-practice and performance recommendations. The tool I like the best is Total .NET Source Book. This tool is a library of code that you can use in your applications. One of the coolest features is that it takes advantage of Web services to retrieve updates and new code for you.

   This tool is great for checking out how to perform various tasks and use code already created for you. Find out more about it at www.fmsinc.com.

❑   **dtSearch — Full Text Retrieval.** This tool is an engine that helps you perform full text searches on various kinds of documents such as Word documents, PDFs, HTML, and even other databases such as SQL Server and Access. Included is an engine that has fully managed code driving it, with classes using properties and methods to help make life simpler. You can find the Web site for dtSearch at www.dtsearch.com.

   dtSearch is a more specialized tool that you may never have a need for, but it is so powerful that it is worthwhile to mention.

❑   **www.dotnetjunkies.com.** This Web site is created specially for .NET developers. There are various authors, including myself, who write for the site because we love the subject matter. You can check out my column called "The First Hit," which is specifically for new .NET developers such as yourself.

   Note that I get no monetary recompense from either of the companies mentioned here. Their products just rock.

Summary

Throughout the book, you have seen various ways to make C# perform tasks the way you need it to. Everything from simply creating a form, to utilizing Web services over the Net, to publishing your applications was covered. And it only gets better from here on out. As you are working with C# and C# Express, you will get more and more comfortable with using the various tools.

In this chapter, you saw how you could publish your C# applications in a number of different ways, either on a CD, the Web, or on a local network. You also saw some of the various tools available out there for your use in your applications. These tools can be located using the Internet and are for different purposes.

Exercises

1. What is it called when your application is ready to be distributed?

2. What product is used for Web development both in Visual Studio .NET 2005 and Visual Web Development Express?

3. What is the name of my column on DotNetJunkies.com?

A

Answers to Exercises

Chapter 1

Exercises

1. What is the difference between C# and Visual C# Express?
2. What are the four sections on the C# Express start page?
3. What does the acronym IDE stand for?
4. Name three of the tools available in the C# Express IDE.
5. What is the difference between a console application and Windows application?

Answers

1. C# is a programming language. Visual C# Express is a development environment.
2. Open an Existing Project, Getting Started, Visual C# Express Headlines, and MSDN: Visual C#.
3. Integrated Development Environment.
4. Solution Explorer, Database Explorer, and Task List.
5. Console applications generally are utilities that are run without user intervention, whereas Windows applications are interactive programs for users with forms.

Chapter 2

Exercises

1. What is the difference between hardware and software?
2. What are the differences between compiled and interpreted languages?
3. Name the three levels of Windows programming mentioned in this chapter.
4. What are dynamic-linked libraries used for?

Answers

1. Hardware is the computer and peripherals, whereas software is instructions that make up applications that run on hardware.

2. Compiled languages arc translated (compiled) from a more human-type language into a machine language all at once. Interpreted languages are translated as the program is run.

3. Application level, Windows level, and system level.

4. These are libraries of routines that can be utilized by other applications.

Chapter 3

Exercises

1. Can you include a Windows form in a console application?

2. What is the extension of the file that is used for a Windows form?

3. What pane in the IDE contains the various controls used on a form?

4. `Height`, `Width`, and `Text` are _____ of a form.

5. What is the property that displays a caption on a button?

Answers

1. Yes

2. .resx

3. Toolbox

4. Properties

5. Text

Chapter 4

Exercises

1. Name the two main parts of the .NET Framework.

2. What is the category in the Solution Explorer that shows the list of namespaces being used?

3. What feature lists parts of namespaces as you are typing the statements in code?

4. You can use _____ _____ to look at the various namespaces, classes and methods.

5. What are the two ways of using namespaces in code?

Answers

1. Common Language Runtime and .NET Framework Class Library

2. References

3. IntelliSense
4. Object Browser
5. Supplying the fully qualified name and the Using directive.

Chapter 5

Exercises

1. What is the difference between variables and constants?
2. How do you add a value to an existing variable?
3. Multiply the value in `intValue1` by 10 and assign the answer to a variable called `intAnswer`.
4. What is the command used to convert a C# type of `double` to `int`.
5. Declare the variable named `intMonth` and assign it the value 10 in a single line.

Answers

1. Variables can be updated in the application, whereas constants are assigned once.
2. Using the equal (=) sign.
3. `intAnswer = intValue * 10;`
4. Convert.ToInt32()
5. int intMonth = 10;

Chapter 6

Exercises

1. Name the three different types of errors you can debug.
2. What are some of the ways to work with breakpoints?
3. Name two of the windows that are used for displaying values in break mode.
4. What is the technology that enables you to hover the mouse over variables and see their values in break mode?
5. What are the three commands for stepping through code?

Answers

1. Syntax and semantic/logical errors.
2. Set breakpoint, disable breakpoint, and remove breakpoint.
3. Immediate window and locals window.
4. IntelliSense.
5. Step Into, Step Over, Run to Cursor.

Chapter 7

Exercises

1. When would you use an if . . . else statement versus a switch . . . case statement?
2. What category of statements does the if . . . else statement fall into?
3. What is the different between the for and foreach statements?
4. Which statement, do or while, does the code execute at least once if the expression starts as false?
5. If the developer wants to have a code block occur whether an exception occurs or not, which statement does the developer use with the try statement?

Answers

1. If there is only one or two choices, using the if . . . else statement.
2. Selection.
3. for is used with an index; foreach iterates though collections and arrays.
4. do
5. finally

Chapter 8

Exercises

1. What do MDI and SDI stand for?
2. What are switchboards used for?
3. What is the difference between a ToolStrip and ToolStripContainer control?
4. How do you add code to the Click event on a MenuStrip control?

Answers

1. Multiple-document interface and single-document interface.
2. Forms that launch other forms, in addition to menus.
3. ToolStrip creates toolbars on forms; ToolStripContainer lets you place other strip controls onto the form.
4. Double-click on the control.

Chapter 9

Exercises

1. What is the name of the enumerator used for setting the SelectionAlignment property of the RichTextBox control.

2. What is one of the methods you can use in code to display all the dialog boxes displayed in this chapters?

3. Which property on the `RichTextBox` do you use to utilize a font from the `FontDialog`?

4. What happens if you choose File ⇨ Open but then click Cancel?

Answers

1. `HorizontalAlignment`

2. `ShowDialog()`

3. `SelectionFont`

4. With the code provided, nothing.

Chapter 10

Exercises

1. What is the process of converting your data from flat-file format to a relational database format called?

2. Name the three types of relationships discussed in the chapter.

3. In Access you have fields and records. What are these elements called in SQL Server?

4. Give a couple of the benefits to using SQL Server databases.

5. Name the extensions of the Access and SQL Server database files.

Answers

1. Normalizing the data.

2. One-to-one, one-to-many, and many-to-many.

3. Columns and rows.

4. Greater volume of data and better to use for the Internet.

5. Acess: *.mdb; SQL Server: *.mdf.

Chapter 11

Exercises

1. What does MSDE stand for?

2. What are the two main tools provided in SQL Server Express?

3. Which tool do you use in C# Express to work with databases in and out of projects?

4. What is the difference between a view and a stored procedure?

Answers

1. Microsoft Desktop Edition

2. Database Explorer and data sources

3. Database Explorer

4. Views are used for displaying data, whereas stored procedures are used for updating data.

Chapter 12

Exercises

1. Which objects do you need to add to your project in order to utilize data in your form?

2. Which control (and underlying class) keeps track of data in memory?

3. What control is used to bind data to controls such as the `TextBox` control, and provide navigation?

4. What is the difference between the `BindingNavigator` and `BindingSource` controls?

Answers

1. `DataSources`.

2. `DataSets`.

3. `BindingSource` and `BindingNavigator`.

4. `BindingSource` binds to a source, and `BindingNavigator` provides navigation after binding to the `BindingSource` control.

Chapter 13

Exercises

1. What were three prior types of access methods provided by Microsoft in the past and mentioned in the chapter?

2. In ADO.NET the main object for working with data is the `DataSet`. What was the main object in the prior version?

3. ADO used connected data methodology. What does ADO.NET use?

4. `DataAdapters` are used to load data into `DataTables` and `DataSets`. What are `Command` objects used for?

Answers

1. DAO, ADO, and RDO.

2. `Recordset`.

3. Disconnected.

4. Performing updates on data using stored procedures, as well as providing the SQL commands for data adapters.

Chapter 14

Exercises

1. What are the two properties for setting the range on a `MonthCalendar` control?

2. What is the control for displaying two different objects in it and letting them be resized separately?

3. Name the four types of controls that can be used in the `StatusStrip` control.

4. Which method on the `System.DateTime` class returns the number of days in a month, and what are the parameters it requires?

Answers

1. `SelectionStart` and `SelectionEnd`

2. `SplitContainer`

3. `StatusLabel`, `ProgressBar`, `DropDownButton`, and `SplitButton`

4. `DaysInMonth()`. It requires the year and month be passed

Chapter 15

Exercises

1. What does UDDI stand for?

2. What are the four sections of Web services infrastructure?

3. Name two of the ways to locate Web services that you can use in your applications.

4. What utility enables you to discover the various classes, methods, and properties once a Web reference has been established for a Web service?

Answers

1. Universal Description, Discovery, and Integration

2. Directory, Discovery, Description, and Wire Format

3. UDDI and Googling

4. Object Browser

Chapter 16

Exercises

1. What is it called when your application is ready to be distributed?

2. What product is used for Web development both in Visual Studio .NET 2005 and Visual Web Development Express?

3. What is the name of my column on DotNetJunkies.com?

Answers

1. Ready for deployment

2. ASP.NET

3. The First Hit

Index